Favorite Recipes from
The Microwave Times

Volume II

Recipes Unlimited INC.

The recipes in this book were tested in 600 to 650-watt countertop microwave ovens. Some recipes include timings in parenthesis or in the Tips for the Combination Microwave Range that operates at about 400 watts of power. For other powered ovens, some adjustment in cooking time may be necessary to achieve the doneness described.

ISBN: 0-918620-30-9

Pictured on Cover: Oriental Scampi, page 18, and Raspberry Delight, page 114.

Favorite Recipes from

The Microwave Times

Contents

Chapter 1
Appetizers & Beverages 5

Chapter 2
Fish & Poultry 11

Chapter 3
Beef and Pork 21

Chapter 4
Main Dishes 37

Chapter 5
Soups & Salads 69

Chapter 6
Vegetables 79

Chapter 7
Breads 93

Chapter 8
Desserts & Pies 103

Chapter 9
Cakes, Cookies & Candies 125

Chapter 10
Potpourri 147
Index ... 152

Dear Reader,

After the success of our first Volume of *Favorite Recipes From The Microwave Times,* it is exciting to bring you this sequel which includes recipes from Volumes 6, 7, 8 and 9.

We are grateful to our subscribers who helped in the selection process. Some responded to our request for favorites with one or two recipes, others sent a list of one or two pages. It not only helped us choose favorites, but also gave us valuable feedback on the types of recipes preferred by our readers. Unfortunately, we were not able to include everyone's favorites, especially where there were several similar recipes.

Our years of publishing "The Times" have been exciting and gratifying. Many readers take the time to send recipes for adapting, ask questions about microwave cooking, share how they have used and enjoyed a recipe or tell how "The Times" has helped them to make better use of their microwave ovens. We appreciate this response, finding it invaluable in planning future issues and cook books to meet your needs.

During the first years of "The Microwave Times", we included directions for the Combination Oven with most recipes, since these units were operating at a lower wattage and required different timings. The Combination Ovens today operate at similar wattages to countertop units so we only include instructions when the combination feature (microwave and bake) will provide a better end product. These directions can be found in the recipe "Tips".

Recent issues have included some special diet sections, and we now regularly include calorie counts with recipes. Where we have calories, cholesterol, sodium, etc. already calculated, we have included the information with the recipes.

Whether you are a subscriber selecting this book for the easy-to-use format or new to "The Times", we are sure you will have many rewarding microwave experiences as you explore the favorites in this book.

Sincerely,

Janet L. Sadlack

Janet L. Sadlack
Box 1271
Burnsville, MN 55337

P.S. Use the form in the back of this book for ordering our microwave cook books and for subscribing to "The Microwave Times".

Chapter 1

Favorite Recipes from

The Microwave Times

Appetizers & Beverages

Pizza Snacks, page 10, Steak Kabobs, page 6, Spinach Herb Balls, page 6, and Chicken Nuggets, page 7.

Miniature kabobs add a hearty, festive touch to any entertaining.

STEAK KABOBS

2 lbs. boneless sirloin steak
½ cup soy sauce
2 tablespoons honey
2 tablespoons catsup
1 tablespoon vinegar
1 clove garlic, minced
½ teaspoon ginger
1 green pepper, cut into ½-inch pieces

1. Trim fat from meat. Freeze until partially frozen. Cut into very thin slices (⅛-inch thick). Place in 2-quart glass casserole.

2. Combine remaining ingredients, except green pepper, in 2-cup glass measure. Pour over meat. Cover with casserole lid.

3. Refrigerate meat at least 2 hours or overnight, turning meat occasionally to coat with marinade. Remove meat from marinade and thread each strip, accordian-style, on a toothpick. Add a piece of green pepper to each end of the toothpick. Divide kabobs between 2 glass plates. Brush with marinade. Cover with waxed paper.

4. MICROWAVE (high), one plate at a time, 4 to 5 minutes or until meat is no longer pink, rotating plate once. Transfer to serving plate.

About 40 Kabobs

TIPS • If meat freezes solid, let stand at room temperature about 1 hour before slicing.
• Green onion or celery pieces can be substituted for green pepper.

This recipe is especially nice for entertaining because it can be made a day or two in advance.

LIVER PATE

2 slices bacon
8 ozs. chicken livers
1 small onion, chopped
1 clove garlic, minced
¼ cup dry white wine
3 drops Tabasco sauce
¼ cup butter or margarine
¼ teaspoon salt
Parsley

1. Arrange bacon in single layer in 1½-quart glass casserole. Cover with paper towel.

2. MICROWAVE (high) 2 to 3 minutes or until crisp, rotating dish once. Remove bacon from drippings and set aside. Add chicken livers, onion, garlic, white wine and Tabasco sauce to bacon drippings. Cover with plastic wrap.

3. MICROWAVE (high) 9 to 10 minutes or until tender, stirring once. Cool. Process until smooth in blender or food processor.

4. MICROWAVE (high) butter in small glass dish ¼ to ½ minute or until softened. Add to liver mixture along with salt; blend well. Refrigerate overnight or up to 4 days. Crumble bacon. Garnish pâté with parsley and bacon. Serve chilled with crackers.

About 2 Cups Pâté

Toasted sesame seed coats these nutritious appetizers. For added convenience, these appetizers can be prepared ahead and frozen or refrigerated.

SPINACH HERB BALLS

2 tablespoons butter or margarine
1 package (1.87 oz.) sesame seed (about ⅓ cup)
1 package (10 oz.) frozen chopped spinach
1 package (8 oz.) cream cheese
1 cup herb-seasoned bread cubes
1 egg
¼ cup Parmesan cheese
1 teaspoon lemon juice

1. MICROWAVE (high) butter in 12 x 8-inch glass baking dish ½ to 1 minute or until melted. Stir in sesame seed.

2. MICROWAVE (high), uncovered, 5 to 6 minutes or until lightly toasted, stirring every minute. Set aside. Place spinach in 1-quart glass casserole. Cover with casserole lid.

3. MICROWAVE (high) 4 to 5 minutes or until spinach is hot, stirring twice. Drain well.

4. MICROWAVE (high) cream cheese in small bowl ½ to 1 minute or until softened. Stir until smooth; add to spinach. Stir in bread cubes, egg, Parmesan cheese and lemon juice. Form into ½-inch balls. Roll in toasted sesame seed, coating evenly. Arrange in baking dish. Cover with waxed paper.

5. MICROWAVE (high) 4 to 5 minutes or until balls are set, rotating dish once.

About 60 Appetizers

A delightfully spicy bean dip that is served with crisp tortilla chips. Adjust the amount of Tabasco sauce to suit your taste.

TORTILLA CHIP FIESTA

- ½ **lb. ground beef**
- 1 **small onion, chopped**
- 1 **can (16 oz.) refried beans**
- 1 **can (8 oz.) tomato sauce**
- ¼ **cup water**
- ¼ **cup chopped green chilies**
- ⅛ **to ¼ teaspoon Tabasco sauce**
- ½ **teaspoon salt**
- ¼ **teaspoon cumin**
- ¼ **teaspoon pepper**
- 1 **cup (4 ozs.) shredded Cheddar cheese**
- 1 **cup shredded lettuce**
- 1 **small tomato, chopped**
- ¼ **cup sour cream**
- 4 **cups tortilla chips**

1. Crumble ground beef in 1½-quart shallow glass casserole. Add onion.

2. MICROWAVE (high), uncovered, 3 to 3½ minutes or until no longer pink, stirring once. Drain. Stir in beans, tomato sauce, water, green chilies, Tabasco sauce, salt, cumin and pepper.

3. MICROWAVE (high), uncovered, 5 to 6 minutes or until mixture is hot, stirring once. Sprinkle with cheese.

4. MICROWAVE (high), uncovered, 1 to 2 minutes or until cheese is melted. Sprinkle with lettuce and tomato. Spoon sour cream in center and arrange chips around edge. Serve warm.

8 to 10 Servings

Cheese and hot peppers top potatoes for a great tasting snack.

POTATO NACHOS

- 3 **slices bacon**
- 3 **medium potatoes**
- 2 **tablespoons water**
- 1½ **cups (6 ozs.) shredded Cheddar cheese**
- ⅓ **cup sliced jalapeno peppers or ripe olives**

1. Place bacon in single layer on bacon rack or in 10 x 6-inch glass baking dish. Cover with paper towel.

2. MICROWAVE (high) 4 to 5 minutes or until crisp, rotating dish once. Set aside.

3. Scrub potatoes; slice ¼-inch thick. Place in 1½-quart glass casserole. Add water. Cover with casserole lid.

4. MICROWAVE (high) 4 to 5 minutes or until almost tender, stirring once. Remove lid. Then, MICROWAVE (high), uncovered, 2 to 3 minutes or until tender.

5. Arrange potatoes in single layer on 3 glass plates. Top potatoes with cheese and peppers or olives. Crumble bacon and sprinkle over potatoes.

6. MICROWAVE (high), one plate at a time, uncovered, ½ to 1 minute or until cheese is melted, rotating plate once. Serve warm.

About 3 Dozen Snacks
35 Calories Each

Tasty chunks of chicken that are finger-licking good.

CHICKEN NUGGETS

- 1 **whole (16 ozs.) chicken breast, halved**
- ½ **cup mayonnaise or salad dressing**
- 3 **tablespoons milk**
- 1 **teaspoon instant minced onion**
- 2 **teaspoons prepared mustard**
- ¾ **cup cornflake crumbs**
- 2 **tablespoons Parmesan cheese**
- 1 **teaspoon paprika**

1. Place chicken breast, skin-side-up on bacon rack. Cover with waxed paper.

2. MICROWAVE (high) 9 to 10 minutes or until tender, rotating rack once. Uncover and cool. Cut chicken into ¾-inch cubes.

3. Combine mayonnaise, milk, onion and mustard in small glass dish; stir well. Combine cornflake crumbs, Parmesan cheese and paprika in plastic bag. Coat chicken cubes with mayonnaise mixture, drop in cornflake crumb mixture and shake lightly to coat. Place coated chicken in baking dish or on glass tray. Cover with paper towel.

4. MICROWAVE (high) 3 to 4 minutes or until pieces are set, rotating dish once. Serve on toothpicks.

About 45 Nuggets

TIP • Two cups of leftover cubed chicken can be substituted for chicken breast. Omit steps 1 and 2.

This tasty bean dip goes perfectly with tortilla chips, nacho peppers and other south-of-the-border specialties.

FONDUE MEXICANA

- 2 slices bacon
- 1 can (8 oz.) tomato sauce
- 2 cans (16 ozs. each) refried beans
- 2 tablespoons chopped chilies
- ½ teaspoon salt
- ¼ teaspoon coriander
- ¼ teaspoon cumin
- 8 drops Tabasco sauce
- 2 cups (8 ozs.) shredded Cheddar cheese

Dippers:
- Avocado strips
- Tortilla chips
- Nacho peppers (chilies)
- Smoked sausage links
- Cubed cooked chicken

1. MICROWAVE (high) bacon, covered with paper toweling in 1½-quart glass casserole 2 to 3 minutes or until crisp. Set aside bacon. Add tomato sauce and beans to drippings; mix well. Stir in chilies, salt, coriander, cumin and Tabasco sauce. Cover with casserole lid.

2. MICROWAVE (high) 6 to 7 minutes or until heated through, stirring once. Stir in cheese.

3. MICROWAVE (high), uncovered, 2 to 3 minutes or until cheese is melted.

4. Serve over warming candle with dippers for dipping in the warm sauce.

8 to 10 Servings

TIPS • For half a recipe, use a 1-quart casserole and microwave bacon 1 to 1½ minutes. Microwave in step 2 for 3 to 4 minutes and in step 3 for 1 to 2 minutes.
• This fondue sauce freezes well. If necessary after thawing, thin with a little water or tomato juice.

This quick and easy appetizer can be assembled ahead and refrigerated until serving time.

STUFFED CELERY

- 1 package (10 oz.) frozen chopped spinach
- 1 cup sour cream
- 1 package (2 oz.) dry vegetable soup mix
- 36 to 40 pieces celery (about 2-inches each)

1. Place spinach in 1-quart glass casserole. Cover with casserole lid.

2. MICROWAVE (high), 5 to 6 minutes or until tender, stirring twice. Drain well. Stir in sour cream and soup mix. Spread a rounded tablespoon of spinach mixture onto each celery piece. Refrigerate at least 1 hour.

36 to 40 Appetizers

This pizza-flavored fondue goes well with a variety of dippers. A perfect casual snack for decorating, caroling, skating or skiing parties.

PIZZA FONDUE

- 1 can (16 oz.) tomato wedges, undrained
- 1 can (8 oz.) tomato sauce
- 1 can (6 oz.) tomato paste
- 1 jar (16 oz.) pasteurized process cheese spread (Cheese Whiz)
- ⅓ cup red wine
- 1 tablespoon finely chopped onion
- ½ teaspoon oregano leaves
- ¼ teaspoon basil leaves
- ¼ teaspoon garlic salt
- ⅛ teaspoon pepper
- 2 cups (8 ozs.) shredded Cheddar cheese
- 1 cup (4 ozs.) shredded Mozzarella cheese

Dippers:
- Cooked bite-sized meatballs
- Sliced Vienna sausages or smokie link sausages
- Cubed French bread
- Partially cooked cauliflower
- Fresh or canned mushrooms
- Green onions
- Green pepper strips
- Crackers or corn chips

1. Cut tomato wedges into small pieces; place in 2-quart glass casserole. Add tomato sauce and paste, cheese spread, wine, onion, oregano, basil, garlic salt and pepper. Cover with casserole lid.

2. MICROWAVE (high) 10 to 11 minutes or until hot and bubbly, stirring once. Stir in cheeses.

3. MICROWAVE (high), uncovered, 2 to 3 minutes or until cheese is melted. Serve warm with an assortment of dippers.

About 10 Servings

TIP • To Make Ahead, prepare through step 1 and refrigerate. Increase microwave time in step 2 to 12 to 13 minutes.

This makes a festive fondue for special occasion hors d'oeuvre tables.

SEAFOOD FONDUE

½ cup water
1 teaspoon instant chicken bouillon
1 package (8 oz.) cream cheese
¼ cup sour cream
1 tablespoon snipped fresh parsley
1 teaspoon Beau Monde seasoning
⅛ teaspoon pepper
1 cup (4 ozs.) shredded Mozzarella cheese
1 can (7 oz.) tiny broken shrimp, drained and rinsed

Dippers:
  Broccoli
  Carrots
  Cauliflower
  Cherry tomatoes

1. MICROWAVE (high) water in 1-cup glass measure 1 to 1½ minutes or until boiling. Stir in chicken bouillon. Set aside.

2. MICROWAVE (high) cream cheese in 3 to 4-cup glass fondue pot or casserole 1 to 1¼ minutes or until softened, stirring once. Stir until creamy; blend in sour cream. Slowly stir in bouillon mixture. Add parsley, seasoning, pepper, cheese and shrimp; mix lightly.

3. MICROWAVE (high), uncovered, 3 to 4 minutes or until cheese is melted, stirring once or twice. Serve with dippers.

8 to 10 Servings

Give your entertaining an international flavor with this sweet and tangy dipping sauce.

ORIENTAL FONDUE

1 can (8 oz.) crushed pineapple, undrained
1 can (8 oz.) tomato sauce
2 tablespoons flour
2 tablespoons brown sugar
1 tablespoon vinegar
1 tablespoon soy sauce
¼ teaspoon dry mustard

Dippers:
  Fried wonton skins
  Water chestnuts
  Partially cooked pea pods
  Cooked chicken or pork cubes
  Cooked shrimp
  Sauteed tofu cubes

1. Combine pineapple, tomato sauce and flour in 3-cup glass fondue pot or casserole. Stir in brown sugar, vinegar, soy sauce and mustard.

2. MICROWAVE (high), uncovered, 4½ to 5 minutes or until mixture boils and thickens slightly, stirring twice. Serve over warming candle with dippers.

About 6 Servings

TIPS • To heat cooked meats, allow about 1 minute per cup of meat.

• Make your own fried wonton skins by cutting skins in half. Roll each piece around finger, bringing edges across at an angle to form a cone shape; pinch edges together with wet fingers. Fry in hot oil (425°) ½ to 1 minute or until lightly browned. These can be made ahead and then reheated ½ to 1 minute in the microwave.

• To partially cook pea pods, microwave a 9-oz. package frozen pea pods 3 to 4 minutes.

Seafood Fondue.

This is one of our all-time favorites. Pizza flavors top crackers for an easy appetizer.

PIZZA SNACKS

- 1 **cup (4 ozs.) finely chopped Canadian bacon**
- 1 **cup (4 ozs.) shredded Mozzarella cheese**
- ½ **cup (2 ozs.) shredded Cheddar cheese**
- ¼ **cup sliced pimiento-stuffed green olives**
- 2 **tablespoons mayonnaise or salad dressing**
- ½ **teaspoon Italian seasoning**
- 50 **to 60 favorite snack crackers**

1. Combine all ingredients except crackers in 1-quart glass mix 'n pour bowl; mix well. Arrange crackers on three glass serving plates. Spoon a teaspoonful of mixture onto each cracker.

2. MICROWAVE (high) one plate at a time, uncovered, ¾ to 1 minute or until cheese starts to melt, rotating plate once. Serve warm.

50 to 60 Snacks

TIPS • To finely chop Canadian bacon, remove outer layer and process in food processor.

• 1 cup finely chopped ham or other favorite pizza topping can be substituted for Canadian bacon.

• Pizza Snacks can be assembled through step 1 several hours ahead and heated just before serving.

Use a microwave pour bowl or pitcher for heating beverages in the microwave.

OLD-FASHIONED GLOGG

- 2 **cinnamon sticks**
- 10 **cardamom seeds, shelled**
- ½ **teaspoon whole cloves**
- ½ **cup raisins**
- ½ **cup whole or slivered almonds**
- ½ **cup orange marmalade**
- ¼ **cup sugar**
- 1 **cup water**
- 4 **cups dry red wine**
- 1 **cup dry to medium sherry**

1. Place cinnamon sticks, cardamom and cloves on a piece of cheesecloth; wrap and tie securely.

2. Combine raisins, almonds, orange marmalade, sugar and water in 2-quart mix 'n pour bowl. Add wrapped spices.

3. MICROWAVE (high), uncovered, 3½ to 4 minutes or until boiling, stirring once. Stir in wine and sherry.

4. MICROWAVE (high), uncovered, 5 to 6 minutes or until heated. Remove cheesecloth-wrapped spices.

About 10 Servings (6 Cups)

TIPS • For a non-alcoholic drink, substitute cranberry juice for wine and apple juice for sherry.

• To make ahead, prepare through step 3. If mixture has cooled, increase cooking time in step 4 to 8 to 9 minutes.

Fruit and fruit juices are the primary ingredients for this icy punch. The club soda gives it a fizz like soda pop.

FRUIT SLUSH

- 1 **package (10 oz.) frozen sweetened strawberries**
- 3 **ripe bananas**
- 1 **can (6 oz.) frozen pink lemonade concentrate**
- 1 **can (6 oz.) frozen pineapple-orange juice concentrate**
- 3 **cups water**
- 4 **cups (1 quart) club soda**

1. MICROWAVE (high) strawberries in package 1½ to 2 minutes or until slushy.

2. Combine strawberries and bananas in food processor or blender container. Process until smooth. Pour into 3-quart container. Mix in fruit juice concentrates and water. Freeze until slushy, about 4 hours, stirring once or twice.

3. To serve, fill glasses ⅔ full with fruit mixture. Add club soda to fill glasses. Stir to combine, (or combine all of club soda with fruit mixture in punch bowl).

About 3 Quarts
65 Calories/Cup

TIP • Other favorite juice concentrates can be substituted for lemonade and pineapple-orange juice.

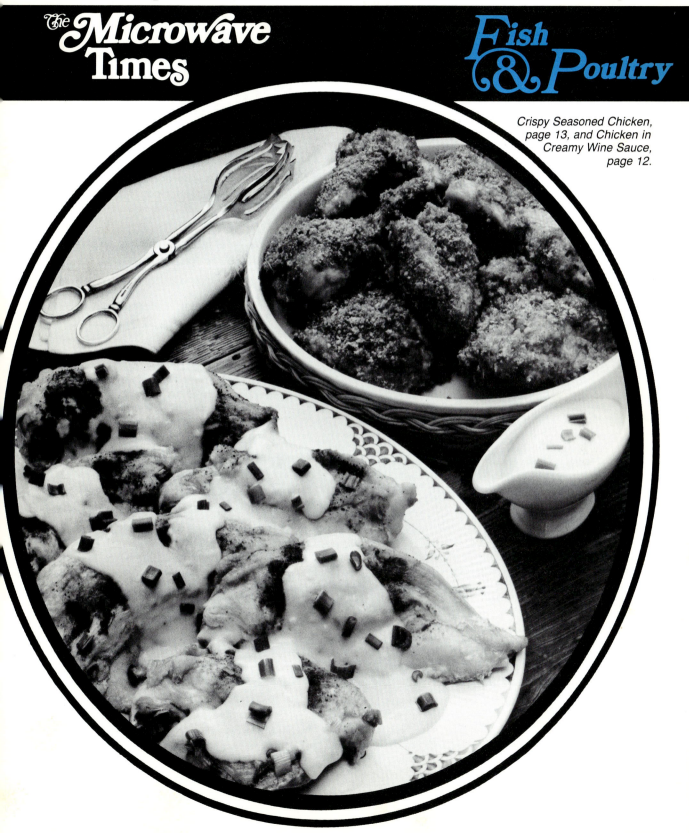

Crispy Seasoned Chicken,
page 13, and Chicken in
Creamy Wine Sauce,
page 12.

Enjoy barbecue flavors year around with this easy-to-fix chicken recipe.

ZESTY BARBECUED CHICKEN

    ¾   cup catsup
    2   tablespoons cornstarch
    3   tablespoons brown sugar
    2   tablespoons vinegar
    2   tablespoons Worcestershire sauce
    1   teaspoon salt
    2   teaspoons prepared mustard
    ½   teaspoon chili powder
    ¼   teaspoon liquid smoke, if desired
    1   small onion, chopped
    1   tablespoon chopped green pepper,
        if desired
 2½ to 3-lb. frying chicken, cut up

1. Combine all ingredients except chicken in 2-cup glass measure.

2. MICROWAVE (high), uncovered, 3 to 3½ minutes or until mixture boils and thickens, stirring once.

3. Arrange chicken skin-side-up in 12 x 8-inch glass baking dish with larger pieces toward edge and smaller pieces in center. Spoon sauce over chicken. Cover with waxed paper.

4. MICROWAVE (high) 25 to 30 minutes or until chicken is tender, rotating dish once.

4 to 6 Servings

TIP • With Combination Oven, in step 4, omit waxed paper covering and microwave-bake at 375° for 25 to 30 minutes.

This low-calorie main dish combines lots of flavor with convenience.

CHICKEN AND CANTONESE VEGETABLES

    1   whole chicken breast, split (about
        16 ozs.)
    1   package (10 oz.) frozen Chinese
        or Japanese-style vegetables
    ¼   cup water
    1   tablespoon soy sauce
    1   teaspoon cornstarch
    ½   teaspoon instant chicken bouillon

1. Arrange chicken breast in 8-inch square glass baking dish. Cover with waxed paper.

2. MICROWAVE (high) 7 to 7½ minutes or until chicken is tender, rotating dish once. Cool enough to handle. Cut meat into bite-sized pieces; set aside. Place vegetables with

sauce or flavoring packet in 1-quart glass casserole. Add water, soy sauce, cornstarch and chicken bouillon; mix lightly. Cover with casserole lid.

3. MICROWAVE (high) 4½ to 5 minutes or until vegetables are just about tender, stirring twice. Add chicken, stirring lightly to coat. Cover.

4. MICROWAVE (high) 2 to 3 minutes or until heated through, stirring once.

About 4 Servings

TIP • 1½ cups leftover cooked chicken or turkey can be used for cooked chicken breast.

A white wine sauce transforms chicken into an elegant company entree.

CHICKEN IN CREAMY WINE SAUCE

    3   whole chicken breasts, split
        (about 3 lbs.)
    1   teaspoon paprika
    ½   teaspoon salt
    ¼   teaspoon pepper
    4   green onions, sliced (reserve tops)
    ½   cup white wine
    3   tablespoons butter or margarine
    ¼   cup unsifted all-purpose flour
    ½   teaspoon salt
    1   cup light cream or milk

1. Arrange chicken skin-side-up in 12 x 8-inch glass baking dish; sprinkle with paprika, salt, pepper and green onions. Pour wine into dish. Cover with waxed paper.

2. MICROWAVE (high) 18 to 20 minutes or until tender, rotating dish twice. Set aside.

3. MICROWAVE (high) butter in 1-quart glass mix 'n pour bowl ½ to 1 minute or until melted; stir in flour and salt. Add pan drippings from chicken; mix well. Stir in cream.

4. MICROWAVE (high), uncovered, 6 to 7 minutes or until mixture boils and thickens, stirring once or twice during last half of cooking. Pour over chicken.

5. MICROWAVE (high), uncovered, 2 to 3 minutes or until heated through. If desired, garnish with sliced green onion tops.

About 6 Servings

This favorite recipe of one of our staff is reminiscent of old-fashioned chicken and dumplings.

CHICKEN WITH DUMPLINGS

- 1 small onion, sliced
- 1 cup sliced carrots
- 2 to 3-lb. frying chicken, cut up
- 1 can (10¾ oz.) condensed cream of chicken soup
  Water
- ½ teaspoon salt
- ⅛ teaspoon pepper
- 1 cup buttermilk baking mix
- ⅓ cup milk
  Parsley, if desired

1. Arrange onion and carrot slices in bottom of 12 x 8-inch glass baking dish. Arrange chicken skin-side-up over vegetables. Cover with waxed paper.

2. MICROWAVE (high) 20 to 25 minutes or until tender, rotating dish once. Remove chicken from juices to cool. Remove chicken from bones and cut into bite-sized pieces.

3. Combine carrots, onion and soup in 2-quart glass casserole. Pour juices from chicken into soup can; add enough water to fill can. Add to vegetables. Stir in salt and pepper. Cover with casserole lid.

4. MICROWAVE (high) 6 to 7 minutes or until mixture boils, stirring once. Stir in chicken.

5. Meanwhile, prepare dumplings by combining baking mix and milk in small mixing bowl. Stir just until combined. Drop tablespoonsful onto hot chicken mixture, leaving center area open. Cover with casserole lid.

6. MICROWAVE (high) 4 to 5 minutes or until dumplings are no longer doughy, rotating dish once. If desired, garnish with fresh parsley.

About 6 Servings
360 Calories Each

This chicken is so crisp and crunchy, it is sure to be a family favorite.

CRISPY SEASONED CHICKEN

- 1 egg
- 2 tablespoons milk
- 1 cup crushed herb-seasoned bread stuffing
- ½ cup Parmesan cheese
- 1 teaspoon paprika
- 3 to 3½-lb. frying chicken, cut up

1. Beat egg and milk together; set aside. Combine crushed stuffing, Parmesan cheese and paprika. Dip chicken pieces into egg; roll in crumb mixture. Arrange skin-side-up in 12 x 8-inch glass baking dish. Cover with paper towel.

2. MICROWAVE (high), uncovered, 25 to 30 minutes or until chicken is done, rotating dish once.

4 to 6 Servings

For smaller family gatherings, capon is ideal. After microwaving, finish it on the grill.

BARBECUED CAPON

- 7 to 8-lb. capon
- 1 medium onion, chopped
- 1 cup finely chopped fresh mushrooms
- ½ cup chopped celery
- ¼ cup butter or margarine
- 4 cups cubed bread
- 1 teaspoon poultry seasoning
- ¼ teaspoon oregano leaves
- ½ teaspoon salt

1. Thaw bird completely. Wash and set aside giblets to use as desired. Let bird drain while preparing stuffing.

2. Combine onion, mushrooms, celery and butter in 2-quart glass mix 'n pour bowl.

3. MICROWAVE (high), uncovered, 4 to 5 minutes or until vegetables are just about tender, stirring once. Stir in bread, poultry seasoning, oregano and salt; mix well.

4. Sprinkle cavity of bird with salt and pepper. Stuff main cavity with stuffing. Secure opening with toothpicks, skewers or thread.

5. Place bird breast-side-down on bacon/meat rack. Cover with a loose tent of waxed paper.

6. MICROWAVE (high) 15 minutes. Turn bird breast-side-up. Cover with waxed paper.

7. MICROWAVE (high) 20 to 25 minutes or until bird is just about cooked. Place bird breast-side-up on grill about 5 inches above hot coals. Cover grill.

8. GRILL 25 to 30 minutes or until thigh joints can be moved easily (about 170° in thigh). Let stand covered 10 to 15 minutes before slicing.

6 to 8 Servings

TIPS • For other sizes of capon, allow 5 minutes microwave time per lb. of bird.
• A 4-oz. can mushroom pieces, drained can be substituted for fresh mushrooms.

The best turkey we've tasted combines the microwave oven with the covered grill

MICRO-BARBECUED TURKEY

1. Select a 10 to 14 lb. turkey. Thaw completely. Remove giblets and use as desired. Rinse turkey; pat dry. Sprinkle cavity with salt and pepper. Fill cavity with favorite stuffing or add 1 to 2 apples, peeled and quartered, and 1 medium onion, quartered, to cavity. Sew opening closed. Tie wings to body and legs together with string.

2. Wrap tips of wings and legs with foil to prevent overcooking. Place turkey breast-side-down in microwave roasting pan or baking dish. Cover with waxed paper.

3. MICROWAVE (high) 25 to 35 minutes (2½ minutes per lb.), rotating dish once. Turn turkey breast-side-up; remove foil and release string on legs. Cover with waxed paper.

4. MICROWAVE (high) 25 to 35 minutes (2½ minutes per lb.), rotating dish once.

5. Place turkey breast-side-up over hot coals on covered grill. Cover grill.

6. GRILL 45 to 60 minutes or until meat is tender (thermometer registers 165° in breast), turning turkey over once. Let stand 20 to 25 minutes before slicing.

10 to 15 Servings

TIP • In step 6, turkey can also be completed in 375° oven for 45 to 60 minutes.

Cornish hens marinate in a soy-flavored sauce before they are microwaved. The grill is used to complete the cooking.

TERIYAKI CORNISH HENS

    4 (16 to 18 ozs. each) Cornish hens, thawed
½ cup soy sauce
¼ cup honey
¼ teaspoon ground ginger
1 clove garlic, minced
    Wild and White Rice Stuffing

1. Remove giblets and neck from each hen. Wash hens; pat dry. Place in plastic bag; set bag in shallow baking dish. Combine soy sauce, honey, ginger and garlic; mix well. Pour over hens, turning to coat evenly. Close bag; refrigerate overnight, turning hens once or twice to marinate evenly.

2. Prepare Rice Stuffing; cool and refrigerate.

3. Remove hens from marinade; place on bacon-meat rack. Spoon ½ to ¾ cup rice mixture into cavity of each hen. Secure openings with toothpicks. Place hens evenly on rack breast-side-down. Cover with waxed paper.

4. MICROWAVE (high) 20 to 22 minutes or until just about done, turning hens breast-side-up halfway through cooking time.

5. Transfer hens to grill, about 5 inches above hot coals. Brush with marinade; cover grill.

6. GRILL 12 to 15 minutes or until hens are nicely browned and tender, turning if necessary and brushing occasionally with additional marinade. Heat remaining rice by microwaving (high) 2½ to 3 minutes. Place rice on serving plate; top with hens.

About 4 Servings

TIPS • If you do not have a covered grill, you can improvise by placing a tent of foil over the hens to hold in the heat. It may be necessary to turn more frequently to prevent overbrowning.
  • Hens can also be baked in 400° oven for 15 to 20 minutes in step 6.

This makes a nice stuffing for Cornish hens, but is also good served as a side dish with other poultry or meats.

WILD AND WHITE RICE STUFFING

    1 package (6 oz.) white and wild rice mix
2⅓ cups water
    1 tablespoon butter or margarine
    1 cup (4 ozs.) sliced fresh mushrooms
¼ cup chopped walnuts, if desired

1. Combine rice, seasoning packet, water, butter and mushrooms in 1½-quart glass casserole. Cover with casserole lid.

2. MICROWAVE (high) 7 to 8 minutes or until mixture boils. Then, MICROWAVE (low — 30%) 25 to 28 minutes or until rice is tender and most of the liquid is absorbed. Stir in walnuts.

About 4½ Cups

TIP • With Full Power, let mixture stand 10 minutes after coming to a boil in step 2. Then microwave 5 minutes, let stand 10 minutes and microwave 3 to 5 additional minutes.

Colorful Pacific salmon steaks team with asparagus spears for an attractive entree. It is sure to bring back the delicate, mellow flavor of freshly caught salmon from the Pacific.

ASPARAGUS-TOPPED PACIFIC SALMON

   8 ozs. fresh asparagus
   1 tablespoon water
   4 fresh salmon steaks, cut 1-inch thick
      (about 2 lbs. total)
   ½ cup sour cream
   ¼ cup mayonnaise
   2 tablespoons white wine, if desired
    Salt
    Dill weed

1. Wash asparagus; break off and discard tough portion of stalk. Place asparagus spears in shallow 1-quart glass casserole. Add water. Cover with casserole lid.

2. MICROWAVE (high) 3 minutes. Let stand covered.

3. Arrange salmon in single layer in shallow glass baking dish with narrow ends of steaks toward center of dish. Cover with plastic wrap.

4. MICROWAVE (high) 6 to 7 minutes or until fish flakes apart easily, rotating dish once. Set aside.

5. Return asparagus to oven and MICROWAVE (high) 1 to 2 minutes or until tender. Drain.

6. Combine sour cream, mayonnaise and wine, mixing well. Arrange asparagus spears on salmon steaks. Sprinkle with salt. Spoon sauce onto asparagus. Sprinkle with dill weed.

7. MICROWAVE (high), uncovered 1 to 2 minutes or until heated through.

About 4 Servings

TIPS • A 9-oz. package frozen asparagus spears can be substituted for fresh. Microwave (high) in paper package 6 to 7 minutes or until tender. Then drain and use in step 6 as directed.

• For half a recipe, microwave in step 2 for about 1½ minutes, in step 4 for about 3 minutes, step 5 for about 1 minute and step 7 for about 1 minute. It is advisable with these smaller quantities to allow the foods to stand 1 to 2 minutes about halfway through the cooking time in steps 2 and 4.

Asparagus-Topped Pacific Salmon.

A quick hollandaise sauce and asparagus spears dress up salmon. Individual loaves are microwaved in custard cups and then removed from cups for serving.

INDIVIDUAL SALMON LOAVES

- 1 **can (15½ oz.) salmon, drained**
- 1 **egg**
- 1 **cup soft bread cubes**
- ⅓ **cup milk**
- 2 **tablespoons finely chopped onion**
- 1 **tablespoon lemon juice**
- ¼ **teaspoon salt**
- **Dash pepper**
- 1 **package (10 oz.) cut asparagus or spears**

Sauce:
- ½ **cup mayonnaise**
- 1 **egg**
- 1 **tablespoon lemon juice**
- ¼ **teaspoon tarragon leaves**
- ¼ **teaspoon prepared mustard**

1. Combine salmon and egg in mixing bowl; mix with fork. Stir in bread, milk, onion, lemon, salt and pepper; mix well. Spoon evenly into 4 or 5 five-oz. glass custard cups. Press firmly into cups. Place cups on glass plate or tray for ease in transferring to oven. Cover with waxed paper.

2. MICROWAVE (high) 5½ to 6 minutes or until center of loaves are set, rotating plate once. Let stand covered while preparing asparagus and sauce.

3. MICROWAVE (high) asparagus in package 5 to 6 minutes or until tender. Set aside.

4. Beat together mayonnaise and egg with fork in 1-cup glass measure. Mix in lemon juice, tarragon and mustard.

5. MICROWAVE (medium — 50%), uncovered, 1¼ to 1½ minutes or until slightly thickened, stirring twice.

6. Unmold salmon onto serving plate. Arrange asparagus in center of or around salmon. Spoon sauce over salmon and asparagus.

7. MICROWAVE (high), uncovered, 1 to 2 minutes or until heated through.

4 to 5 Servings

TIPS • Salmon loaves can be made ahead and refrigerated 1 to 2 days. Increase microwave time in step 2 to 7 to 7½ minutes.

If cooking only half the loaves, decrease the time to 3 to 4 minutes.

• With Full Power, microwave in step 5 for 30 to 45 seconds, stirring 3 to 4 times.

• A 15-oz. can cut asparagus, drained, can be substituted for frozen. In step 3, microwave asparagus 2 minutes before arranging with salmon loaves.

The microwave is ideal for steam-cooking fish and this Rocky Mountain trout is no exception. A lightly seasoned stuffing enhances the mild fresh water fish flavor.

STUFFED MOUNTAIN TROUT

- 2 **tablespoons butter or margarine**
- 2 **tablespoons chopped onion**
- ¼ **cup chopped celery**
- 1 **cup chopped fresh mushrooms**
- 1 **cup soft bread cubes (about 1½ slices)**
- ½ **teaspoon salt**
- ¼ **teaspoon thyme leaves**
- **Dash pepper**
- 2 **teaspoons lemon juice**
- 2½ **to 3 lbs. dressed rainbow trout (4 to 6 trout**

1. Combine butter, onion, celery and mushrooms in glass mixing bowl.

2. MICROWAVE (high), uncovered, 2½ to 3 minutes or until vegetables are just about tender. Stir in bread cubes, salt, thyme, pepper and lemon juice.

3. Arrange trout in 12 x 8-inch glass baking dish or other shallow microwave baking dish. Spoon stuffing into each trout cavity. Cover with waxed paper.

4. MICROWAVE (high) 9 to 11 minutes or until fish flakes apart easily, rotating dish once or twice. Let stand a few minutes before serving.

4 to 6 Servings

TIPS • To halve recipe, microwave in step 2 for 1 to 1½ minutes and in step 4 microwave 4½ to 5 minutes. Also in step 4, allow a 1 to 2-minute standing time about halfway through the microwave time.

• Since trout vary in size and weight, it is important to consider the total weight when determining the cooking time. Generally, allow about 4 minutes per lb.

For optimum cooking of the salmon mixture, the ingredients are stirred part way through the cooking time. The Florentine-type topping makes it extra special and nutritious.

SALMON LOAF FLORENTINE

   1 package (10 oz.) frozen chopped
       spinach
   1 can (15½ oz.) salmon, drained and
       flaked
   3 slices bread, crumbled
   2 eggs
   ½ cup milk
   ½ teaspoon salt
   ⅛ teaspoon pepper
   1 tablespoon lemon juice
   ¼ cup sour cream
   ¼ cup mayonnaise or salad dressing
   1 egg
   ¼ teaspoon seasoned salt
       Dash Tabasco sauce

1. MICROWAVE (high) spinach in package 4½ to 5 minutes or until completely thawed. Drain and set aside.

2. Combine salmon, bread, 2 eggs, the milk, salt and pepper until thoroughly mixed. Stir in lemon juice.

3. Spoon into 8 or 9-inch round glass cake dish, spreading evenly. Cover with waxed paper.

4. MICROWAVE (high) 3 minutes. Stir lightly; spread evenly in dish. Cover.

5. MICROWAVE (high) 2½ to 3 minutes or until just about set.

6. Combine spinach with sour cream, mayonnaise, 1 egg, the seasoned salt and Tabasco sauce. Spoon onto salmon loaf, spreading evenly. Cover with waxed paper.

7. MICROWAVE (high) 3 to 4 minutes or until topping is just about to set, rotating dish once.

About 6 Servings

Salmon Loaf Florentine.

Shrimp and vegetables in a savory sauce are prepared to perfection in the microwave. Cooking times are kept short so the shrimp remain tender and the vegetables retain their tender-crispness.

ORIENTAL SCAMPI

¼ **cup butter or margarine**
2 **cups sliced fresh mushrooms**
¼ **cup sliced green onions**
1 **clove garlic, minced**
1 **tablespoon arrowroot or 2 tablespoons cornstarch**
2 **tablespoons soy sauce**
½ **teaspoon salt**
12 **ozs. frozen uncooked shrimp**
1 **package (6 oz.) frozen pea pods**
1 **cup fresh bean sprouts**

1. Combine butter, mushrooms, green onions and garlic in 1½-quart glass casserole.

2. MICROWAVE (high), uncovered, 2 to 3 minutes or until vegetables are just about tender. Stir in arrowroot, soy sauce, salt and shrimp. Cover with casserole lid.

3. MICROWAVE (high) 5 to 6 minutes or until shrimp are no longer icy, stirring once. Run warm water over pea pods until separated. Stir in pea pods and bean sprouts. Cover.

4. MICROWAVE (high) 6 to 7 minutes or until vegetables are tender and shrimp are firm, stirring once or twice. If desired, serve over rice.

5 to 6 Servings

This recipe was shared by one of our readers. We found it super easy and very good tasting.

NO HASSLE BAKED FISH

⅓ **cup butter or margarine**
¾ **cup fresh bread crumbs (about 2 slices)**
¾ **cup cracker crumbs (about 20 squares)**
1 **lb. frozen perch fillets, thawed**
Salt and pepper
⅔ **cup milk**

1. MICROWAVE (high) butter in 8-inch square glass baking dish 1 to 1½ minutes or until melted. Stir in bread crumbs and cracker crumbs; mix well. Remove about half of crumbs.

2. Arrange fish in even layer over crumbs. Sprinkle with salt and pepper. Top with remaining crumbs. Pour milk evenly over crumbs. Cover with paper towel.

3. MICROWAVE (high) 7 to 8 minutes or until fish flakes apart easily.

4 to 5 Servings

TIP • Other favorite fresh or salt water fish fillets can be used.

Fish usually requires 4 minutes microwave cooking per pound. In this recipe, the time is increased because of the addition of the sauce.

SOLE FLORENTINE

1 **package (10 oz.) frozen chopped spinach**
12 **ozs. sole or other favorite fish fillets**
1 **cup milk**
2 **tablespoons flour**
1 **teaspoon salt**
½ **teaspoon tarragon leaves**
2 **tablespoons butter or margarine**
1 **tablespoon lemon juice**
¼ **cup Parmesan cheese**
Paprika

1. MICROWAVE (high) spinach in package 5 to 6 minutes or until thawed; drain. Arrange in 8-inch round glass baking dish. Arrange fillets on spinach. Set aside.

2. Combine milk, flour, salt and tarragon; mix well. Add butter.

3. MICROWAVE (high), uncovered, 3 to 4 minutes or until mixture boils and thickens, stirring twice during last half of cooking time. Stir in lemon juice; pour over fillets. Sprinkle with Parmesan cheese and paprika. Cover with waxed paper.

4. MICROWAVE (high) 5 to 6 minutes or until fish flakes apart easily with fork, rotating dish once.

About 4 Servings

TIP • The spinach can be thawed and sauce prepared several hours ahead. Assemble with fish just before cooking and serving.

This favorite was part of an economy meals feature. Utilize older bread for the toasted bread cubes that add color and crunch to the milk poached fish.

FISH DIVINE

- 2 tablespoons butter or margarine
- 2 slices bread, cubed
- 2 tablespoons Parmesan cheese
- 1 teaspoon parsley flakes
- ¼ teaspoon garlic salt
- 1 lb. frozen fish fillets, thawed (cod, perch, halibut or flounder)
- ½ teaspoon salt
  Dash pepper
- ¼ teaspoon tarragon leaves
- ¼ cup light cream

1. MICROWAVE butter in 9-inch glass pie plate ½ to 1 minute or until melted. Add bread cubes; stir to coat evenly with butter. Stir in Parmesan cheese, parsley and garlic salt.

2. MICROWAVE (high), uncovered, 4 to 5 minutes or until bread is dry and lightly toasted, stirring 3 or 4 times. Cool.

3. Arrange fillets in 8-inch round glass serving dish, rolling up fillets as necessary to fit dish. Sprinkle with salt, pepper and tarragon. Pour cream evenly over fillets. Cover with waxed paper.

4. MICROWAVE (high) 4 to 4½ minutes or until fish flakes apart easily with fork. Crush bread cubes with fork. Sprinkle over fillets.

About 5 Servings

TIPS • To thaw frozen fish, place wrapped fish in microwave and microwave (low—30%) about 8 minutes or until partially thawed. Separate fillets into serving pieces and rinse with cold water. Place on paper toweling and microwave (low — 30%) 1 to 3 minutes or until thawed.

• If tarragon is not a common herb on your shelf, use dill weed or other favorite fish seasoning.

• If you don't keep light cream on hand, substitute 3 tablespoons milk and 1 tablespoon melted butter.

Serve this favorite with wild rice and parsley buttered carrots for an extra special meal.

SEAFOOD SUPREME

- 1 cup water
- 1 teaspoon instant chicken bouillon
- 1 bay leaf
- 1 clove garlic, halved
- 1 medium onion, sliced
- 1 stalk celery with leaves, sliced
- 2 sprigs parsley
- 5 peppercorns
- 1 carrot, peeled and cut into 1-inch pieces
- 8 ozs. frozen uncooked shrimp
- 8 ozs. frozen bay scallops
- ⅓ cup unsifted all-purpose flour
- ½ teaspoon salt
- ½ cup whipping or light cream
- ¼ cup butter or margarine
- 1 teaspoon lemon juice
  Parsley

1. Combine water, bouillon, bay leaf, garlic, onion, celery, parsley, peppercorns and carrot in 1½-quart glass casserole. Cover with casserole lid.

2. MICROWAVE (high) 7 to 8 minutes or until vegetables are tender. Remove vegetables from liquid with slotted spoon; discard vegetables. Add shrimp and scallops to liquid. Cover.

3. MICROWAVE (high) 5 to 6 minutes or until seafood is opaque, stirring once. Set aside.

4. Combine flour and salt in 4-cup glass measure. Stir in cream. Drain liquid from shrimp and scallops into flour mixture; mix well. Add butter.

5. MICROWAVE (high), uncovered, 4 to 5 minutes or until mixture thickens and boils, stirring 2 or 3 times.

6. Stir in lemon juice. Add sauce to shrimp and scallops; mix lightly. Divide mixture among 5 or 6 shells; sprinkle with parsley.

7. MICROWAVE (high), uncovered, 1 to 2 minutes or until heated through.

About 5 Servings
275 Calories Each

TIPS • If using sea scallops, cut into ½-inch pieces.

• Mixture is also good served over rice.

If you like seafood and soup, you are sure to enjoy this hearty combination.

LOUISIANA GUMBO

- 1 package (10 oz.) frozen cut okra
- 3 tablespoons butter or margarine
- ½ cup chopped onion
- ½ cup chopped green pepper
- ½ cup chopped celery
- 1 clove garlic, minced
- 1 can (16 oz.) tomatoes, undrained
- 1 can (14 oz.) chicken broth
- 1 teaspoon sugar
- ⅛ teaspoon pepper
- ⅛ teaspoon thyme leaves
- 1 small bay leaf
- 10 ozs. frozen cooked shrimp, thawed
- 1 can (8 oz.) oysters, drained

1. MICROWAVE (high) okra in package 4 to 5 minutes or until hot; set aside.

2. Combine butter, onion, green pepper, celery and garlic in 2-quart glass casserole. Cover with casserole lid.

3. MICROWAVE (high) 6 to 7 minutes or until vegetables are tender. Add undrained okra, tomatoes (cut into pieces), broth, sugar, pepper, thyme and bay leaf. Cover.

4. MICROWAVE (high) 6 to 7 minutes or until mixture boils. Add shrimp and oysters; cover.

5. MICROWAVE (high) 3 to 4 minutes or until mixture is steaming hot and seafood is heated. Remove bay leaf. Serve by placing spoonfuls of cooked rice in each serving bowl; fill bowls with gumbo.

About 6 Servings

TIPS • If desired, substitute 1 cup sliced fresh okra for the frozen. In step 1, precook the okra with ¼ cup water in a covered casserole 6 to 7 minutes.

• Fresh shrimp and oysters can be used. Use about 8 ozs. each shrimp and oysters. Increase microwave time in step 5 to 9 to 10 minutes or until the seafood is done.

This delectable stew features chunks of fish and shrimp. Select a firm-textured fish so the pieces will retain their shape.

BOUILLABAISSE

- 1 medium onion, chopped
- 1 clove garlic, minced
- 1 tablespoon oil
- 1 can (28 oz.) whole tomatoes, undrained
- 1 bay leaf
- 1 teaspoon instant chicken bouillon
- ½ teaspoon salt
- ½ teaspoon thyme leaves
- ⅛ teaspoon ground allspice, if desired
- 6 drops Tabasco sauce
- 1 lb. fish fillets (red snapper, turbot or pike)
- 6 ozs. frozen uncooked shrimp
- 3 tablespoons snipped parsley
- 3 lemon slices

1. Combine onion, garlic and oil in 2-quart glass casserole.

2. MICROWAVE (high), uncovered, 3 to 4 minutes or until tender, stirring once.

3. Stir in tomatoes, bay leaf, bouillon, salt, thyme, allspice and Tabasco sauce.

4. MICROWAVE (high), uncovered, 13 to 15 minutes or until flavors are blended, stirring once.

5. Cut fish fillets into 1-inch pieces. Add fish and shrimp to tomato mixture. Cover.

6. MICROWAVE (high) 7 to 7½ minutes or until fish flakes apart easily and shrimp are firm, stirring twice. Remove bay leaf. Garnish with parsley and lemon slices.

5 to 6 Servings

TIPS • Other favorite seafoods can be combined with fish. Crab, lobster or clams are delicious. For added interest leave them in the shell.

• Frozen cooked shrimp can be substituted for uncooked. Timing will be very similar.

Pork Chops and Dressing, page 34.

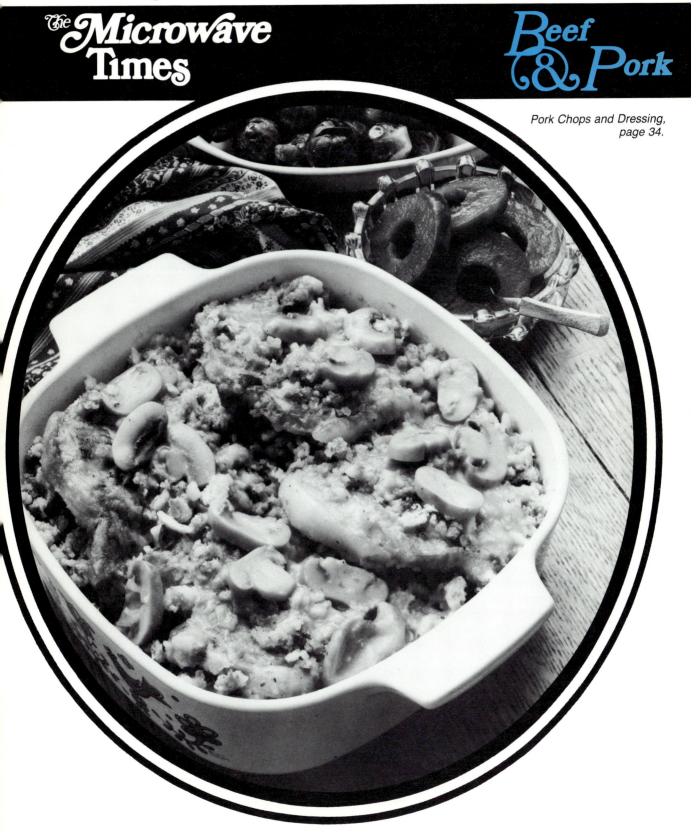

This meat loaf recipe was shared by one of our readers. She found it to be well received when doing microwave demonstrations.

BEEF & PORK MEAT LOAF

- 1 lb. ground beef
- ½ lb. ground pork
- 1 envelope dry onion soup mix
- 1 slice bread, crumbled
- 1 egg
- ¼ cup tomato juice or milk

1. Combine all ingredients in large mixing bowl; mix thoroughly. Press evenly into 8 x 4-inch plastic or glass loaf dish. Cover with paper towel.

2. MICROWAVE (medium-high — 70%) 8 minutes. Drain fat; cover.

3. MICROWAVE (medium-high — 70%) 6 to 8 minutes or until no longer pink in center (160°), rotating dish once. Let stand 5 minutes. Remove from pan; slice and serve.

About 6 Servings

TIPS • All ground beef can be used if desired.
• With full power, microwave in steps 2 and 3 for a total of 14 to 16 minutes, rotating dish 3 or 4 times.
• With Combination Oven, microwave-bake at 350° for 20 to 22 minutes.

This easy, dependable meat loaf is perked up with an Italian accent.

ITALIAN MEAT LOAF

- 1 can (8 oz.) tomato sauce
- ½ teaspoon sugar
- ½ teaspoon Italian seasoning
- ¼ teaspoon garlic powder
- 1½ lbs. ground beef
- ½ cup fine bread crumbs (½ slice)
- 1 small onion, finely chopped
- ½ teaspoon salt
- ¼ teaspoon pepper
- 1 egg
- ½ cup (2 ozs.) shredded Mozzarella cheese

1. Combine tomato sauce, sugar, Italian seasoning and garlic powder to make a sauce. Set aside.

2. Combine meat, bread crumbs, onion, salt, pepper, egg and ½ cup of sauce; mix well. Press into 8 x 4 or 9 x 5-inch plastic or glass loaf dish. Cover with waxed paper.

3. MICROWAVE (high) 13 to 15 minutes or until just about set in center, rotating dish twice.

4. Drain meat loaf and transfer to serving tray. Spoon remaining sauce over meat loaf; sprinkle with cheese.

5. MICROWAVE (high), uncovered, 1 to 1½ minutes or until cheese begins to melt.

5 to 6 Servings
485 Calories Each

Hash browns are rolled inside of a meat mixture for these interesting rolls that were part of an "economy meals" feature.

BEEF ROLLS

- 1 package (12 oz.) frozen hash browns (2 patties)
- 1 lb. ground beef
- 1 egg
- 1 small onion, chopped
- ¼ cup dry bread crumbs
- ¼ cup milk
- 1 teaspoon salt
- 1 teaspoon Worcestershire sauce
- ¼ teaspoon pepper
- ¼ teaspoon sage
- ½ teaspoon seasoned salt
- ½ cup catsup or chili sauce

1. MICROWAVE (high) hash browns in paper package 5 to 6 minutes or until steaming hot, turning package over once. Set aside.

2. Combine ground beef, egg, onion, bread crumbs, milk, salt, Worcestershire sauce, pepper and sage in mixing bowl. Mix until combined.

3. Place meat between 2 pieces of waxed paper; roll or pat into a 12 x 8-inch rectangle. Break apart hash browns and spread evenly over meat; sprinkle with seasoned salt. Roll up as you would jelly roll, starting with 12-inch side and lifting the waxed paper to help roll meat. Seal edges. Cut into eight 1½-inch slices. Place slices cut-side-down on bacon or meat rack. Cover with waxed paper.

4. MICROWAVE (high) 7 to 8 minutes or until meat is no longer pink, rotating dish once or twice. Top each roll with about a tablespoon of catsup.

About 8 Servings

TIP • Two large potatoes, peeled and shredded, can be substituted for frozen hash browns. Rinse shredded potatoes well and microwave as directed in step 1 in covered glass casserole, stirring once.

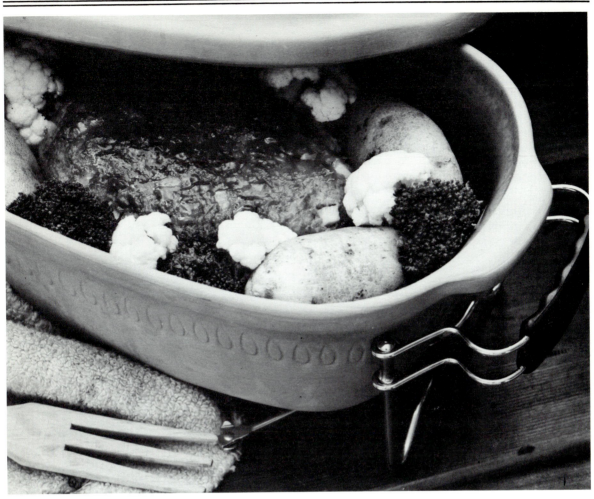

Meat Loaf Dinner.

Meat loaf, potatoes and vegetable combine in a simmer pot for a simple to cook, easy to clean up meal.

MEAT LOAF DINNER

1	lb. ground beef
⅓	cup dry bread crumbs
1	small onion, chopped
¼	cup milk
¼	cup catsup
1	egg
½	teaspoon salt
⅛	teaspoon pepper
4	medium baking potatoes, washed
1	tablespoon brown sugar
1	tablespoon catsup
¼	teaspoon prepared mustard
3	cups fresh broccoli and/or cauliflower pieces

1. Presoak 2-quart clay simmer pot and lid 10 minutes. Combine ground beef, bread crumbs, onion, milk, ¼ cup catsup, the egg, salt and pepper; mix well.

2. Spoon mixture into center of simmer pot. Form into a loaf, about 5½ x 3 inches. Arrange potatoes in corners of simmer pot. Cover with simmer pot lid.

3. MICROWAVE (high) 16 to 18 minutes or until meat and potatoes are just about done. Turn potatoes over. Combine brown sugar, catsup and mustard. Spoon onto meat loaf. Place vegetables around loaf. Cover.

4. MICROWAVE (high) 6 to 7 minutes or until vegetables are tender. Slice meat loaf; serve from simmer pot or transfer to serving platter.

About 4 Servings

TIP • A 3-quart glass casserole can be substituted for simmer pot. Prepare as directed, rotating dish twice in step 3 and once in step 4.

Incredibly delicious! The zucchini is the secret ingredient in these basic meatballs.

ZUCCHINI MEATBALLS IN SOUR CREAM SAUCE

- 1 lb. ground beef
- 1 small onion, chopped
- 1 egg
- ⅓ cup dry bread crumbs
- 1½ cups shredded, unpeeled zucchini
- ¾ teaspoon salt
- ⅛ teaspoon pepper

Sauce:
- 1 can (10¾ oz.) condensed cream of chicken soup
- ⅓ cup sour cream
- ¼ cup milk
- Dash nutmeg

1. Combine ground beef, onion, egg, bread crumbs, zucchini, salt and pepper; mix well. form into 24 meatballs, about 1½ inches in size. Arrange in 8 or 9-inch round glass baking dish. Cover with paper towel.

2. MICROWAVE (high) 6 to 7 minutes or until meat is set, rotating dish once. Drain fat. Mix together sauce ingredients; pour over meatballs. Cover with waxed paper.

3. MICROWAVE (high) 5 to 6 minutes or until hot and bubbly, rotating dish once.

4 to 5 Servings

TIP • One reader suggests making extra meatballs when zucchini is plentiful. After cooking in step 2, she freezes them. Then, to serve she simply thaws them, adds sauce and heats.

Sauerkraut hidden in the center of these meatballs adds flavor and reduces calories.

SAUERKRAUT BALLS

- 1 cup (8 ozs.) sauerkraut, drained
- 1 teaspoon brown sugar
- ½ teaspoon caraway seed
- 1 lb. ground beef
- 1 egg
- 1 slice fresh bread, crumbled
- ¼ cup chopped onion
- 2 tablespoons milk
- ¼ teaspoon garlic salt
- ⅛ teaspoon pepper
- 1½ tablespoons natural meat browning and seasoning powder

1. Combine sauerkraut, brown sugar and caraway seed in small mixing bowl. Toss until combined; set aside.

2. Combine ground beef, egg, bread, onion, milk, garlic salt and pepper; mix well. Flatten 1-inch balls of meat mixture into patties. Place 1½ tablespoons of sauerkraut mixture on each patty. Shape meat around sauerkraut forming 12 meatballs. Roll each meatball in browning powder. Arrange in 8-inch round glass or plastic baking dish. Cover with waxed paper.

3. MICROWAVE (high) 5 to 6 minutes or until meat is set, rotating dish once.

About 12 Meatballs
120 Calories Each

TIP • With Combination Oven, omit browning powder. Microwave-bake, uncovered, in preheated 375° oven 8 to 10 minutes.

Ground beef forms the easy crust for this lower calorie main dish pie. The filling features sauerkraut and Swiss cheese with a sprinkling of caraway.

REUBEN PIE

- 1 lb. lean ground beef
- ½ cup rolled oats
- 1 egg
- ¼ cup chopped onion
- ¼ cup low-calorie Thousand Island dressing
- ½ teaspoon salt
- ½ teaspoon garlic salt
- ⅛ teaspoon pepper
- 1 can (16 oz.) sauerkraut, drained and rinsed
- 1 teaspoon caraway seed
- ¾ cup (3 ozs.) shredded Swiss cheese

1. Combine ground beef, rolled oats, egg, onion, dressing, salts and pepper in large bowl; mix well. Press mixture into bottom and up sides of 9-inch glass pie plate.

2. MICROWAVE (high), uncovered, 5 to 6 minutes or until meat is set and no longer pink, rotating pie plate once. Absorb extra juices with paper toweling.

3. Combine sauerkraut, caraway and cheese. Spoon onto meat, spreading evenly.

4. MICROWAVE (high), uncovered, 4 to 5 minutes or until cheese is melted. Let stand 5 minutes before cutting into wedges for serving.

6 Servings
About 230 Calories Each

TIP • If calories are not a concern, use regular dressing and increase the cheese to 1½ to 2 cups.

The surprise cheese centers make these meatballs a family favorite.

CHEESE-FILLED MEATBALLS

- 1 lb. ground beef
- 1 small onion, chopped
- 1 egg
- ⅓ cup milk
- ¼ cup dry bread crumbs
- ½ teaspoon salt
- ⅛ teaspoon pepper
- 1 slice pasteurized process cheese spread, cut 1-inch thick
  Natural meat browning and seasoning powder

1. Combine ground beef, onion, egg, milk, bread crumbs, salt and pepper; mix well. Cut cheese into 12 cubes. Form meat mixture around cheese cubes to make 12 meatballs, about 1½ inches in diameter. Arrange in 8-inch round glass or plastic baking dish. Sprinkle with browning powder. Cover with waxed paper.

2. MICROWAVE (high) 5 to 6 minutes or until meat is no longer pink, rotating dish once. Let stand covered a few minutes before serving.

4 to 5 Servings

Individual meat loaves topped with a zippy barbecue sauce — a quick, economical entree.

BARBECUED MINI-LOAVES

- ⅔ cup catsup
- 2 tablespoons brown sugar
- 1 teaspoon Worcestershire sauce
- ¼ teaspoon garlic salt
- ½ teaspoon prepared mustard

Loaves:
- 1 lb. ground beef
- 1 slice bread, crumbled
- ¼ cup milk
- 1 egg
- ½ teaspoon salt
  Dash pepper

1. Combine catsup, brown sugar, Worcestershire sauce, garlic salt and mustard; set aside.

2. Combine ground beef, bread, milk, egg, salt and pepper. Add two tablespoons of catsup mixture. Mix thoroughly; shape into 5 oval loaves about 3 inches long. Arrange on microwave meat rack. Cover with waxed paper.

3. MICROWAVE (high) 6½ minutes, rotating dish once. Spoon sauce evenly onto mini-loaves.

4. MICROWAVE (high), uncovered, 1 to 2 minutes or until meat is desired doneness.

About 5 Servings

Reuben Pie, page 24.

Use your microwave to precook vegetables before threading on skewers for barbecuing or broiling.

BEEF SHISH KABOBS

- 1¼ lbs. boneless sirloin or round steak, cut 1-inch thick
- ½ cup cooking oil
- ½ cup red wine
- 1 small onion, sliced
- 1 clove garlic, minced
- 2 teaspoons Worcestershire or steak sauce
- ½ teaspoon salt
- 3 medium potatoes, scrubbed
- ¼ cup water
- 2 medium ears corn, husked
- 12 broccoli pieces (about 8 ozs.)
- 12 cherry tomatoes

1. Trim excess fat from meat. Cut meat into 1-inch pieces. Place in plastic bag set in bowl. Combine oil, wine, onion, garlic, Worcestershire sauce and salt; mix well. Pour over meat. Turn meat over to coat evenly. Close bag and refrigerate overnight.

2. Cut potatoes into 1-inch pieces. Combine potatoes and water in 2-quart glass casserole. Cover with casserole lid.

3. MICROWAVE (high) 8 minutes. Break ears of corn in half; add corn and broccoli to potatoes. Cover.

4. MICROWAVE (high) 4 to 5 minutes or until vegetables are just about tender. Let stand covered 5 minutes.

5. Thread meat and vegetables alternately on metal skewers with corn placed near center of kabob and skewer running lengthwise through corn.

6. Place skewers on grill, about 5 inches above hot coals. Brush with marinade mixture.

7. GRILL OR BROIL 12 to 15 minutes or until meat is desired doneness, turning skewers occasionally and brushing with additional marinade.

About 4 Servings

TIP • Other vegetables can be used on kabobs. Some vegetables such as mushrooms and zucchini will require no precooking. Others such as cauliflower and carrots should be precooked until just about tender.

Taco filling in bell peppers makes an attractive family treat.

TACO BELLS

- 3 medium green peppers
- 1 lb. ground beef
- 1 small onion, chopped
- 1 can (8 oz.) tomato sauce
- 2 tablespoons chopped green chilies
- ½ teaspoon garlic salt
- ¼ teaspoon ground coriander
- ¼ teaspoon cumin
- ⅛ teaspoon red pepper (cayenne)
- 10 drops Tabasco sauce
- 1 tomato, chopped
- 1 cup shredded lettuce
- ¼ cup shredded Cheddar cheese
- 6 tablespoons taco sauce
- ½ cup crushed taco chips

1. Cut peppers in half. Remove core and seeds; rinse. Place peppers cut-side-up in 12 x 8-inch glass baking dish. Cover with waxed paper.

2. MICROWAVE (high) 4 to 5 minutes or until heated through, rotating dish once. Let stand covered.

3. Crumble ground beef into 1½-quart glass casserole; add onion.

4. MICROWAVE (high), uncovered, 5 to 6 minutes or until meat is no longer pink, stirring once. Stir to break meat into small pieces; drain. Stir in tomato sauce, chilies, garlic salt, coriander, cumin, red pepper and Tabasco sauce. Gently stir in tomato and lettuce. Drain peppers; spoon filling into pepper halves, mounding mixture as necessary. Sprinkle with cheese.

5. MICROWAVE (high), uncovered, 3 to 4 minutes or until cheese is melted and meat is heated, rotating dish once. Top each pepper with a tablespoon of taco sauce and sprinkle with taco chips.

About 6 Servings

This delightful stuffing for green peppers makes them as nutritious as they are delicious.

SAUSAGE-STUFFED GREEN PEPPERS

  3 **large or 4 medium green peppers**
½ **lb. Italian sausage**
½ **lb. ground beef**
  1 **cup herb-seasoned stuffing mix**
  1 **cup shredded carrot**
  1 **egg**
¼ **cup water**
¼ **cup catsup**

1. Cut peppers in half; remove core and seeds and rinse. Place peppers cut-side-up in 12 x 8-inch glass baking dish. Cover with waxed paper.

2. MICROWAVE (high) 3 to 4 minutes or until heated through. Let stand covered.

3. Combine sausage, beef, stuffing mix, carrot, egg, water and catsup; mix well. Spoon into pepper halves, mounding mixture as necessary. Cover with waxed paper.

4. MICROWAVE (high) 11 to 12 minutes or until meat is done, rotating dish once. If desired, top each with additional catsup.

About 6 Servings

TIPS • For more tender peppers, use the maximum time in step 2; for a crunchier texture, use minimum time.

• If you are short of peppers or not everyone likes them, just form meat into balls about the same size as the stuffed peppers and place in dish with peppers. The meat is flavored by the other peppers as it cooks.

Sausage-Stuffed Green Peppers.

If you've questioned the tenderness of meat from the microwave, we think you'll be excited about the fork-tender results you get from this recipe.

BEEF STROGANOFF

1½ **lbs. family or round steak**
  2 **teaspoons natural meat browning and seasoning powder**
  1 **medium onion, sliced**
  2 **cups (8 ozs.) sliced fresh mushrooms**
1¾ **cups water**
  1 **tablespoon parsley flakes**
  2 **tablespoons catsup**
  2 **teaspoons instant beef bouillon**
½ **teaspoon salt**
  1 **teaspoon prepared mustard**
¼ **cup water**
  4 **tablespoons flour**
½ **cup sour cream**

1. Cut meat into thin, bite-sized pieces. Place in 2-quart glass casserole. Sprinkle with browning powder. Top with onion.

2. MICROWAVE (high), uncovered, 6 to 7 minutes or until no longer pink, stirring once.

3. Add mushrooms, 1¾ cups water, the parsley, catsup, bouillon, salt and mustard. Stir lightly; cover with casserole lid.

4. MICROWAVE (high) 6 to 7 minutes or until mixture begins to boil. Stir. Then, MICROWAVE (low — 30%) 55 to 60 minutes or until meat is tender, stirring once.

5. Blend together ¼ cup water and the flour. Stir into meat mixture.

6. MICROWAVE (high), uncovered, 2 to 3 minutes or until mixture boils and thickens, stirring once. Stir in sour cream. Garnish with additional parsley, if desired. Serve over noodles or rice.

5 to 6 Servings

TIPS • About ¼ cup dry red wine can be substituted for part of the water added in step 3.

• With Full Power, use segments of 10 minute stand time and 5 minute microwave time for the simmer time in step 4.

• If you don't have the browning powder, prebrown the meat and onion on the range over medium-high heat in a pyroceramic skillet or shallow casserole. Omit cooking time in step 2.

For optimum flavor, we suggest prebrowning the meat.

OVEN STROGANOFF

1½ lbs. boneless round steak or sirloin tip
½ can (10½-oz. size) condensed onion
   soup*
1 can (10½ oz.) golden mushroom soup
1 can (4 oz.) mushroom pieces, drained
1 can (8 oz.) tomato sauce

1. Cut meat into thin, bite-sized pieces. Brown meat in its own juices in 2-quart pyroceramic casserole over medium-high heat. Add soups, mushrooms and tomato sauce. Cover with casserole lid.

2. MICROWAVE (high) 4 to 5 minutes or until mixture boils. Then, MICROWAVE (medium — 50%) 50 to 60 minutes or until meat is tender, stirring 2 or 3 times. Serve with rice or noodles.

About 6 Servings

TIP • *If you don't have a use for the extra soup, add the entire can.
• With Full Power, use segments of 5 minute microwave and 5 minute stand periods for the total simmer time in step 3.

Strips of round steak simmer slowly in a savory bacon-flavored sauce. Prebrowning the meat on a surface unit enhances the flavor and helps seal in the juices.

SAUCY BEEF STRIPS

3 slices bacon
1 lb. boneless round steak
1 medium onion, sliced
1 clove garlic, minced
3 tablespoons flour
1 can (10½ oz.) condensed beef broth

1. Arrange bacon slices in 8-inch square (1½-quart) pyroceramic glass skillet or casserole. Cover with paper towel.

2. MICROWAVE (high) 3 to 4 minutes or until bacon is crisp. Remove bacon; set aside.

3. Cut steak into thin, bite-sized strips. Add to bacon drippings along with onion and garlic. Place over medium-high heat on range and brown evenly, stirring occasionally. Stir in flour and broth. Crumble bacon; add to meat mixture. Cover with casserole lid.

4. MICROWAVE (high) 3 to 4 minutes or until mixture boils. Then MICROWAVE (low — 30%) 25 to 30 minutes or until meat is tender, stirring 2 or 3 times.

4 to 5 Servings

TIP • With Full Power in step 4, use segments of 3 minutes microwave and 5 minute standing times for a total of 25 to 30 minutes.

This recipe is from one of our staff. She prepares mashed potatoes to accompany the delicious steak roll and sauce that serves as gravy.

STUFFED FLANK STEAK

2 tablespoons butter or margarine
1½ cups herb-seasoned bread stuffing
2 tablespoons Parmesan cheese
1½ to 2-lb. flank steak
1 package (.98 oz.) brown gravy mix
   Water
¼ cup dry red wine
2 tablespoons sliced green onion

1. Presoak 2-quart clay simmer pot and lid about 10 minutes.

2. MICROWAVE (high) butter in 4-cup glass measure, ½ to 1 minute or until melted. Stir in bread stuffing and cheese. Place stuffing lengthwise down center of steak. Bring long sides of steak up to overlap on top, enclosing stuffing. Secure with wooden toothpicks and fasten with string by lacing around picks down the length of steak roll; tie securely. Place in simmer pot, seam-side up.

3. Combine gravy mix and water as directed on package, substituting wine for ¼ cup of water; mix well. Stir in onion. Pour over steak roll. Cover with simmer pot lid.

4. MICROWAVE (high) 10 to 15 minutes or until mixture boils. Turn meat over and MICROWAVE (medium — 50%) 25 to 35 minutes or until tender, turning meat 2 or 3 times.

About 6 Servings
445 Calories Each

TIP • With Full Power, microwave 15 minutes in step 4. Then use segments of 10 minutes standing time and 5 minutes microwave for a total of 25 to 35 minutes or until meat is tender.

Enjoy the tantalizing aroma of barbecued beef ribs by slowly simmering with the microwave in a clay simmer pot or cooking-roasting bag.

BARBECUED BEEF RIBS

    3 to 4 lbs. beef ribs (about 10 to 12 ribs)
    1 small onion, chopped
    1 clove garlic, minced
    1 cup catsup
    3 tablespoons brown sugar
    2 tablespoons flour
    2 tablespoons lemon juice
    1 tablespoon Worcestershire sauce
    ½ teaspoon salt
    ½ teaspoon chili powder
    ½ teaspoon liquid smoke, if desired

1. Cut meat into individual rib pieces. Place regular sized cooking-roasting bag in 12 x 8-inch glass baking dish. Add meat, onion and garlic. Combine remaining ingredients; spoon over ribs. Close bag with rubber band, making small slit in bag close to rubber band.

2. MICROWAVE (high) 10 minutes. Rearrange ribs. Then, MICROWAVE (low — 30%) 1¼ to 1½ hours or until ribs are tender, turning and rearranging ribs 2 or 3 times.

4 to 6 Servings

TIPS • A clay simmer pot can be used for cooking the ribs. Presoak pot 10 minutes in cold water. Drain pot, add ingredients, cover and cook as directed.

• With Full Power, use segments of 5 minutes microwave and 10 minutes stand for the low setting called for in step 2.

Marinating overnight and cooking at a lower power setting, produces very tender results with this less tender steak. The lean nature of flank steak and minimal calories in the marinade ingredients make this recipe ideal when calorie counting.

MARINATED FLANK STEAK

    ¼ cup soy sauce
    ¼ cup orange or pineapple juice
    1 tablespoon dry sherry
    1 clove garlic, minced
    ¼ teaspoon whole peppercorns
    ¼ teaspoon whole cloves
    1½ -lb. flank steak, scored

1. Combine soy sauce, orange juice, sherry, garlic, peppercorns and cloves. Place steak in 10 x 6-inch glass baking dish. Pour marinade over steak. Turn to coat both sides. Cover with plastic wrap. Refrigerate 6 to 12 hours.

2. Drain off marinade, removing any cloves and peppercorns from meat. Return meat to baking dish. Cover with plastic wrap.

3. MICROWAVE (high) 7 minutes. Then, MICROWAVE (low — 30%) 50 to 60 minutes or until meat is tender, turning meat over once. Cut meat across grain into thin slices for serving. If desired, serve with strained marinade.

6 Servings
About 230 Calories Each

TIP • With Full Power, use segments of 10 minute stand and 5 minute microwave for the 50 to 60 minutes simmer time.

Wieners, teamed with a spicy barbecue sauce, make popular family meals, and can be quite economical, too.

BARBECUED WIENERS

    ¼ cup chopped green peppers
    1 small onion, chopped
    2 tablespoons water
    ¾ cup catsup
    2 tablespoons brown sugar
    ½ teaspoon chili powder
    12 ozs. wieners (about 10)

1. Combine green pepper, onion and water in 1-quart glass casserole. Cover with casserole lid.

2. MICROWAVE (high) 2½ to 3 minutes or until onion is about tender, stirring once. Stir in catsup, brown sugar and chili powder. Add wieners, stirring gently to coat each with sauce. Cover.

3. MICROWAVE (high) 3½ to 4½ minutes or until wieners are hot and plump, rearranging once.

5 to 7 Servings

TIP • Wieners can also be cut into pieces before adding to the sauce.

This is an adapted recipe from a subscriber. The chili sauce makes a flavorful, simple sauce.

BARBECUED BEEF

  1 large onion, sliced or chopped
2 -lb. beef brisket
1 bottle (12 oz.) chili sauce

1. Place onion in bottom of oven cooking bag. Place meat over onion; pour chili sauce evenly over all. Tie bag securely with string; do not pierce bag. Place in 12 x 8-inch glass baking dish.

2. MICROWAVE (medium — 50%) 30 minutes. Turn meat over. Then, MICROWAVE (low — 30%) 60 to 75 minutes or until meat is tender, turning meat over 2 or 3 times. Let stand 10 to 15 minutes.

3. Carefully remove meat from cooking bag. Slice meat across grain into very thin pieces. Place meat in 1½-quart glass casserole. Pour sauce over meat. Cover with casserole lid.

4. MICROWAVE (high) 2 to 3 minutes or until heated through. Spoon onto split buns or hard rolls.

6 to 8 Servings

TIP • A presoaked simmer pot can also be used for cooking the meat. Place onion, meat and sauce in pot; cover with lid. Microwave as directed. If desired, return sliced meat to simmer pot for final heating.

  • For other sizes of brisket, allow about 45 minutes total cooking time per pound. Cook ⅓ of the time at 50% power and the remaining ⅔ time at 30% power.

  • Any extras are good for refrigerating or freezing for later heating. Planned-overs like this are especially handy when you are expecting overnight guests.

If your family enjoys liver, you are sure to find this recipe a favorite.

LIVER WITH STROGANOFF SAUCE

  3 slices bacon
1 lb. sliced beef liver
¼ cup chopped onion
2 tablespoons butter or margarine
1 can (4 oz.) mushroom pieces, drained
1 teaspoon instant beef bouillon
1 teaspoon chopped chives
¼ teaspoon salt
½ teaspoon Worcestershire sauce
2 tablespoons flour
½ cup water
½ cup sour cream

1. Arrange bacon slices in 8-inch square glass baking dish. Cover with paper towel.

2. MICROWAVE (high) 3 to 4 minutes or until bacon is crisp. Remove bacon and set aside. Add liver slices to drippings, turning to coat evenly; arrange evenly in dish. Cover with paper towel.

3. MICROWAVE (high) 5 to 6 minutes or until liver is no longer pink, turning liver over and rearranging once. Drain; set aside.

4. .Combine onion and butter in 4-cup glass measure.

5. MICROWAVE (high), uncovered 3 to 3½ minutes or until onion is tender. Stir in mushrooms, bouillon, chives, salt, Worcestershire sauce and flour. Blend in water.

6. MICROWAVE (high), uncovered, 2 to 3 minutes or until mixture boils and thickens, stirring once during last half of cooking time. Stir in sour cream. Spoon onto cooked liver. Crumble bacon and sprinkle over sauce. If desired, sprinkle with additional chopped chives.

7. MICROWAVE (high), uncovered, 1 to 2 minutes or until heated through.

About 5 Servings

The presoaked simmer pot makes an ideal container for the slow, moist cooking required for corned beef. Cabbage is added the last part of the cooking time.

CORNED BEEF AND CABBAGE

2½ **to 3-lb. corned beef brisket**
1 **clove garlic, minced**
1 **medium onion, quartered**
  Water
1 **small head cabbage, cut into wedges**

1. Presoak simmer pot and lid about 10 minutes. Place corned beef in simmer pot. Add seasoning packet from corned beef (see Tip if there is not a seasoning packet). Add garlic and onion; cover meat with water. Cover with simmer pot lid.

2. MICROWAVE (medium — 50%) 60 minutes. Turn meat over. Then, MICROWAVE (low — 30%) 60 minutes. Add cabbage. Cover.

3. MICROWAVE (low — 30%) 40 to 45 minutes or until cabbage is tender. Let stand a few minutes before removing meat and cabbage to serving plate. Slice meat diagonally across grain.

5 to 6 Servings

TIPS • If the corned beef brisket does not have a seasoning packet, substitute 1 bay leaf, crushed and 1 teaspoon peppercorns.

• A regular-sized oven cooking bag can be substituted for the simmer pot. Add 2½ cups water in step 1. Tie bag loosely with string; place in 12 x 8-inch glass baking dish. Pepare as directed, turning bag over twice in step 2 and once in step 3.

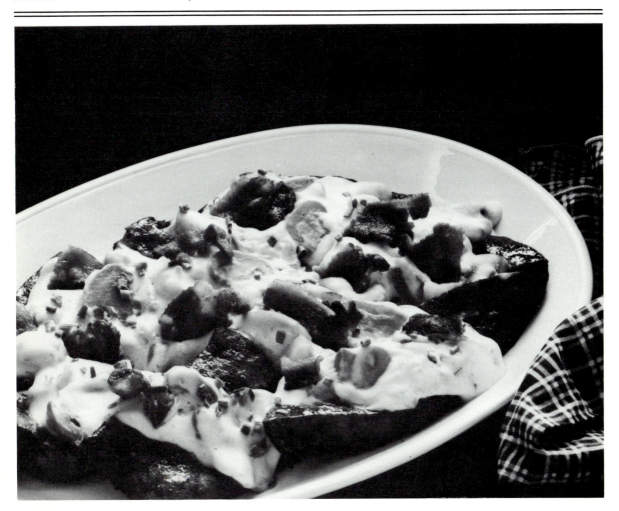

Liver With Stroganoff Sauce, page 30.

This favorite was adapted from a reader's recipe. Slow, moist cooking is best with less tender cuts of meat.

BEEF ROULADEN

6 ozs. beef bacon (about 5 slices)
2 medium onions, chopped
1 large dill pickle, chopped
6 thinly sliced beef shoulder steaks
  (about 2 lbs.)
 Prepared mustard
 Salt and pepper
1 tablespoon cooking oil
1 can (10½ oz.) condensed beef
  consommé
¼ cup water
¼ cup all-purpose flour

1. Place beef bacon slices evenly in 8-inch or 9-inch pyroceramic skillet. Cover with paper towel.

2. MICROWAVE (high) 4 to 5 minutes or until partially cooked, rotating dish once. Remove bacon from dish; cut into small pieces.

3. Combine onions, pickle and chopped bacon in small bowl. Trim excess fat from meat. Pound meat with meat mallet until very thin. Spread each piece of meat lightly with mustard; sprinkle with salt and pepper. Spoon onion mixture onto each piece of meat. Roll up with onion mixture inside; fasten with toothpicks.

4. Add cooking oil to drippings in skillet. Heat oil on range over medium-high heat. Add meat rolls and brown on all sides. Add consommé. Cover with skillet lid.

5. MICROWAVE (high) 5 minutes. Then, MICROWAVE (low — 30%) 60 to 70 minutes or until tender, turning meat over 2 or 3 times. Remove meat rolls and cover to keep warm. Combine water and flour; blend until smooth. Stir into meat liquid.

6. MICROWAVE (high), uncovered, 2½ to 3 minutes or until mixture boils and thickens, stirring 2 or 3 times. Add meat rolls to sauce or pour sauce over rolls.

6 Servings

TIPS • The browning procedure in step 4 can be omitted if the rolls are sprinkled with natural meat browning and seasoning powder.

• The onion can also be thinly sliced and the pickle cut into thin sticks; this makes the rolling a little easier.

Apples go well with pork. Here we've combined them with chops for a flavorful meat dish.

PORK CHOPS AND APPLES

4 pork chops, cut ½-inch thick (1 to 1½ lbs.)
1 tablespoon butter or margarine
2 apples, peeled and sliced
1 tablespoon brown sugar
½ teaspoon salt
¼ teaspoon poultry seasoning
½ cup water
2 tablespoons flour

1. Brown chops in butter in shallow pyroceramic skillet over medium heat.

2. Arrange chops evenly in skillet. Top chops with apple slices. Sprinkle evenly with brown sugar, salt and poultry seasoning. Combine water and flour. Pour over chops. Cover with skillet lid or waxed paper.

3. MICROWAVE (high) 3 to 3½ minutes or until steaming hot. Then MICROWAVE (low— 30%) 45 to 60 minutes or until meat is tender rotating dish once.

About 4 Servings

TIPS • If you don't have a pyroceramic skillet, brown chops in frying pan and then transfer to shallow dish for microwaving.

• A microwave browning dish can be used for the browning in step 1. Preheat the dish 5 to 7 minutes or as recommended by manufacturer for pork chops. Add chops and microwave 2 minutes or until browned. Turn chops over and microwave 4 to 5 minutes or until lightly browned. Continue with step 2.

This colorful "meal in a pot" includes rolled pork tenderloin, carrots and mashed potatoes.

PORK TENDERLOIN PLATTER

    3 carrots, peeled, quartered and cut
       into 3-inch pieces
    2 tablespoons water
  ¾ to 1 lb. pork tenderloin
    1 small onion, sliced
  ¼ cup Parmesan cheese
       Natural meat browning and seasoning
       powder
  ⅓ cup water
  ⅓ cup white wine
    2 tablespoons flour
  ¼ teaspoon salt
  ¼ teaspoon thyme leaves
 1⅓ cups water
  ⅓ cup milk
    2 tablespoons butter or margarine
  ½ teaspoon salt
 1½ cups instant mashed potato granules
    1 teaspoon chopped chives
    1 egg

1. Presoak simmer pot and lid about 10 minutes. Combine carrots and 2 tablespoons water in 2-cup glass measure. Cover with plastic wrap.

2. MICROWAVE (high) 3 to 3½ minutes or until partially cooked. Let stand covered.

3. If meat is not already in thin pieces, cut tenderloin into 4 or 5 pieces. Place cut-side-down between waxed paper and pound with rolling pin until about ¼ inch thick. Divide onion among meat pieces. Sprinkle each piece with Parmesan cheese. Roll up with onion and cheese inside; fasten with toothpicks. Sprinkle pieces with browning powder. Place in center of simmer pot.

4. MICROWAVE (high), uncovered, 3 to 3½ minutes or until meat is no longer pink. Drain carrots and add to simmer pot along lengthwise sides. Combine ⅓ cup water, the wine, flour, salt and thyme; blend well. Pour over meat and carrots. Cover.

5. MICROWAVE (medium — 50%) 20 to 22 minutes or until meat is tender. Let stand covered. Combine 1⅓ cups water, the milk, butter and salt in 4-cup glass measure.

6. MICROWAVE (high), uncovered, 3½ to 4 minutes or until mixture boils. Stir in potato granules until thickened. Beat in chives and egg. Spoon potato mixture into ends of simmer pot. Cover.

7. MICROWAVE (high) 4½ to 5 minutes or until heated through.

About 4 Servings

TIPS • If you do not have the browning powder, prebrown the rolls in a little butter in a skillet over medium-high heat.

• Boneless pork chops can be substituted for pork tenderloin.

• The wine can be omitted and a total of ⅔ cup water added to the meat.

• A 2-quart glass casserole can be substituted for the simmer pot. Prepare as directed, rotating dish once or twice during cooking in step 5.

Rice and pork chops require simmering to become tender. Here apple juice, onion and raisins are used to enhance the flavors.

PORK CHOPS AND RICE

  ¾ cup long or medium grain white rice
  ½ cup raisins
  ¼ cup packed brown sugar
    1 large onion, sliced
  ⅛ teaspoon nutmeg
    1 cup apple or orange juice
  ½ cup water
    6 pork chops, cut ½-inch thick
       (about 2 lbs.)
    5 whole cloves
       Natural meat browning and seasoning
       powder

1. Presoak simmer pot and lid about 10 minutes. Combine rice, raisins, brown sugar, onion, nutmeg, juice and water in simmer pot. Cover with simmer pot lid.

2. MICROWAVE (high) 6½ to 7½ minutes or until mixture begins to boil. Insert a clove in the fat portion of each chop. Sprinkle chops liberally with browning powder. Arrange chops on rice mixture. Cover.

3. MICROWAVE (low — 30%) 45 to 55 minutes or until meat is tender, rearranging chops once.

About 6 Servings

TIPS • If you do not have the browning powder, prebrown the chops in a skillet over medium-high heat. Add 1 teaspoon salt to rice.

• A 3-quart glass casserole can be substituted for the simmer pot. Decrease water to ¼ cup; prepare as directed, rotating dish once or twice in step 3.

Guests will enjoy this unique combination and the cook will appreciate the ease of preparation.

HONG KONG CHOPS

 6 **pork chops, cut ½-inch thick (about 2 lbs.)**
   Natural meat browning and seasoning powder
 1 **lemon**
 ¼ **cup sherry or orange juice**
 3 **tablespoons soy sauce**
 ¼ **teaspoon ground ginger**
 ¼ **teaspoon garlic powder**
 1 **can (4 oz.) mushroom stems and pieces, drained**
 1 **small onion, sliced**
 1½ **tablespoons cornstarch**
 ¼ **cup water**
 1 **green pepper, sliced**
 1 **can (8 oz.) sliced water chestnuts, drained**

1. Trim excess fat from meat. Moisten meat and sprinkle both sides with browning powder. Arrange in single layer in 12 x 8-inch glass baking dish. Halve lemon and squeeze 1 tablespoon juice; slice other half and set aside. Combine lemon juice, sherry, soy sauce, ginger and garlic powder; pour over chops. Add mushrooms and onion. Cover with plastic wrap.

2. MICROWAVE (high) 7 to 8 minutes or until mixture boils; rotate dish, then MICROWAVE (low — 30%) 30 to 35 minutes or until chops are tender, rotating dish once. Combine cornstarch and water; mix into pan juices. Add green pepper and water chestnuts. Cover.

3. MICROWAVE (high) 5 to 6 minutes or until sauce boils and thickens. Garnish with lemon slices.

About 6 Servings

TIPS • If you do not have browning powder, prebrown chops over medium-high heat before arranging in baking dish.
   • With Full Power in step 2, microwave 10 minutes. Then microwave 5 minutes and let stand 5 to 10 minutes or until tender.

Pork chops are sandwiched between savory dressing and topped with a creamy mushroom sauce. For added flavor, the chops are prebrowned before microwaving with a lower power setting.

PORK CHOPS AND DRESSING

 4 **pork chops (about 1 lb.)**
 1 **can (4 oz.) mushroom pieces, undrained**
 ½ **cup water**
 2 **tablespoons flour**
 ½ **teaspoon salt**
 2 **cups herb-seasoned stuffing mix (crumb-type)**
 ½ **cup water**

1. Brown chops on both sides in 8-inch (2-quart) pyroceramic glass skillet on range over medium-high heat. Set aside chops; stir mushrooms into pan drippings.

2. Combine water, flour and salt in 2-cup glass measure. Stir in mushrooms and drippings.

3. MICROWAVE (high), uncovered, 1 to 2 minutes or until mixture boils, stirring once.

4. Place half of stuffing mix in the pyroceramic skillet. Mix in ¼ cup of water. Arrange pork chops evenly over stuffing mixture. Combine remaining stuffing with ¼ cup water; spoon over chops. Pour mushroom sauce over stuffing. Cover with casserole lid.

5. MICROWAVE (high) 5 minutes. Then, MICROWAVE (medium — 50%) 20 to 25 minutes or until meat is tender, rotating dish once.

About 4 Servings

TIP • With Full Power in step 5, use segments of 5 minutes microwave and 5 minute standing time for a total of 25 to 30 minutes.

Strips of pork simmer to perfection in a flavorful sour cream sauce. Stuffing balls add an interesting and flavorful topping.

PORK STROGANOFF WITH STUFFING BALLS

1½ lbs. boneless pork
2 teaspoons natural meat browning and seasoning powder
1 large onion, sliced
1 cup (4 ozs.) sliced fresh mushrooms
¼ cup all-purpose flour
¼ teaspoon salt
⅛ teaspoon pepper
1 can (10¾ oz.) condensed cream of chicken soup
1 cup water
¼ cup butter or margarine
1 cup water
1 package (8 oz.) herb-seasoned stuffing mix
1 tablespoon parsley flakes
2 eggs
1 cup sour cream

1. Presoak simmer pot and lid about 10 minutes. Trim excess fat from meat. Cut into thin, bite-sized pieces. Place in simmer pot. Sprinkle with browning powder. Top with onion.

2. MICROWAVE (high), uncovered, 7 to 7½ minutes or until meat is no longer pink, stirring once. Mix in mushrooms, flour, salt, pepper and soup. Stir in 1 cup water. Cover with simmer pot lid.

3. MICROWAVE (high) 10 to 11 minutes or until mixture boils. Stir and then, MICROWAVE (low — 30%) 45 to 50 minutes or until meat is tender. Let stand covered.

4. Combine butter and 1 cup water in 2-quart glass mix 'n pour bowl.

5. MICROWAVE (high), uncovered, 2¼ to 2½ minutes or until boiling. Stir in stuffing mix and parsley; mix well. Mix in eggs until combined. Stir sour cream into meat mixture. Form stuffing mixture into 12 balls; arrange on meat. Cover.

6. MICROWAVE (high) 5 to 6 minutes or until heated through.

6 to 8 Servings

TIPS • About ¼ cup white wine can be substituted for part of the water added to the meat.
• When reheating leftovers, remove the stuffing balls before heating the meat mixture.

Then, add the stuffing balls to the hot meat and heat a few minutes longer.
• When time is short, boil the water on a surface unit for the stuffing so the balls are ready to add after the simmering in step 3.
• If you do not have the browning powder, prebrown the pork in 2 tablespoons oil in a skillet over medium-high heat. Increase salt to ½ teaspoon.
• A 2-quart glass casserole can be substituted for simmer pot. Prepare as directed, stirring 2 or 3 times in step 3.

This recipe is simple enough for quick family meals. It tastes so good you'll want to share it with guests, too.

COUNTRY BARBECUED RIBS

2 lbs. country-style ribs
1 cup catsup
⅓ cup (half a 6-oz. can) frozen lemonade concentrate
3 tablespoons brown sugar
2 tablespoons chopped onion
¼ teaspoon celery seed

1. Arrange ribs bone-side-up in 8-inch square glass baking dish. Cover with waxed paper.

2. MICROWAVE (high) 13 to 15 minutes or until no longer pink, turning ribs bone-side-down halfway through cooking time. Drain fat.

3. Combine remaining ingredients. Spoon over ribs.

4. MICROWAVE (high), uncovered, 11 to 12 minutes or until tender, rotating dish twice.

About 4 Servings

TIP • Ribs can be placed over hot coals for cooking in step 4. Brush occasionally with sauce during cooking.

Here is a recipe from a feature on combining the grill and microwave. If you've not tried the method, we think you will be pleasantly surprised.

MINT-GLAZED LEG OF LAMB

- ½ cup (half a 10-oz. jar) mint-flavored jelly
- 1 teaspoon garlic salt
- 1 teaspoon lemon juice
- 4 to 4½-lb. leg of lamb (half a leg)

1. Combine jelly, garlic salt and lemon in small glass dish.

2. MICROWAVE (high), uncovered, 1 to 1½ minutes or until just about melted.

3. Place lamb on bacon-meat rack. Brush with melted jelly mixture. Shield small end of roast, if necessary, by wrapping in foil. Cover loosely with waxed paper.

4. MICROWAVE (high) 15 minutes. Remove foil; turn roast over and brush with additional jelly. Cover with waxed paper.

5. MICROWAVE (high) 10 to 15 minutes or until just about done (150°).

6. Transfer lamb to grill, about 5 inches above hot coals. Brush with jelly mixture; cover grill.

7. Grill 18 to 20 minutes or until meat is done (165°), turning meat over once if necessary. Let stand covered 10 to 15 minutes before slicing. Serve remaining jelly mixture with lamb.

8 to 10 Servings

TIP • For other sizes of leg of lamb, allow about 7 minutes microwave time per lb. of meat.

• To complete in oven, transfer to clean baking pan in step 7 and bake at 375° for 30 to 45 minutes.

Marinated Shish Kabobs.

Let your guests join in the fun by assembling their own kabobs. For an outdoor gathering, kabobs can be grilled as directed in the Tips.

MARINATED SHISH KABOBS

- 1½ to 2-lb. boned leg of lamb
- ¼ cup olive oil or cooking oil
- 1 tablespoon vinegar
- 1 teaspoon instant onion
- 1 teaspoon garlic powder
- 3 medium carrots, cut into 1-inch pieces
- 2 tablespoons water
- 2 tablespoons natural meat browning and seasoning powder
- 1 jar (16 oz.) whole onions, drained
- 8 ozs. (about 1½ cups) whole fresh mushrooms

1. Trim excess fat from meat. Cut into 1-inch cubes. Place in plastic bag. Combine oil, vinegar, onion and garlic powder; mix well. Pour over meat. Turn meat over to coat evenly. Close bag and refrigerate at least overnight or up to 2 days.

2. Combine carrots and water in 1-quart glass casserole. Cover with casserole lid.

3. MICROWAVE (high) 4 to 5 minutes or until carrots are almost tender.

4. Coat meat cubes with browning powder. Thread meat, carrots, onions, and mushrooms alternately on 10-inch bamboo skewers. Place kabobs on meat rack. Cover with waxed paper. (Refrigerate if not microwaving immediately.)

5. MICROWAVE (high) 9 to 10 minutes or until meat is desired doneness and vegetables are tender, rearranging kabobs once.

About 8 Servings
195 Calories Each

TIPS • Kabobs can also be grilled. Omit browning pwoder, use metal skewers and omit step 5. Grill 12 to 15 minutes.

• 1½ to 2 lbs. boneless sirloin or round steak, cut 1-inch thick can be substituted for lamb.

• Other vegetables can be used on kabobs. Some vegetables like zucchini and cherry tomatoes will require no precooking. Others such as cauliflower and potatoes should be precooked until just about tender.

Ham and Wild Rice, page 40,
and Chicken and Pasta,
page 55.

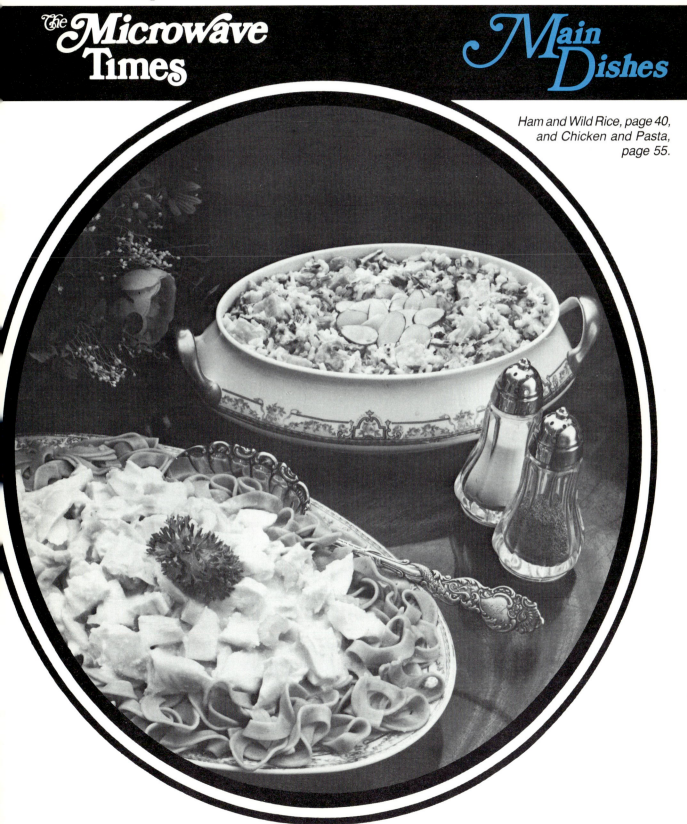

Chili powder enhances the sauce for this hearty pasta dish. Thin pieces of meat (partially frozen for ease in slicing) and a lower power setting give fork-tender results.

SPAGHETTI WITH SPICY ROUND STEAK SAUCE

- 8 ozs. spaghetti
- 1½ lbs. boneless round steak, partially frozen
- 3 tablespoons flour
- 1 teaspoon salt
- ⅛ teaspoon pepper
- 2 tablespoons cooking oil
- 1 can (15 oz.) tomato sauce
- 1 clove garlic, minced
- ⅔ cup water
- ⅓ cup catsup
- ½ to 1 teaspoon chili powder
  Dash cayenne pepper, if desired

1. Cook spaghetti as directed on package. Drain and rinse in cold water. Set aside.

2. Trim excess fat from meat. Cut into very thin 2-inch strips. Combine flour, salt and pepper on waxed paper. Coat beef with flour mixture.

3. Heat oil in 10-inch pyroceramic skillet on range over medium-high heat. Add meat; stir occasionally to brown all sides. Stir in remaining ingredients and any remaining flour mixture; mix well. Cover with casserole lid.

4. MICROWAVE (high) 10 minutes or until mixture is boiling. Stir and then, MICROWAVE (low — 30%) 20 to 30 minutes or until tender, stirring twice.

5. MICROWAVE (high) spaghetti in glass serving bowl 3 to 4 minutes or until heated. Serve sauce with spaghetti.

5 to 6 Servings

TIPS • This sauce reheats well so extras can be refrigerated or frozen until ready to serve. Just cook the amount of spaghetti desired while the sauce is heating.
 • For added flavor, use the special tomato sauce that contains onions and green peppers.
 • With Full Power in step 4, microwave (high) 10 minutes. Then use segments of 6 minutes stand and 3 minutes microwave for the 20 to 30 minutes simmer time.

Round steak cooks nicely in the microwave when a slower cooking method is used. Pieces of meat simmer in a tasty wine sauce at the same time the potatoes are cooking...a good way to make meat, potatoes and gravy something special.

BAKED POTATOES WITH BEEF BURGUNDY SAUCE

- ¾ lb. round steak, cut into bite-sized pieces
- 1 small onion, sliced
- 1 clove garlic, minced
- 2 tablespoons butter or margarine
- 3 tablespoons flour
- 2 teaspoons instant beef bouillon
- ¼ teaspoon salt
- ¼ teaspoon marjoram leaves
- 1 cup water
- ¼ cup Burgundy wine
- 1 can (4 oz.) mushroom pieces, undrained
- 5 medium potatoes
  Sour cream, if desired

1. Brown meat, onion and garlic in butter in 1½-quart pyroceramic casserole on range over medium-high heat. Add flour, bouillon, salt, and marjoram; mix well. Stir in water, wine and mushrooms. Cover with casserole lid.

2. Place casserole dish in center of oven and potatoes at sides.

3. MICROWAVE (high) 4 to 5 minutes or until meat mixture boils. Stir meat and rearrange and turn over potatoes.

4. MICROWAVE (medium-high — 70%) 40 to 50 minutes or until meat is tender and potatoes are done, turning potatoes over once.

5. Make cross cuts in each potato. Press sides to open potato. Sprinkle each with salt. Spoon meat mixture into each. If desired, top with spoonfuls of sour cream.

About 5 servings

TIPS • With Full Power, microwave (high) potatoes and meat together using segments of 10 minutes microwave and 5 minutes standing times for a total of 40 to 50 minutes.
 • When not cooking potatoes along with the meat, use a low — 30% power setting for the time in step 4.

Here frozen vegetables provide both the vegetable and base for the sauce. The flavor combination of this dish was well liked by all our tasters.

SAUSAGE-RICE ORIENTAL

- ½ cup chopped green pepper
- 1 cup chopped celery
- 1 small onion, chopped
- 1 lb. bulk pork sausage
- ¼ cup soy sauce
- 2 cups uncooked quick-cooking rice
- 2 cups water
- 1 package (10 oz.) frozen Japanese-style vegetables with soy sauce

1. Combine green pepper, celery and onion in 2-quart glass casserole. Crumble sausage and add to casserole.

2. MICROWAVE (high), uncovered 7 to 8 minutes or until sausage is no longer pink, stirring once. Stir to break meat into pieces; drain.

3. Stir soy sauce, rice and water into sausage

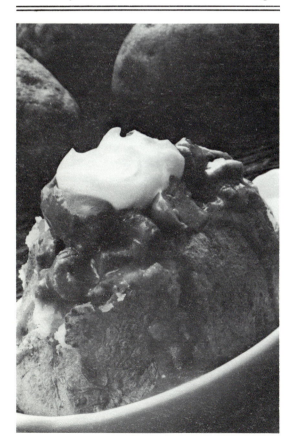

Baked Potatoes with Beef Burgundy Sauce.

mixture. Remove frozen vegetables from pouch and place on rice mixture. Cover with casserole lid.

4. MICROWAVE (high) 10 to 12 minutes or until liquid is absorbed and mixture is hot, stirring twice. Let stand about 5 minutes before serving.

About 6 Servings

Chow mein meat, fresh bean sprouts and broccoli cook in a soy-flavored sauce for a nutritious and colorful combination.

ORIENTAL SPROUTS 'N BROCCOLI HOT DISH

- 1 medium onion, sliced
- 1 clove garlic, minced
- 1 tablespoon water
- 1 lb. chow mein meat (coarsely ground pork and veal)
- ¾ cup water
- ¼ cup soy sauce
- 2 tablespoons cornstarch
- 2 teaspoons instant chicken bouillon
- ¼ teaspoon ginger
- 2 cups sliced fresh broccoli, cut into 1-inch pieces
- 1 can (8 oz.) water chestnuts, drained and sliced
- 8 ozs. (4 cups) fresh bean sprouts, rinsed and drained

1. Combine onion, garlic and 1 tablespoon water in 2-quart glass casserole. Cover with casserole lid.

2. MICROWAVE (high) 2 to 2½ minutes or until vegetables are tender. Crumble chow mein meat and add to onion.

3. MICROWAVE (high), uncovered, 4½ to 5 minutes or until no longer pink, stirring once.

4. Stir in remaining ingredients, except bean sprouts. Cover.

5. MICROWAVE (high) 6½ to7½ minutes or until mixture boils, stirring once.

6. Add bean sprouts; stir gently. Cover.

7. MICROWAVE (high) 3½ to 4 minutes or until sprouts are tender crisp.

5 to 6 Servings

TIP • Canned bean sprouts can be substituted for fresh. Drain a 16-oz. can and add as directed in step 6.

Wild rice adds a festive touch to any company dish. Remember, it requires presoaking and slow simmering to become tender and fluffy.

HAM AND WILD RICE

- 1 **cup wild rice**
- 2 **cups water**
- 1 **cup long grain white rice**
- 2 **cups water**
- 1 **teaspoon salt**
- 1 **medium onion, chopped**
- 2 **cups (8 ozs.) sliced fresh mushrooms**
- ¼ **cup butter or margarine**
- 1 **cup sour cream**
- 1 **teaspoon salt**
- ⅛ **teaspoon thyme leaves**
- ⅛ **teaspoon marjoram leaves**
- 3 **cups cubed cooked ham**
- ½ **cup half & half cream**
- ½ **cup sliced almonds**
- 1 **tablespoon butter or margarine**

1. Combine wild rice and 2 cups water in 3-quart glass casserole. Cover with casserole lid.

2. MICROWAVE (high) 8 to 10 minutes or until mixture boils. Let stand covered 1 hour.

3. Add white rice, 2 cups water and 1 teaspoon salt. Cover.

4. MICROWAVE (high) 9 to 10 minutes or until mixture starts to boil.

5. MICROWAVE (medium — 50%) 13 to 14 minutes or until rice is just about tender. Uncover and set aside.

6. Combine onion, mushrooms and butter in 1-quart glass mix 'n pour bowl.

7. MICROWAVE (high), uncovered, 4 to 4½ minutes or until vegetables are tender, stirring once. Add to rice along with sour cream, salt, thyme, marjoram and ham; mix lightly. Pour cream over rice; cover.

8. MICROWAVE (high) 9 to 10 minutes or until heated through, stirring once. Let stand covered.

9. Combine almonds and butter in shallow glass baking dish.

10. MICROWAVE (high), uncovered, 4 to 5 minutes or until lightly toasted, stirring twice. Sprinkle over casserole.

8 to 10 Servings

TIPS • Rice and vegetables can be cooked early in day; then combine and refrigerate. To serve, just mix in other ingredients and

increase microwave time in step 8 to 12 to 14 minutes. (Toast almonds early in day, too.)

• Cooked chicken or turkey can be substituted for half or all the ham.

• For half a recipe, use 1½-quart casserole and microwave in step 2 for 4 to 5 minutes; step 4 for 4½ to 5 minutes; step 5 for 10 to 11 minutes; step 7 for 2 to 3 minutes; step 8 for 4 to 5 minutes and step 10 for 2 to 3 minutes.

Here is a flavorful combination with an Oriental flare that goes from the microwave to the table in just minutes.

SWEET-SOUR LINKS OVER RICE

- 2 **tablespoons chopped onion**
- 2 **tablespoons chopped green pepper**
- 1 **tablespoon butter or margarine**
- 1 **can (8 oz.) pineapple chunks, undrained**
- ¼ **cup packed brown sugar**
- 1 **tablespoon cornstarch**
- 2 **tablespoons vinegar**
- 1 **tablespoon soy sauce**
- 6 **ozs. fully cooked smokie sausages, cut into 1-inch pieces**
-   **Cooked rice**
- ½ **orange, sliced and quartered**

1. Combine onion, green pepper and butter in 1-quart glass casserole.

2. MICROWAVE (high), uncovered, 1½ to 2 minutes or until vegetables are just about tender. Add pineapple, brown sugar, cornstarch, vinegar and soy sauce. Mix until cornstarch is dissolved.

3. MICROWAVE (high), uncovered, 3 to 3½ minutes or until mixture boils and thickens, stirring twice. Stir in sausages.

4. MICROWAVE (high) 1½ to 2 minutes or until heated through, stirring once. Serve over hot cooked rice; garnish with orange slices, if desired.

About 4 Servings

TIP • Sauce can be prepared ahead through step 3. To serve, increase time in step 4 to 5 to 6 minutes.

This recipe from a reader had won her a prize for conventional preparation. Here is our microwave version which is also prize worthy.

FRANK 'N BEAN BISCUIT BAKE

    2 tablespoons chopped onion
    2 tablespoons chopped green pepper
    2 tablespoons butter or margarine
    1 lb. wieners
    1 can (15 oz.) ranch-style beans,
      undrained
    1 can (11½ oz.) condensed bean with
      bacon soup
    1 can (12 oz.) vacuum-packed whole
      kernel corn, undrained
    1 can (10 oz.) refrigerated biscuits
      (10 biscuits)
      Prepared mustard

1. Combine onion, green pepper and butter in 2-quart glass casserole. Cover with casserole lid.

2. MICROWAVE (high) 2 to 3 minutes or until partially cooked. Cut ten 1-inch pieces of wiener; set aside. Thinly slice remaining wieners into casserole dish. Add beans, soup and corn; mix lightly. Cover.

3. MICROWAVE (high) 10 to 11 minutes or until mixture boils, stirring once or twice. Flatten each biscuit with fingers to form 3-inch rounds; spread each with mustard. Place a piece of wiener in the center of each biscuit round. Wrap dough around wiener and seal. Arrange biscuits, seam-side-down on top of hot bean mixture. Cover with paper towel.

4. MICROWAVE (high) 4 minutes, rotating dish once. Turn biscuits over and rearrange inner and outer edges, using fork to carefully lift biscuits. Cover with paper towel.

5. MICROWAVE (high) 3 to 4 minutes or until biscuits are no longer doughy, rotating dish once. Let stand 5 minutes before serving.

About 6 Servings

A zesty dish, perfect when the entertaining includes children.

ITALIAN HOT DOGS

    10 manicotti shells (1-inch diameter)
     1 egg
     1 cup (8 ozs.) cottage cheese
    ½ teaspoon Italian seasoning
       Dash pepper
    10 wieners (16 ozs.)
     1 jar (15½ oz.) spaghetti sauce
    ½ cup water
     1 cup (4 ozs.) shredded
       Mozzarella cheese

1. Cook manicotti shells as directed on package until tender. Drain and rinse in cold water. Set aside.

2. Beat egg; mix in cottage cheese, Italian seasoning and pepper.

3. Split wieners almost in half, lengthwise. Fill with cottage cheese mixture; slip each into a cooked manicotti shell.

4. Arrange in 12 x 8-inch glass baking dish. Pour spaghetti sauce and water over manicotti. Cover with waxed paper.

5. MICROWAVE (high) 15 to 17 minutes or until heated through (160°), rotating dish twice. Sprinkle with Mozzarella cheese.

6. MICROWAVE (high), uncovered, 1 to 1½ minutes or until cheese is melted.

6 to 8 Servings

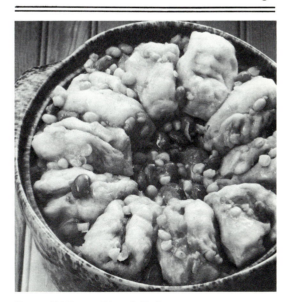

Frank 'N Bean Biscuit Bake.

Here is an interesting combination ot noodles, meatballs and a slightly tangy sauce.

BAVARIAN MEATBALLS AND NOODLES

- 4 **cups wide noodles, cooked**
- 2 **slices bacon**
- 1 **large onion, sliced (1 cup)**
- 1 **lb. ground beef**
- 1 **egg**
- ¼ **cup dry bread crumbs**
- ¼ **cup milk**
- ½ **teaspoon salt**
- 1 **teaspoon Worcestershire sauce**
  Natural meat browning and seasoning powder, if desired
- 4 **tablespoons flour**
- 1 **tablespoon instant beef bouillon**
- 2 **teaspoons brown susgar**
- ½ **teaspoon salt**
- ⅛ **teaspoon pepper**
- 1½ **cups water**
- 1 **tablespoon vinegar**

1. Cook noodles as directed on package. Drain, rinse and set aside.

2. Place bacon in single layer in 8 or 9-inch round glass baking dish. Cover with paper towel.

3. MICROWAVE (high) 1½ to 2½ minutes or until crisp. Remove bacon and set aside. Add onion slices to drippings. Cover with paper towel.

4. MICROWAVE (high) 3½ to 4 minutes or until just about tender.

5. Combine ground beef, egg, bread crumbs, milk, salt and Worcestershire sauce; mix well. Remove onions from baking dish and set aside. Form meat mixture into 1½-inch meatballs. Add to dish used for onions. Sprinkle lightly with browning powder. Cover with waxed paper.

6. MICROWAVE (high) 5 to 6 minutes or until no longer pink, rotating dish once.

7. Combine flour, bouillon, brown sugar, salt, pepper, water and vinegar in 4-cup glass measure; mix well.

8. MICROWAVE (high), uncovered, 3½ to 4 minutes or until mixture boils and thickens, stirring 2 or 3 times.

9. Spread noodles in shallow 2-quart glass casserole. Top with meatballs and onions. Pour sauce over meatballs. Crumble bacon and sprinkle over top.

10. MICROWAVE (high), uncovered, 7 to 9 minutes or until heated through.

4 to 5 Servings

TIP • Casserole can be prepared ahead through step 9. If refrigerated, cover with casserole lid or waxed paper and increase microwave time to 10 to 12 minutes, rotating dish once.

Meatballs combined with fresh and frozen vegetables and a rich gravy sauce make an economical main dish. Carrots require longer cooking than potatoes so are cut smaller than the potatoes.

MEATBALL STEW

- 4 **to 5 medium potatoes, peeled and cut into 1-inch cubes**
- 3 **to 4 large carrots, peeled and sliced**
- 1 **small onion, sliced**
- 2 **tablespoons instant beef bouillon**
- 1½ **cups water**
- 1 **lb. ground beef**
- 1 **egg**
- ⅓ **cup dry bread crumbs**
- ⅓ **cup milk**
- ½ **teaspoon salt**
- ½ **teaspoon Worcestershire sauce**
- 1 **package (10 oz.) frozen peas**
- ½ **cup water**
- 3 **tablespoons flour**
- ½ **teaspoon salt**
- ½ **teaspoon browning and bouquet sauce**

1. Combine potatoes, carrots, onion, bouillon and water in 2½ or 3-quart glass casserole. Cover with casserole lid.

2. MICROWAVE (high) 13 to 15 minutes or until vegetables are just about tender, stirring once. Set aside.

3. Combine ground beef, egg, bread crumbs, milk, salt and Worcestershire sauce. Form into meatballs about 1 inch in size. Place in 9 or 10-inch glass pie plate. Cover with waxed paper.

4. MICROWAVE (high) 6 to 7 minutes or until meat is set. Drain. Add meatballs and frozen peas to vegetables.

5. Combine water, flour, salt and browning sauce. Stir into meatball mixture. Cover.

6. MICROWAVE (high) 8 to 10 minutes or until mixture boils and thickens, stirring twice.

About 6 Servings

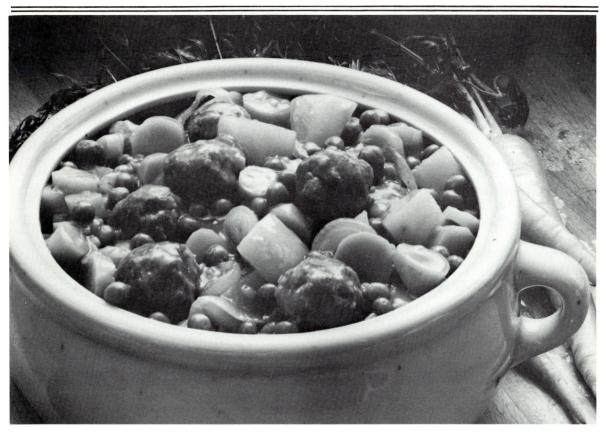

Meatball Stew.

Italian flavors bring out the best in this stuffed eggplant. Soaking the eggplant in salt water prevents a strong acidic taste.

EGGPLANT BAKE

- 1 **medium eggplant**
- ½ **lb. ground beef**
- 1 **small onion, chopped**
- 1 **clove garlic, minced**
- ½ **unpeeled cucumber, chopped**
- ½ **green pepper, chopped**
- 1 **can (8 oz.) tomato sauce**
- ½ **teaspoon salt**
- ½ **teaspoon Italian seasoning**
- ¼ **teaspoon basil leaves**
- ⅛ **teaspoon pepper**
- ½ **cup shredded Monterey Jack cheese**

1. Cut eggplant in half lengthwise. Soak in salt water* about 30 minutes.

2. Crumble ground beef into 1½-quart glass casserole.

3. MICROWAVE (high), uncovered, 2 to 3 minutes or until meat is set, stirring once. Stir to break meat into small pieces; drain.

4. Drain eggplant and scoop out center leaving a ¼-inch shell. (Grapefruit knife works well.) Chop center of eggplant and reserve 1½ cups.

5. Combine 1½ cups chopped eggplant, onion, garlic, cucumber and green pepper in 4-cup glass measure. Cover with plastic wrap.

6. MICROWAVE (high) 4 to 5 minutes or until almost tender; drain. Stir into ground beef. Add tomato sauce, salt, Italian seasoning, basil and pepper; mix well. Spoon into eggplant halves, mounding as necessary. Place in 8-inch square glass baking dish. Cover with waxed paper.

7. MICROWAVE (high) 7 to 8 minutes or until eggplant is tender, rotating dish once. Sprinkle with cheese.

8. MICROWAVE (high), uncovered, ½ to 1 minute or until cheese is melted.

3 to 4 Servings

TIP • *Add 1 tablespoon salt to 2 quarts water in which to soak eggplant.

Precooking the cabbage is necessary when preparing cabbage rolls in the microwave. This recipe is a favorite of one of our staff.

STUFFED CABBAGE ROLLS

- 2 cups water
- 12 cabbage leaves
- 1 lb. lean ground beef
- ¼ lb. ground pork
- 1 small onion, chopped
- 1 can (8 oz.) tomato sauce
- ¾ cup cooked rice
- 2 teaspoons salt
- ½ teaspoon pepper

Sauce:
- 1 can (8 oz.) tomato sauce
- ¼ cup packed brown sugar
- ¼ cup lemon juice
- ¼ cup cold water
- 2 tablespoons cornstarch

1. MICROWAVE (high) water in 2-quart glass mix 'n pour bowl 5 to 6 minutes or until boiling. Add cabbage leaves, cup-side-up, covering with water as much as possible. Cover with plastic wrap.

2. MICROWAVE (high) 5 to 6 minutes, or until almost tender, rearranging leaves once. Let stand covered while preparing meat filling.

3. Combine ground beef, ground pork, onion, 1 can tomato sauce, rice, salt and pepper; mix well.

4. Drain cabbage leaves. Rinse with cold water until easy to handle; drain. Place ⅓ cup meat mixture in each cabbage leaf. Fold in sides and roll up around filling. Place in 12 x 8-inch glass baking dish.

5. Combine 1 can tomato sauce, brown sugar and lemon juice; mix well. Pour sauce over cabbage rolls. Cover with plastic wrap.

6. MICROWAVE (high) 5 to 6 minutes or until sauce is steaming hot. Then, MICROWAVE (medium — 50%) 30 to 35 minutes or until cabbage rolls are tender, rotating dish once. Place cabbage rolls on serving tray. Combine water and cornstarch; stir into sauce in baking dish.

7. MICROWAVE (high), uncovered, 1 to 2 minutes or until sauce boils and thickens, stirring once. Serve over cabbage rolls.

12 Cabbage Rolls
190 Calories Each

TIPS • With Full Power, microwave 10 minutes in step 6. Then use segments of 10 minutes standing time and 5 minutes microwave for a total of 30 to 35 minutes or until cabbage rolls are tender.

Convenience is always appreciated, especially for family meals. This recipe combines the beef mixture with uncooked macaroni for a quick and easy hot dish.

EASY BEEF AND RONI HOT DISH

- 1 lb. ground beef
- ½ cup chopped celery
- ¼ cup chopped onion
- 1½ cups (7 ozs.) uncooked macaroni
- 1 can (10¾ oz.) condensed golden mushroom soup
- 1¼ cups water
- 2 teaspoons parsley flakes
- ¾ teaspoon salt
- ⅛ teaspoon pepper
- ½ cup half & half or milk
- 1 cup (4 ozs.) shredded Cheddar cheese

1. Crumble ground beef into 1½-quart glass casserole. Add celery and onion.

2. MICROWAVE (high), uncovered, 5 to 6 minutes or until meat is no longer pink, stirring once. Drain. Stir in macaroni, soup, water, parsley, salt and pepper. Cover with casserole lid.

3. MICROWAVE (high) 14 to 15 minutes or until macaroni is just about tender, stirring twice. Stir in half & half and cheese. Cover.

4. MICROWAVE (high) 2 to 3 minutes or until heated through.

5 to 6 Servings

TIPS • For half a recipe, use a 1-quart glass casserole. In step 2, microwave 2½ to 3 minutes, in step 3 microwave 9 to 10 minutes and in step 4, microwave 1 to 1½ minutes.

• Mushroom soup can be substituted for golden mushroom soup.

The pleasing flavor of this casserole makes it enjoyable for the whole family.

CABBAGE CASSEROLE

   1 **lb. lean ground beef**
   1 **small onion, chopped**
   1 **medium carrot, shredded**
   1 **tablespoon Worcestershire sauce**
   4 **cups shredded cabbage (about ½ medium head)**
   1 **can (10¾ oz.) condensed tomato soup**
      Chopped chives, if desired

1. Crumble ground beef into 1½-quart glass casserole. Add onion and carrot.

2. MICROWAVE (high), uncovered, 5 to 6 minutes or until no longer pink, stirring once; drain.

3. Stir in Worcestershire sauce and cabbage. Spoon soup over top; spread evenly. Cover with casserole lid.

4. MICROWAVE (high) 14 to 15 minutes or until cabbage is tender, stirring once or twice. Sprinkle with chives, if desired.

About 8 Servings
140 Calories Each

TIP • Leftovers freeze well. For a 1-cup serving, microwave (high), covered, 2 to 3 minutes or until heated, stirring once.

This family casserole was sent in to be adapted by one of our readers. Potato slices are topped with a meat loaf mixture for an interesting one-dish meal.

BEEF AND POTATO CASSEROLE

   4 **cups peeled and sliced potatoes (about 4 large)**
   1 **small onion, chopped**
   ½ **cup water**
   1 **lb. ground beef**
   1 **can (10¾ oz.) condensed mushroom soup**
   ½ **cup crushed soda crackers (8 squares)**
   ½ **cup sour cream**
   1 **teaspoon salt**
   ¼ **to ½ teaspoon pepper**
   ½ **cup (2 ozs.) shredded Cheddar cheese**

1. Combine potatoes, onion and water in 8-inch square glass baking dish. Cover with plastic wrap.

2. MICROWAVE (high) 7 to 8 minutes or until potatoes are just about tender, stirring once. Let stand covered.

3. Combine ground beef, soup, cracker crumbs, sour cream, salt and pepper. Drain potatoes; sprinkle with cheese. Spoon meat mixture onto potatoes, spreading evenly. Cover with paper towel.

4. MICROWAVE (high), 10 to 12 minutes or until meat is done, rotating dish once.

5 to 6 Servings

Enjoy the convenience of casseroles you make ahead and store in the freezer to later pop in your microwave and heat.

INDIVIDUAL MEAT AND TATOR CASSEROLES

   1 **lb. ground beef**
   1 **small onion, chopped**
   1 **egg**
   ½ **cup dry bread crumbs**
   ¼ **cup milk**
   ½ **teaspoon salt**
   ¼ **teaspoon oregano leaves**
   ⅛ **teaspoon pepper**
   1 **can (10¾ oz.) condensed mushroom soup**
   40 **frozen potato puffs**

1. Combine ground beef, onion, egg, bread crumbs, milk, salt, oregano and pepper in mixing bowl; mix well. Divide into 4 portions. Press each portion into bottom and up sides of 1½-cup individual casserole. Spoon about ⅓ cup soup into center of each meat-lined dish. Top each with about 10 potato puffs.

2. Use casseroles immediately or wrap individually and refrigerate or freeze. (Casseroles can also be frozen and then combined in one larger container to store.)

3. To heat, MICROWAVE (high) one casserole at a time, covered with paper toweling:
   Freshly prepared: 4 to 5 minutes
   Refrigerated: 6 to 7 minutes
   Frozen: 8 to 9 minutes
Let stand covered a few minutes before serving.

4 Individual Casseroles

TIPS • To reheat 2 frozen casseroles, microwave 13 to 14 minutes.
• With Variable power, microwave one frozen casserole on medium-high (70%) 10 to 11 minutes.

Fettuccini noodles make the crust for this unusual pie. Rich tomato sauce, topped with Parmesan cheese, makes the delicious filling. The attractive wedges add a special touch to any meal.

FETTUCCINI PIE

- **8 ozs. fettuccini noodles**
- **1 lb. ground beef**
- **1 medium onion, chopped**
- **¼ cup chopped celery**
- **1 tablespoon sugar, if desired**
- **½ teaspoon oregano leaves**
- **½ teaspoon basil leaves**
- **1 can (16 oz.) tomato wedges, undrained**
- **1 can (6 oz.) tomato paste**
- **1 can (4 oz.) mushroom pieces, drained**
- **1 package (3 oz.) cream cheese**
- **½ teaspoon garlic salt**
- **¼ teaspoon salt**
- **¾ cup Parmesan cheese**

1. Cook fettuccini noodles as directed on package. Drain and rinse in cold water. Set aside.

2. Crumble ground beef into 1½-quart glass casserole. Add onion and celery.

3. MICROWAVE (high), uncovered, 5 to 6 minutes or until meat is no longer pink, stirring once. Stir to break meat into small pieces; drain. Add sugar, oregano, basil, tomato wedges, tomato paste and mushrooms. Stir to combine and break tomatoes into small pieces. Cover with casserole lid.

4. MICROWAVE (high) 7 to 8 minutes or until bubbly throughout, stirring once. Set aside.

5. MICROWAVE (high) cream cheese 30 to 45 seconds or until softened. Blend until smooth; stir in salts. Add cooked noodles; mix to coat evenly. Stir in ¼ cup Parmesan cheese.

6. Turn noodles into 10-inch glass pie plate or 9-inch deep-dish glass pie plate. Press evenly into bottom and up sides of pie plate, forming crust. Top with meat mixture; sprinkle with remaining Parmesan cheese.

7. MICROWAVE (high), uncovered, 7 to 8 minutes or until heated through, rotating dish once. Let stand 5 minutes. Cut into wedges.

About 8 Servings

TIPS • Regular noodles can be substituted for fettuccini noodles.

• Mixture can be prepared ahead through step 6. In step 7, microwave (medium-high — 70%) 11 to 13 minutes, rotating dish once.

Fettuccini Pie.

This tamale pie recipe boasts a spicy meat sauce, topped with a cornmeal and cheese topping.

TAMALE PIE

    1 lb. ground beef
    1 medium onion, chopped
    1 green pepper, chopped
    1 clove garlic, minced
    1 can (15 oz.) tomato sauce
    1 can (12 oz.) cut corn, drained
  ½ cup sliced pitted ripe olives
    1 tablespoon sugar
1½ to 2 teaspoons chili powder
    1 teaspoon salt
    1 cup (4 ozs.) shredded Cheddar cheese
1¾ cups water
  ¾ cup yellow cornmeal
  ¼ teaspoon salt
    2 tablespoons butter or margarine
       Paprika

1. Crumble ground beef into 2-quart glass casserole. Add onion, green pepper and garlic.

2. MICROWAVE (high), uncovered, 5 to 6 minutes or until meat is no longer pink. Stir to break meat into pieces; drain. Stir in tomato sauce, corn, olives, sugar, chili powder and 1 teaspoon salt. Cover with paper towel.

3. MICROWAVE (high) 13 to 15 minutes or until slightly thickened and flavors are blended, stirring once. Stir in ½ cup of cheese; set aside.

4. Combine water, cornmeal and ¼ teaspoon salt in 4-cup glass measure.

5. MICROWAVE (high), uncovered, 4 to 5 minutes or until mixture boils and thickens, stirring 2 or 3 times. Stir in butter. Drop teaspoonfuls onto meat mixture. Sprinkle with remaining cheese and the paprika.

6. MICROWAVE (high), uncovered, 7 to 8 minutes or until bubbly throughout, rotating dish once.

5 to 6 Servings

TIP • The liquid from the corn can be used for part of the water that is combined with the cornmeal.

Pizza variations are always favorites. This recipe features an easy spaghetti base with pizza toppings.

PIZZA-GHETTI CASSEROLE

1½ cups ready-cut spaghetti
    1 jar (15½ oz.) spaghetti sauce
  ½ teaspoon garlic salt
1½ cups (6 ozs.) shredded Mozzarella cheese
    4 ozs. thinly sliced Canadian bacon
1¾ ozs. thinly sliced pepperoni
  ¼ cup chopped onion
  ¼ cup chopped green pepper
  ½ cup sliced ripe or green olives
    1 can (4 oz.) mushroom pieces, drained

1. Cook spaghetti as directed on package. Drain and rinse in cold water.

2. Combine cooked spaghetti with spaghetti sauce, garlic salt and ¾ cup of Mozzarella cheese in shallow 1½-quart glass casserole. Spread evenly in dish. Top with even layers of Canadian bacon, pepperoni, onion, green pepper, olives and mushrooms. Cover with waxed paper or casserole lid.

3. MICROWAVE (high) 7 to 8 minutes or until heated through, rotating dish once. Sprinkle with remaining ¾ cup Mozzarella cheese.

4. MICROWAVE (high), uncovered, 1½ to 2 minutes or until cheese is melted.

4 to 5 Servings

TIPS • Other favorite pizza topping ingredients can be substituted or added to the topping.

• Casserole can be prepared ahead through step 2. If refrigerated, increase time in step 3 to 10 to 11 minutes.

• If desired, onion can be partially precooked by microwaving (high) in small covered dish about 2 minutes.

Lasagna without precooking the noodles! You'll be pleasantly suprised how easy it is to assemble and how tasty the results are.

LAZY DAY LASAGNA

  1 **lb. ground beef**
  1 **can (14½ oz.) tomatoes, undrained**
  1 **can (6 oz.) tomato paste**
1½ **teaspoons salt**
1½ **teaspoons basil leaves**
  ½ **teaspoon oregano leaves**
  ⅛ **teaspoon garlic powder**
  ½ **cup water**
  2 **cups cottage cheese**
  ¼ **cup Parmesan cheese**
  1 **egg**
  1 **tablespoon parsley flakes**
  8 **uncooked lasagna noodles**
  2 **cups (8 ozs.) shredded Mozzarella cheese**

1. Crumble ground beef into 1½-quart glass casserole.

2. MICROWAVE (high), uncovered, 5 to 6 minutes or until no longer pink, stirring once. Stir to break meat into pieces. Drain. Stir in tomatoes, tomato paste, salt, basil, oregano, garlic powder and water. Cover with casserole lid.

3. MICROWAVE (high) 4 to 5 minutes or until mixture boils. Combine cottage cheese, Parmesan cheese, egg and parsley; mix well.

4. Pour 1½ cups tomato sauce mixture into 12 x 8-inch glass baking dish; spread evenly in dish. Place 4 uncooked noodles evenly over sauce. (They may overlap slightly.)

5. Top with half the cottage cheese mixture, spreading evenly. Sprinkle with half the Mozzarella cheese. Spoon 1 cup sauce evenly over cheese. Place 4 or more noodles on sauce. Top with even layers of remaining cottage cheese mixture, Mozzarella cheese and tomato sauce. Cover tightly with plastic wrap.

6. MICROWAVE (high) 15 minutes. Rotate dish.

7. MICROWAVE (medium — 50%) 15 to 20 minutes or until noodles are tender. Remove plastic wrap. Sprinkle lasagna with an additional 2 tablespoons Parmesan cheese.

8. MICROWAVE (high), uncovered, 1½ to 2 minutes or until cheese is melted. Let stand about 10 minutes before cutting into squares for serving.

About 6 Servings

TIPS • With Full Power in steps 6 and 7, microwave (high) 15 minutes; let stand 5 minutes. Then, microwave (high) 5 minutes. Let stand 5 minutes. Add Parmesan cheese and microwave as directed in step 8.

  • Casserole can be assembled ahead through step 5. If refrigerated, increase time in step 7 to 20 to 25 minutes.

A luscious cheese filling is rolled inside of lasagna noodles making a memorable meal for two.

LASAGNA ROLLS

  2 **lasagna noodles**
  ½ **cup (2 ozs.) shredded Mozzarella cheese**
  ¼ **cup Ricotta cheese or dry-curd cottage cheese**
  2 **tablespoons Parmesan cheese**
  ½ **teaspoon fresh snipped parsley**
  ⅓ **lb. ground beef**
  1 **cup favorite spaghetti sauce**

1. Cook noodles as directed on package. Drain and rinse in cold water.

2. Combine cheeses and parsley, mixing well. Lay noodles on flat surface; spoon cheese onto noodles. Gently press cheese evenly onto noodles with back of spoon. Roll up each with cheese inside. Set aside.

3. Crumble ground beef into 2-cup glass casserole.

4. MICROWAVE (high), uncovered, 1½ to 2 minutes or until no longer pink, stirring once; drain. Stir in spaghetti sauce. Cover with casserole lid.

5. MICROWAVE (high) 1½ to 2 minutes or until heated through. Place lasagna rolls in meat mixture; and spoon some of mixture over rolls.

6. MICROWAVE (high), uncovered, 2 to 3 minutes or until rolls are heated through, rotating dish once. Spoon sauce over rolls for serving; sprinkle with additional Parmesan cheese.

About 2 Servings
810 Calories Each

Cooked pasta layered with a creamy cheese filling and zesty meat topping really does taste a lot like lasagna. It is an ideal do-ahead supper dish.

A-LOT-LIKE LASAGNA

1	package (7 oz.) spaghetti
1	medium onion, chopped
1	clove garlic, minced
2	tablespoons water
1	lb. ground beef
1	can (15 oz.) tomato sauce
1	teaspoon basil leaves
½	teaspoon oregano leaves
½	teaspoon salt
1	teaspoon sugar
1	package (3 oz.) cream cheese
1½	cups (12 ozs.) cottage cheese
¼	cup milk
1	tablespoon parsley flakes
2	tablespoons dry bread crumbs
2	tablespoons Parmesan cheese

1. Prepare spaghetti as directed on package; drain and rinse. Set aside.

2. Combine onion, garlic and water in 1½-quart glass casserole. Cover with casserole lid.

3. MICROWAVE (high) 3 to 4 minutes or until tender. Crumble ground beef; add to casserole.

4. MICROWAVE (high), uncovered, 5 to 6 minutes or until no longer pink, stirring once. Stir to break meat into pieces; drain.

5. Stir in tomato sauce, basil, oregano, salt and sugar. Cover with casserole lid.

6. MICROWAVE (high) 5 to 6 minutes or until hot and bubbly, stirring once.

7. MICROWAVE (high) cream cheese in glass dish ½ to ¾ minute or until softened. Blend in cottage cheese, milk and parsley.

8. Spread cooked spaghetti in bottom of 8-inch square glass baking dish or 2-quart glass casserole. Spoon cheese mixture over spaghetti; mix lightly. Top with meat mixture, spreading evenly. Cover with waxed paper.

9. MICROWAVE (high) 10 to 12 minutes or until heated through (150°), rotating dish once.

10. Combine crumbs and Parmesan cheese; sprinkle evenly over casserole.

11. MICROWAVE (high), uncovered, 2 to 3 minutes.

6 to 8 Servings

Lasagna Rolls.

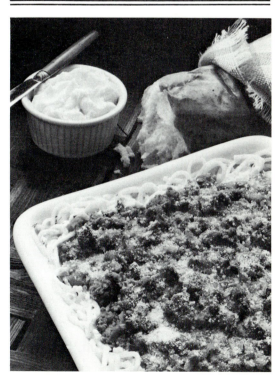

A-Lot-Like-Lasagna.

This company casserole is reminiscent of enchiladas, but with an easier preparation method.

ENCHILADA CASSEROLE

- 1 lb. ground beef
- 1 medium onion, chopped
- 1 clove garlic, minced
- 1 can (12 oz.) tomato paste
- 1 cup water
- 1 can (4 oz.) chopped green chilies, drained
- ½ cup sliced ripe olives
- ½ teaspoon salt
- 2 eggs
- 2 cups cottage cheese
- 1 package (8 oz.) Monterey Jack cheese, sliced
- 1 package (10 oz.) corn tortillas, quartered
- 1 cup (4 ozs.) shredded Cheddar cheese
  Sour cream

1. Crumble ground beef into 1½-quart glass casserole; add onion and garlic.

2. MICROWAVE (high), uncovered, 5 to 6 minutes or until meat is set, stirring once. Stir to break meat into small pieces; drain. Stir in tomato paste, water, green chilies, olives and salt. Cover with casserole lid.

3. MICROWAVE (high) 9 to 10 minutes or until flavors are blended and sauce is bubbly, stirring twice. Set aside.

4. Beat eggs; mix in cottage cheese. Set aside. Spread ⅓ of meat mixture in 3-quart glass casserole; top with half of Monterey Jack cheese, half of cottage cheese mixture and half of tortillas. Repeat layers ending with meat mixture and half of tortillas. Repeat layers ending with meat mixture. Cover with casserole lid.

5. MICROWAVE (medium-high—70%) 15 to 17 minutes (160°) or until center is heated, rotating dish once or twice. Sprinkle with Cheddar cheese.

6. MICROWAVE (high), uncovered, 1 to 1½ minutes or until cheese is melted. Let stand 10 minutes before serving. Garnish with additional sliced olives, if desired. Serve with sour cream.

8 to 10 Servings

TIP • With Full Power in step 5, microwave 10 to 12 minutes; let stand covered 5 minutes before completing step 6.

South-of-the-border flavors are always favorites and this casserole is no exception. Fruit salad and corn muffins would be tasty additions.

MEXICAN LAYER CASSEROLE

- 1 lb. ground beef
- 1 medium onion, chopped
- 1 can (16 oz.) refried beans
- 1 can (8 oz.) tomato sauce
- 1 package (1½ oz.) enchilada sauce mix
- ½ cup water
- 7 cups (about 8 ozs.) tortilla chips
- 1 cup (4 ozs.) shredded Cheddar cheese
- ¼ cup sliced ripe olives
- 2 cups shredded lettuce
- 1 medium tomato, chopped

1. Crumble ground beef into 2-quart glass mix 'n pour bowl. Add onion.

2. MICROWAVE (high), uncovered, 5 to 6 minutes or until meat is set, stirring once. Stir to break meat into small pieces; drain. Stir in beans, tomato sauce, sauce mix and water.

3. MICROWAVE (high), uncovered, 6 to 7 minutes or until hot and bubbly, stirring once.

4. Place chips in 12 x 8-inch glass baking dish; crush slightly. Spoon hot meat mixture evenly onto chips. Sprinkle with cheese and olives.

5. MICROWAVE (high), uncovered, 2 to 2½ minutes or until cheese is melted. Garnish with lettuce and tomato.

6 to 8 Servings

TIP • This recipe can be prepared ahead through step 2 and refrigerated. Heat meat mixture and assemble casserole just before serving.

This interesting casserole combines contrasting flavors and textures for delicious tasting results—crunchy, salty chips, creamy mushroom sauce and a spicy tomato sauce.

MEXICALI HOT DISH

- 1 lb. ground beef
- 1 small onion, chopped
- 1 can (10¾ oz.) condensed mushroom soup
- 1 can (4 oz.) diced green chilies
- 1 can (16 oz.) tomatoes, undrained
- 2 to 3 teaspoons chili powder
- ½ teaspoon oregano leaves
- ⅛ teaspoon garlic powder
- 1 package (8 oz.) corn or tortilla chips
- 2 cups (8 ozs.) shredded Monterey Jack or Longhorn cheese

1. Crumble ground beef into 1-quart glass casserole; add onion.

2. MICROWAVE (high), uncovered, 5 to 6 minutes or until meat is no longer pink, stirring once. Stir to break meat into pieces; drain fat. Blend in soup and chilies. Set aside.

3. Combine tomatoes (cut each into pieces), chili powder, oregano and garlic powder in 4-cup glass measure.

4. MICROWAVE (high), uncovered, 2½ to 3½ minutes or until sauce is bubbly, stirring once.

5. In 12 x 8-inch glass baking dish, layer a third of the corn chips and half each of meat mixture, tomato sauce and cheese. Repeat with another third of corn chips and remaining meat mixture, sauce and cheese. Top with remaining corn chips. Cover with paper towel.

6. MICROWAVE (high) 10 to 12 minutes or until hot and bubbly (160°), rotating dish once.

6 to 8 Servings

A hearty, colorful supper dish. For easy meal accompaniments, serve with crusty bread and a tossed salad.

ZUCCHINI-BEEF COMBO

- 6 cups sliced, unpeeled zucchini
- 1 lb. ground beef
- 1 small onion, chopped
- 1 clove garlic, minced
- ¼ cup unsifted all-purpose flour
- 1 cup water
- 1 teaspoon instant beef bouillon
- ¾ teaspoon salt
- ½ teaspoon oregano leaves
- ½ cup sour cream
- 2 tomatoes, thinly sliced
- ⅓ cup chopped green pepper
- 1 cup (4 ozs.) shredded Cheddar cheese

1. Place zucchini in 12 x 8-inch glass baking dish. Cover with plastic wrap.

2. MICROWAVE (high) 7 to 8 minutes or until tender-crisp. Let stand covered.

3. Crumble ground beef into 1-quart glass casserole. Add onion and garlic.

4. MICROWAVE (high), uncovered, 5 to 6 minutes or until no longer pink, stirring once. Drain. Stir in flour, water, bouillon, salt and oregano; mix well.

5. MICROWAVE (high), uncovered, 2½ to 3 minutes or until mixture boils, stirring once. Stir in sour cream.

6. Drain zucchini. Arrange evenly in baking dish. Top with tomato slices and green pepper. Spoon meat mixture onto vegetables, spreading evenly. Cover with waxed paper.

7. MICROWAVE (high) 6 to 8 minutes or until heated through, rotating dish once. Sprinkle with cheese.

8. MICROWAVE (high), uncovered, 1 to 2 minutes or until cheese is melted.

5 to 6 Servings

This bean combination is ideal for picnics because it makes such a large quantity.

BEAN CASSEROLE

2 lbs. hot Italian sausage
2 slices bacon
1 can (16 oz.) baked beans, undrained
1 can (15 oz.) kidney beans, undrained
1 can (15¾ oz.) hot chili beans, undrained
1 can (15½ oz.) wax beans, drained
1 can (16 oz.) baby lima beans, drained
1 can (16 oz.) green beans, drained
1 can (10¾ oz.) condensed tomato soup
1 can (6 oz.) tomato paste
1 cup packed brown sugar
½ cup barbecue sauce

1. Crumble Italian sausage into 5-quart glass casserole.

2. MICROWAVE (high), uncovered, 10 to 12 minutes or until meat is set, stirring twice; drain. Place bacon in single layer in 9-inch glass pie plate. Cover with paper towel.

3. MICROWAVE (high) 3 to 4 minutes or until crisp. Set aside.

4. Add remaining ingredients except bacon and barbecue sauce to sausage. Mix well. Cover with casserole lid.

5. MICROWAVE (high) 15 minutes stirring once. Stir beans; top with barbecue sauce. Crumble bacon and sprinkle over top.

6. MICROWAVE (high), uncovered, 15 to 18 minutes or until flavors are blended, rotating dish 2 or 3 times.

16 Servings
355 Calories Each

TIPS • This recipe freezes well.
   • For half a recipe, microwave (high) in step 2 for 5 to 6 minutes, 1 to 2 minutes in step 3, 6 to 8 minutes in step 5 and 10 to 12 minutes in step 6.

Stretch a half pound of ground beef into 5 servings by combining with a variety of beans. Pineapple adds an interesting flavor.

SAUCY TRIPLE BEAN BAKE

4 slices bacon
½ lb. ground beef
½ cup chopped onion
2 tablespoons chopped green pepper
1 can (16 oz.) pork and beans
1 can (16 oz.) kidney beans, drained
1 can (16 oz.) butter beans, drained
1 can (16 oz.) chunk pineapple, drained
¼ cup packed brown sugar
¼ cup catsup
2 tablespoons molasses
1 tablespoon vinegar
1½ teaspoons prepared mustard
1 teaspoon Worcestershire sauce

1. Place bacon in 2-quart glass casserole. Cover with paper towel.

2. MICROWAVE (high) 3½ to 4½ minutes or until crisp. Remove bacon and set aside. Crumble meat into drippings. Add onion and green pepper.

3. MICROWAVE (high), uncovered, 2½ to 3 minutes or until meat is no longer pink. Stir to break meat into pieces. Drain. Stir in remaining ingredients. Crumble bacon and sprinkle onto bean mixture. Cover with casserole cover.

4. MICROWAVE (high) 10 to 11 minutes or until hot and bubbly (170°), stirring once.

About 5 Servings

TIP • This dish freezes well so you need not be concerned about too many leftovers. Just package in 1-serving quantities and plan to reheat by microwaving 3 to 4 minutes, stirring once.

An easy-to-make casserole with a delightful blend of flavors. Keep ingredients on hand for last-minute company meals.

SEAFOOD STUFFING CASSEROLE

- 1 **package (6 oz.) frozen crabmeat**
- 1½ **cups water**
- ¼ **cup butter or margarine**
- 1 **package (6 oz.) chicken-flavored saucepan stuffing mix**
- 1 **cup (4 ozs.) sliced fresh mushrooms**
- 2 **tablespoons butter or margarine**
- 1 **can (4½ oz.) tiny shrimp, drained**
- 1 **tablespoon lemon juice**
- ½ **cup mayonnaise or salad dressing**
- ½ **cup shredded Swiss or Cheddar cheese**

1. Place pouch of frozen crabmeat in hot water to partially thaw.

2. Combine water, ¼ cup butter and the vegetable packet from stuffing mix in 1½-quart glass casserole.

3. MICROWAVE (high), uncovered, 3 to 3½ minutes or until steaming hot. Add stuffing mix and mix with fork until moistened. Cover and set aside. Combine mushrooms and 2 tablespoons butter in 4-cup glass measure.

4. MICROWAVE (high), uncovered, 2½ to 3 minutes or until mushrooms are tender. Break partially thawed crabmeat into pieces; add to mushrooms along with shrimp, lemon juice, mayonnaise and cheese. Mix lightly.

5. Remove about ⅓ of stuffing mixture from casserole. Arrange remaining stuffing evenly in dish. Top with crabmeat mixture. Spoon remaining stuffing over crabmeat.

6. MICROWAVE (high), uncovered, 6 to 7 minutes or until heated through, rotating dish once. Let stand 10 minutes before serving.

5 to 6 Servings

TIPS • With Combination Oven in step 6, microwave-bake, uncovered, in preheated 350° oven 6 to 6½ minutes.

• This recipe can be assembled several hours ahead through step 5. If refrigerated, increase time in step 6 to 8 to 9 minutes.

A creamy sauce and shredded potatoes stretch seafood into a special family meal or quick company dish.

SEAFOOD COMBO

- 1 **package (6 oz.) frozen crabmeat and shrimp**
- 2 **cups shredded potato or 12 ozs. frozen hash brown potatoes**
- 1 **tablespoon butter or margarine**
- 2 **green onions, sliced (including tops)**
- 1 **can (10¾ oz.) condensed cream of celery soup**
- ¾ **cup sour cream**
- 1 **tablespoon lemon juice**
- ¼ **teaspoon garlic salt**
- ½ **cup (2 ozs.) shredded Cheddar cheese**
- 2 **tablespoons sliced green olives, if desired**
  Paprika

1. Place pouch of frozen seafood in warm water to partially thaw.

2. Combine potatoes, butter and onions in 1½-quart glass casserole. Cover with casserole lid.

3. MICROWAVE (high) 4½ to 5½ minutes or until potatoes are just about tender, stirring once. Stir in soup, sour cream, lemon juice, garlic salt and seafood. Cover.

4. MICROWAVE (high) 4 to 5 minutes or until hot. Stir well. Sprinkle with cheese, olives and paprika.

5. MICROWAVE (high), uncovered, 2 to 2½ minutes or until cheese is melted.

4 to 5 Servings

A well-liked combination of broccoli, tuna and cheese sauce. With the cheese topping, a lower power setting is recommended, but in the Tips you will see how to use a full power setting if the cheese is added later.

CHARLIE'S SUPER SUPPER

- **2 packages (10 ozs. each) frozen chopped broccoli**
- **1 can (10¾ oz.) condensed mushroom soup**
- **1 cup (4 ozs.) shredded Cheddar cheese**
- **½ cup sour cream**
- **1 teaspoon Worcestershire sauce**
- **1 can (7 oz.) white tuna, drained**
- **½ cup (2 ozs.) shredded Cheddar cheese**

1. MICROWAVE (high) broccoli in packages on paper toweling 8 to 10 minutes or until hot. Drain and spread in 10 x 6-inch glass baking dish.

2. Combine soup, 1 cup cheese, the sour cream and Worcestershire sauce. Break tuna into pieces and arrange on broccoli. Spoon soup mixture evenly over tuna; spread to cover. Sprinkle with ½ cup cheese.

3. MICROWAVE (medium-high — 70%), uncovered, 12 to 14 minutes or until heated through (150°), rotating dish once.

4 to 5 Servings

TIP • With Full Power, omit sprinkling with cheese in step 2. Microwave 6 minutes. Let stand 4 minutes. Add cheese and microwave 2 to 3 minutes.

Easy, creamy and delicious best describe this recipe. It is sure to be a popular combination.

CREAMY TUNA AND NOODLES

- **3 cups (4 ozs.) uncooked egg noodles**
- **1 cup water**
- **1 can (10¾ oz.) condensed mushroom soup**
- **¼ teaspoon salt**
- **⅛ teaspoon pepper**
- **¼ cup milk**
- **1 cup (4 ozs.) cubed pasteurized process American cheese**
- **1 can (7 oz.) tuna, drained**
- **1 package (10 oz.) frozen peas**
- **½ cup coarsely crushed potato chips**

1. Combine noodles, water, soup, salt and pepper in 1½-quart glass casserole. Cover with casserole lid.

2. MICROWAVE (high) 10 minutes, stirring once. Stir in milk, cheese, tuna and peas. Cover.

3. MICROWAVE (high) 5 to 6 minutes or until noodles are tender and mixture is heated, stirring once. Sprinkle with potato chips before serving.

About 5 Servings

Corn and oysters have become a flavorful combination that are a tradition for many families.

SCALLOPED CORN AND OYSTERS

- **¼ cup butter or margarine**
- **1 medium onion, chopped**
- **1 can (17 oz.) cream-style corn**
- **½ cup milk**
- **1 cup coarsely crushed cracker crumbs (about 16 squares)**
- **1 egg**
- **⅛ teaspoon pepper**
- **1 can (8 oz.) oysters, drained**

1. MICROWAVE (high) butter and onion in 1-quart glass casserole 2 to 3 minutes or until onion is just about tender. Add remaining ingredients, mixing well. Cover with casserole lid.

2. MICROWAVE (high) 4 minutes. Stir and then MICROWAVE (high) 3 to 4 minutes or until center is just about set, stirring once.

4 to 6 Servings

TIPS • If using fresh oysters, precook by microwaving in covered glass dish about 2 minutes. Add to corn and cook as directed.

• With Combination Oven in step 2, microwave-bake, uncovered, in preheated 375° oven 15 to 17 minutes.

A deliciously flavored sauce with chunks of chicken to serve over your favorite pasta. We especially liked it with spinach noodles or linguini.

CHICKEN AND PASTA

- 2 whole chicken breasts (about 2 lbs.)
- 1 small onion, sliced
- 1 rib celery, sliced
- 1 sprig parsley
- 1½ cups water
- 8 ozs. spinach noodles or spaghetti
- ¾ cup half & half cream
- ⅓ cup flour
- 1½ teaspoons salt
  Dash pepper
- 1 teaspoon Dijon-style mustard
- 3 drops Tabasco sauce
- 2 tablespoons Parmesan cheese
- 2 tablespoons dry white wine, if desired
  Parsley and paprika for garnish

1. Cut chicken breasts in half. Combine onion, celery, parsley, chicken and water in 2-quart glass mix 'n pour bowl. Cover with plastic wrap; make a small slit in plastic for escape of steam.

2. MICROWAVE (high) 18 to 20 minutes or until chicken is done, rearranging chicken once. Remove chicken from broth; cool. (Cook noodles as directed on package.) Remove and discard parsley. Blend together cream, flour, salt, pepper, mustard and Tabasco sauce. Blend into hot broth, mixing well.

3. MICROWAVE (high), uncovered, 5 to 6 minutes or until boiling hot, stirring once. Discard skin on chicken and cut chicken from bones and into bite-sized pieces; add to sauce along with Parmesan cheese and wine.

4. MICROWAVE (high), uncovered, 1 to 2 minutes or until heated through. Serve over cooked noodles; garnish with parsley and paprika.

5 to 6 Servings

TIP • To make ahead, prepare through step 3. Increase time in step 4 to 10 to 12 minutes, stirring once.

With canned or ready-cooked chicken you can put together this attractive chicken dish in under 30 minutes. By keeping the noodles and chicken sauce separate, it's easy to reheat leftovers for another day.

GUACAMOLE-CHICKEN OVER NOODLES

- 1 cup chicken broth
- 1 cup half & half cream
- 6 tablespoons flour
- ½ teaspoon salt
- ⅛ teaspoon rosemary leaves
- ⅛ teaspoon basil leaves
- ¼ cup butter or margarine
- 1 cup (4 ozs.) shredded Cheddar cheese
- 2 cans (5 ozs. each) chicken (2 cups)
- 1 carton (6 oz.) frozen avocado dip, thawed
- ½ cup sour cream
- 4 drops Tabasco sauce
- 4 to 5 cups chow mein noodles

1. Combine broth, cream, flour, salt, rosemary and basil in 1-quart glass mix 'n pour bowl; blend well. Add butter.

2. MICROWAVE (high), uncovered, 5 to 5½ minutes or until mixture boils and thickens, stirring 2 or 3 times. Stir in cheese and chicken.

3. MICROWAVE (high), uncovered, 1½ to 2 minutes or until cheese is melted. Set aside.

4. Combine avocado dip, sour cream and Tabasco sauce in small serving dish. If desired, heat noodles by microwaving (high) 1 to 1½ minutes.

5. Serve chicken mixture over noodles, topping with guacamole (avocado) mixture.

About 5 Servings

TIPS • To thaw dip in microwave oven, remove lid and microwave mixture 2 minutes. Stir and break apart mixture. Microwave 1 to 1½ minutes or until thawed.

• This recipe can easily be halved. Just reduce microwave times to about ½ the original.

• Fresh avocado can be substituted for frozen dip. Mash one ripe avocado and mix with 1 tablespoon lemon juice and ¼ teaspoon onion salt.

This chicken salad is served in cream puffs, but would also be good served on lettuce.

BROCCOLI-CHICKEN SALAD PUFFS

- 2 **whole chicken breasts, split**
- 1 **bunch (12 ozs.) fresh broccoli**
- 1 **tablespoon water**
- 2 **hard-cooked eggs, chopped**
- 1 **small onion, finely chopped**
- ½ **cup chopped celery**
- 2 **tablespoons chopped pimiento**
- 1 **cup mayonnaise**
- 1 **tablespoon lemon juice**
- 1 **teaspoon salt**
- ½ **teaspoon dill weed**
- ⅛ **teaspoon curry powder**
- 20 **to 24 Luncheon Puffs (recipe this page)**

1. Arrange chicken breasts skin-side-up in 8-inch square glass baking dish. Cover with waxed paper.

2. MICROWAVE (high) 13 to 15 minutes or until chicken is done, rotating dish once. Set aside to cool.

3. Wash and drain broccoli. Cut top 4-inches off broccoli; discard remainder. Cut broccoli into small pieces (about 5 cups). Place in 2-quart glass mix 'n pour bowl. Add water. Cover with plastic wrap.

4. MICROWAVE (high) 4 to 5 minutes or until bright green and tender-crisp, stirring once. Drain; uncover and cool.

5. Cut chicken into small pieces; add to broccoli. Add eggs, onion, celery and pimiento; mix lightly. Add mayonnaise, lemon juice, salt, dill and curry; mix just until evenly coated. Cover and refrigerate overnight if possible.

6. To serve, slice off top of each puff; spoon about ¼-cup salad mixture into each puff. Replace each top. Refrigerate until served.

10 to 12 Servings

TIP • If desired, two packages frozen chopped broccoli can be substituted for fresh. Microwave in step 4 for 7 to 8 minutes or until thawed.

These cream puffs are baked in the conventional oven after using the microwave to aid the preparation.

LUNCHEON PUFFS

- ½ **cup butter or margarine**
- 1 **cup water**
- 1 **cup unsifted all-purpose flour**
- ½ **teaspoon salt**
- 4 **eggs**

1. Preheat oven to 400°. Combine butter and water in 2-quart glass mix 'n pour bowl.

2. MICROWAVE (high), uncovered, 3½ to 4½ minutes or until mixture boils hard. Carefully add flour and salt all at once. Stir until mixture leaves sides of bowl and forms a ball. Add eggs, one at a time, beating until well-blended after each.

3. Drop mixture by tablespoon 2 inches apart onto ungreased baking sheet to form 20 to 24 puffs.

4. Bake 25 to 30 minutes or until golden brown. Turn off heat. Prick each puff once with sharp knife for steam to escape; leave in oven 10 minutes. Carefully remove from baking sheet. Cool, split and fill with Broccoli-Chicken Salad (this page).

20 to 24 Puffs

TIPS • Dough may be covered and stored in refrigerator up to 3 days.
• Puffs can be filled and refrigerated up to 4 hours.
• Unfilled puffs should be stored loosely covered.
• With Combination Oven, use a metal baking pan and bake in preheated 400° oven 15 minutes; then microwave - bake 8 to 10 minutes.

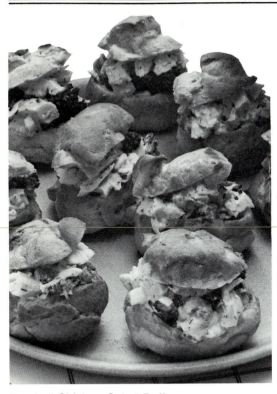

Broccoli-Chicken Salad Puffs.

This casserole features chicken with traditional crisp Cantonese vegetables for a flavorful, colorful and delightful foreign cuisine dish.

CHICKEN CANTONESE CASSEROLE

2½ cups cubed, cooked chicken
2 cups sliced celery
1 medium green pepper, chopped
1 can (10¾ oz.) condensed cream of chicken soup
1 can (8 oz.) sliced water chestnuts, drained
1 can (2 oz.) mushroom pieces, drained
1 jar (2 oz.) diced pimiento, drained
2 teaspoons soy sauce
½ cup chopped cashews
1 can (3 oz.) chow mein noodles

1. Combine chicken, celery, green pepper, soup, water chestnuts, mushrooms, pimiento and soy sauce in 2-quart glass casserole; mix well. Cover with casserole lid.

2. MICROWAVE (high) 7 to 8 minutes or until heated through. Add cashews and chow mein noodles; mix lightly.

3. MICROWAVE (high), uncovered, 2½ to 3 minutes or until heated through.

About 5 Servings

TIPS • A 3-lb. frying chicken can be used for the 2½ cups cooked chicken. To microwave, place cut-up chicken in 12 x 8-inch glass baking dish. Cover with waxed paper. Microwave (high) 20 to 25 minutes or until tender.

• You may wish to substitute turkey or other favorite cooked meat or fish for the chicken.

• Save a few chow mein noodles to use for a garnish.

Tender-crisp vegetables help minimize the cholesterol level of each portion.

CHICKEN ALMOND DING

1 small head cauliflower (about 2 cups)
1 small onion, sliced
2 cups small broccoli pieces
1 cup thinly sliced carrots
2 tablespoons water
¼ cup water
1 tablespoon cornstarch
3 tablespoons soy sauce
1 teaspoon instant chicken bouillon
2 cups cubed cooked chicken
½ cup slivered almonds
2 tablespoons butter or margarine

1. Separate cauliflower into flowerettes; cut each into ¼-inch slice. Place in 2-quart glass casserole. Add onion, broccoli, carrots and 2 tablespoons water. Cover with casserole lid.

2. MICROWAVE (high) 6 to 7 minutes or until vegetables are just about tender, stirring once or twice.

3. Combine ¼ cup water, cornstarch, soy sauce and chicken bouillon in 1-cup glass measure. Stir into vegetables. Add chicken; cover.

4. MICROWAVE (high) 3 to 3½ minutes or until sauce thickens, stirring once or twice. Let stand covered.

5. Combine almonds and butter in 9-inch glass pie plate.

6. MICROWAVE (high), uncovered, 4 to 5 minutes until lightly toasted, stirring 2 or 3 times. Stir into chicken. If desired, serve with rice.

5 Servings
Calories: 160
Cholesterol: 28 mg.

TIP • One package (20 oz.) frozen vegetable combination can be substituted for cauliflower, broccoli and carrots. Increase microwave time in step 2 to 9 to 10 minutes.

This popular combination of broccoli and chicken was sent to us for adapting by one of our readers.

BROCCOLI AND CHICKEN

   3 **whole chicken breasts (about 2½ lbs.)**
   2 **packages (10 ozs. each) frozen chopped broccoli**
   2 **cans (10¾ ozs. each) condensed cream of chicken soup**
   1 **cup mayonnaise**
   1 **tablespoon lemon juice**
  ¼ **teaspoon salt**
1½ **cups (6 ozs.) shredded Cheddar or other favorite cheese**
   1 **tablespon butter or margarine**
   1 **cup herb-seasoned stuffing cubes**

1. Place chicken, skin-side-up, in 12 x 8-inch glass baking dish. Cover with waxed paper.

2. MICROWAVE (high) 11 to 13 minutes or until tender, rotating dish once. Uncover and cool.

3. MICROWAVE (high) broccoli in packages 10 to 12 minutes or until just about tender; set aside. Drain cooking juices from chicken into 4-cup glass measure. Cube chicken and place in 12 x 8-inch glass baking dish. Top with broccoli.

4. Add soup, mayonnaise, lemon juice and salt to juices in 4-cup measure; mix well. Pour over chicken mixture. Sprinkle with cheese.

5. MICROWAVE (high) butter in small glass dish ½ to 1 minute or until melted. Toss with stuffing cubes. Sprinkle over casserole.

6. MICROWAVE (high), uncovered, 8 to 10

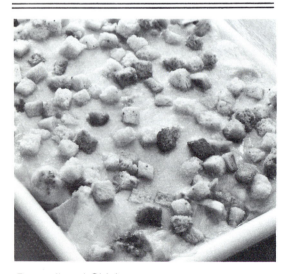

Broccoli and Chicken.

minutes or until heated through, rotating dish once.

About 8 Servings

TIPS • For half a recipe, use an 8-inch round or square baking dish. Microwave in step 2 for 8 to 9 minutes, in step 3 for 6 to 7 minutes and in step 6 for 5 to 6 minutes.

• If prepared ahead, omit stuffing cube topping and refrigerate up to 12 hours. Microwave (high), covered with waxed paper, 10 to 12 minutes. Sprinkle topping on casserole. Microwave (high), uncovered, 2 to 3 minutes or until center is heated.

Slices of ham and turkey top a cheesy broccoli sauce in this dish which is just right to serve for any occasion.

HAM 'N TURKEY ROLL-UPS

   2 **packages (10 ozs. each) frozen chopped broccoli**
  ¼ **cup flour**
  ½ **teaspoon salt**
  ⅛ **teaspoon pepper**
  ⅛ **teaspoon dry mustard**
1½ **cups milk**
  ¼ **cup butter or margarine**
   1 **cup (4 ozs.) shredded Cheddar cheese**
   8 **slices (1 lb.) fully cooked ham (about ¼-inch thick)**
   8 **slices (8 ozs.) cooked turkey (about ⅛-inch thick)**

1. MICROWAVE (high) broccoli in packages 10 to 12 minutes or until almost tender, turning packages over once. Set aside.

2. Combine flour, salt, pepper and dry mustard in 2-quart glass mix 'n pour bowl. Slowly stir in milk; add butter.

3. MICROWAVE (high), uncovered, 5 to 6 minutes or until sauce boils and thickens, stirring 2 or 3 times. Stir in cheese. Drain liquid from broccoli; stir broccoli into cheese sauce.

4. Spoon broccoli mixture into 12 x 8-inch glass baking dish. Place a turkey slice on top of each ham slice. Roll up each with ham on outside. Fasten each with toothpick. Arrange on broccoli, turning each roll to coat with sauce. Cover with waxed paper.

5. MICROWAVE (high) 6 to 7 minutes or until ham is heated, rotating dish once or twice. Remove toothpicks before serving.

About 8 Servings

This casserole has a special blend of flavors and you need not wait for leftover turkey to make it. Turkey parts are in most food markets and can be cooked easily in the microwave as suggested in the "Tips". Also, leftover cooked chicken works equally well.

SHERRIED TURKEY CASSEROLE

    2 cups cubed, cooked turkey
    3 cups dry bread cubes
    ½ cup butter or margarine
    2 tablespoons finely chopped onion
    ½ teaspoon poultry seasoning
    ½ teaspoon salt
    ¼ teaspoon pepper
    1 teaspoon parsley flakes
    2 tablespoons flour
 1½ cups turkey stock or broth
    ½ cup dry sherry

1. Combine turkey and bread cubes in 1-quart glass casserole; set aside.

2. MICROWAVE (high) butter in 1-quart glass mix 'n pour bowl ¾ to 1 minute or until melted. Pour all but about 2 tablespoons over bread cubes. Add onion to butter remaining in dish.

3. MICROWAVE (high), uncovered, 2 to 2½ minutes or until onion is tender. Blend in poultry seasoning, salt, pepper, parsley and flour. Stir in stock and sherry.

4. MICROWAVE (high), uncovered, 5 to 6 minutes or until mixture boils and thickens, stirring twice during last half of cooking time. Pour sauce over turkey mixture. Cover with paper towel.

5. MICROWAVE (high) 9 to 10 minutes or until center is just about to set. Let stand a few minutes before serving.

                              4 to 5 Servings

TIPS • Canned chicken broth can be substituted for turkey stock; just omit salt.
• A 1¼-lb. turkey breast yields about 2 cups cooked turkey. Place in baking dish with 1¼ cups water. Cover with waxed paper and microwave (medium-high — 70%) 13 to 15 minutes.

Turkey leftovers team with broccoli and sprouts to make a nutritious main dish.

TURKEY AND SPROUTS CASSEROLE

    1 package (20 oz.) frozen chopped broccoli
    3 cups cut up, cooked turkey (thin strips)
 1½ cups (8 ozs.) cubed pasteurized process cheese
    2 tablespoons chopped onion
    ⅓ cup chopped celery
    2 tablespoons butter or margarine
    3 tablespoons flour
    1 cup milk
    ½ teaspoon salt
    ¼ teaspoon rosemary leaves
    ⅛ teaspoon pepper
    1 teaspoon Worcestershire sauce
 1½ cups alfalfa sprouts
    2 tablespoons Parmesan cheese

1. Place broccoli in shallow 1½-quart glass casserole. Cover with casserole lid or plastic wrap.

2. MICROWAVE (high) 11 to 12 minutes or until almost tender. Drain. Top with even layers of turkey and cheese; set aside.

3. Combine onion, celery and butter in 2-cup glass measure.

4. MICROWAVE (high), uncovered, 2½ to 3 minutes or until vegetables are just about tender. Blend in flour. Stir in milk, salt, rosemary, pepper and Worcestershire sauce.

5. MICROWAVE (high), uncovered, 2½ to 3 minutes or until mixture boils and thickens, stirring twice. Pour sauce over turkey mixture.

6. MICROWAVE (high), uncovered 6 to 7 minutes or until bubbly and heated through. Top with sprouts and Parmesan cheese.

7. MICROWAVE (high), uncovered, 1½ to 2 minutes or until heated through.

                              About 6 Servings

TIPS • A 1¾-lb. turkey breast yields about 3 cups cooked turkey.
• A 10¾-oz. can condensed celery soup can be substituted for onion, celery, butter, flour, milk and salt.
• A combination of cooked turkey and ham is also very delicious. Or, use all ham.

Spinach, mushrooms and sour cream make a flavorful sauce for spaghetti or other noodles. The flavor is perfect for a meatless dish or served with roast, ham or poultry.

SPAGHETTI FLORENTINE

 8 ozs. spaghetti
 1 package (10 oz.) frozen chopped
    spinach
 1 medium onion, chopped
 2 tablespoons butter or margarine
 1 cup (8 ozs.) sour cream
 ¾ cup milk
 2 cans (4 ozs. each) sliced mushrooms,
    drained
 ¼ cup dry white wine, if desired
1½ teaspoons instant chicken bouillon
 1 teaspoon salt

1. Cook spaghetti as directed on package. Drain and rinse in cold water. Set aside.

2. MICROWAVE (high) spinach in package 3½ to 4 minutes or until thawed. Set aside.

3. Combine onion and butter in 2-quart glass casserole.

4. MICROWAVE (high), uncovered, 3 to 4 minutes or until onion is tender, stirring once. Stir in sour cream, milk, mushrooms, wine, chicken bouillon, salt and spinach; mix well. Cover with casserole lid.

5. MICROWAVE (medium-high — 70%) 13 to 15 minutes or until heated through, stirring twice. Heat spaghetti if necessary by microwaving (high) 3 to 5 minutes. Serve sauce over cooked spaghetti.

About 6 Servings

TIPS • Sauce and spaghetti can be combined before heating in step 5. Cover with casserole lid and microwave (high) 7 to 8 minutes or until heated through, stirring 2 or 3 times.

• Cooked noodles also combine well with the sauce. Just substitute noodles for spaghetti and prepare as directed, mixing the noodles with the sauce before heating.

• Liquid from the mushrooms can be used in place of milk.

• With Full Power in step 5, microwave 7 to 8 minutes, stirring 3 or 4 times.

Bacon and sour cream turn macaroni and cheese into something special. It can be quickly prepared in under 30 minutes or made ahead for reheating.

MOSTACCIOLI AND CHEESE SUPREME

 8 ozs. Mostaccioli macaroni
 4 slices bacon
 1 small onion, chopped
 2 tablespoons flour
 ½ teaspoon salt
    Dash pepper
 1 cup milk
 ½ cup sour cream
1½ cups (6 ozs.) shredded Cheddar
    cheese

1. Cook macaroni as directed on package. Drain.

2. Meanwhile layer bacon in shallow 1½-quart glass casserole. Cover with paper towel.

3. MICROWAVE (high) 4 to 4½ minutes or until crisp. Set aside bacon. Add onion to drippings.

4. MICROWAVE (high), uncovered, 2 to 3 minutes or until onion is tender. Blend in flour, salt and pepper. Stir in milk.

5. MICROWAVE (high), uncovered, 2½ to 3½ minutes or until mixture boils and thickens, stirring once. Stir in sour cream, cheese and cooked macaroni. Mix well. Crumble bacon and sprinkle over top.

6. MICROWAVE (high), uncovered, 5 to 6 minutes or until heated through.

4 to 5 Servings

TIPS • Elbow macaroni can be substituted for Mostaccioli.

• This recipe can be prepared ahead through step 5 except for topping with bacon. Refrigerate up to 2 days. Increase microwave time in step 6 to 7 to 8 minutes, stirring once. Add bacon and microwave 1 to 2 minutes.

• When omitting the bacon, cook the onion in 3 tablespoons butter or margarine.

This recipe combines economical ingredients as well as a time-saving cooking method that eliminates the need to precook the macaroni.

DRIED BEEF CASSEROLE

- 1½ cups (7 ozs.) uncooked macaroni
- 2 cups water
- 1 tablespoon chopped onion
- ½ package (10-oz. size) frozen chopped spinach
- 1 cup milk
- 2 tablespoons flour
- 1 teaspoon prepared mustard
- ½ teaspoon salt
- 4 ozs. processed cheese spread, crumbled
- 1 package (2½ oz.) dried beef, cut into pieces

1. Combine macaroni, water and onion in 2-quart glass casserole. Cover with casserole lid.

2. MICROWAVE (high) 5 to 6 minutes or until mixture boils. Let stand, covered, 5 minutes.

3. To thaw half a package of spinach, wrap half the package with foil. Place in microwave and microwave (high) 2 to 3 minutes or until thawed. Squeeze thawed end to drain. Add thawed spinach to macaroni; wrap and return remaining half of package to freezer.

4. Stir in milk, flour, mustard, salt, cheese and dried beef. Cover.

5. MICROWAVE (high) 8 to 9 minutes or until mixture is bubbly and macaroni is tender, stirring twice.

About 5 Servings

TIP • When a casserole like this starts with uncooked macaroni, it will become quite stiff when cold. To reheat, thin with additional milk or water.

Looking for a special meal accompaniment for the holidays? Try this flavorful combination of wild rice and mushrooms.

WILD RICE PILAF

- ½ cup wild rice (about 3 ozs.)
- 1 cup water
- ½ cup long grain white rice
- 1¼ cups water
- 1 teaspoon salt
- 1 teaspoon instant beef bouillon
- 1 medium onion, chopped
- 1 clove garlic, minced
- 2 cups (8 ozs.) sliced fresh mushrooms
- 1 cup chopped celery
- ¼ cup butter or margarine
- 1 cup frozen peas

1. Rinse and drain wild rice. Combine with 1 cup water in 1½-quart glass casserole. Cover with casserole lid.

2. MICROWAVE (high) 4 to 5 minutes or until mixture boils. Let stand covered 1 hour.

3. Add white rice, 1¼ cups water, salt and beef bouillon. Cover.

4. MICROWAVE (high) 5 to 6 minutes or until mixture boils. Then, MICROWAVE (medium — 50%) 13 to 14 minutes or until rice is just about tender. Let stand covered 10 minutes.

5. Combine onion, garlic, mushrooms, celery and butter in 1-quart glass mix 'n pour bowl. Cover with plastic wrap.

6. MICROWAVE (high) 5 to 6 minutes or until vegetables are tender, stirring once. Stir into rice along with peas. Cover.

7. MICROWAVE (high) 5 to 6 minutes or until peas are tender, stirring once.

6 to 8 Servings

Noodles in a creamy sauce make an easy-to-serve accompaniment for patio dining. The mild flavor is a nice contrast to spicy barbecue-glazed meats.

EASY NOODLE BAKE

  8 ozs. noodles (about 4 cups)
¼ cup butter or margarine
2 tablespoons chopped onion
2 tablespoons flour
1 teaspoon prepared mustard
½ teaspoon salt
½ teaspoon Worcestershire sauce
⅛ teaspoon pepper
1½ cups milk
½ cup sour cream
2 tablespoons dry bread crumbs
¼ teaspoon barbecue seasoning or paprika

1. Cook noodles as directed on package; drain. Rinse well in cold water; drain and set aside.

2. Combine butter and onion in 1½-quart glass casserole.

3. MICROWAVE (high), uncovered, 2½ to 3 minutes or until tender. Blend in flour and seasonings. Stir in milk.

4. MICROWAVE (high), uncovered, 3½ to 4½ minutes or until mixture boils and thickens, stirring once or twice.

5. Stir in sour cream and cooked noodles. Spread evenly in dish. Combine bread crumbs and seasoning. Sprinkle over noodles.

6. MICROWAVE (high), uncovered, 7 to 9 minutes or until heated through (170°).

                      5 to 6 Servings

TIP • If noodles have been refrigerated before heating in step 6, cover with paper towel and increase microwave time to 9 to 11 minutes.

Soaking and slow cooking are the secrets to tender, flavorful wild rice prepared in the microwave.

GREAT PLAINS WILD RICE

  1 cup wild rice
1 cup water
2 tablespoons butter or margarine
¼ cup chopped celery
¼ cup chopped onion
½ cup chopped fresh mushrooms, if desired
1 can (10½ oz.) condensed beef consommé

1. Wash wild rice in cold water; drain. Combine rice and water in 2-quart glass casserole. Cover with casserole lid.

2. MICROWAVE (high) 5 to 6 minutes or until mixture boils. Allow to stand covered at least 3 hours.

3. Add remaining ingredients. Cover with casserole lid.

4. MICROWAVE (high) 7 to 8 minutes or until mixture boils. Then, MICROWAVE (low — 30%) 45 to 60 minutes or until liquid is absorbed and rice is tender.

                      4 to 6 Servings

TIPS • With Full Power, use segments of 3 minutes microwave and 6 minutes stand for the 45 to 60 minutes low power time in step 4.

  • Crumbled, cooked bacon compliments wild rice dishes. Cook 4 slices bacon by microwaving (high) 4 to 5 minutes. Use drippings for butter in step 3 and add crumbled, cooked bacon just before serving.

Serve this as a meatless main dish or side dish for a roast. Freshly grated Parmesan cheese is worth the extra step.

FETTUCCINI

  8 ozs. fettuccini noodles
¼ cup butter or margarine
1 package (3 oz.) cream cheese
¼ cup half & half or milk
½ teaspoon garlic salt
¼ teaspoon salt
¼ teaspoon onion salt
½ cup (2 ozs.) Parmesan cheese

1. Cook noodles as directed on package. Drain and rinse in cold water. Set aside.

2. MICROWAVE (high) butter and cream cheese in 1½-quart glass serving bowl 20 to 30 seconds or until softened.

3. Mix until creamy. Blend in half & half and salts. Mix in cooked noodles. Cover with bowl or overturned plate.

4. MICROWAVE (high) 4 to 5 minutes or until heated through, stirring twice. Mix in Parmesan cheese.

5. MICROWAVE (high), uncovered, 1 to 2 minutes or until heated.

                      4 to 6 Servings

TIPS • Noodles can be prepared ahead through step 3. Complete steps 4 and 5 when ready to serve.

  • Try this recipe with other favorite noodles.

A delicate flavored quiche is welcome at any meal and when filled with crab, it makes a special entree for company. Yellow food coloring enhances the color of the microwaved crust.

CRAB QUICHE

Crust:
- 1 cup unsifted all-purpose flour
- ½ teaspoon salt
- ⅓ cup shortening
- 2 drops yellow food coloring
- 2 to 3 tablespoons cold water

Filling:
- 1 cup half & half cream
- 4 eggs
- 1 teaspoon chopped chives
- 1 teaspoon Dijon-style mustard
- ½ teaspoon salt
- Dash pepper
- Dash nutmeg
- 1 package (6 oz.) frozen crabmeat, thawed and drained
- ¾ cup (3 ozs.) shredded Swiss cheese

1. Combine flour and salt. Cut in shortening until it resembles coarse crumbs. Add food coloring to water; gradually stir into flour mixture until dough clings together. Form into a smooth ball.

2. Roll out on floured cloth-covered surface to circle 1 inch larger than 9-inch glass pie plate. Fit into pie plate. Fold under edge, forming standing rim; flute. Prick bottom and sides with fork.

3. MICROWAVE (high), uncovered, 4 to 5 minutes or until crust is no longer doughy, rotating plate twice.

4. MICROWAVE (high) cream in 1-cup glass measure 2 to 2½ minutes or until steaming hot. Beat together eggs and seasonings; slowly beat in hot cream.

5. Layer crabmeat and cheese in crust. Pour egg mixture in crust; cover with waxed paper.

6. MICROWAVE (high) 7 to 9 minutes or until center is just about set, rotating dish two or three times.

About 6 Servings

TIPS • Other favorite 9-inch unbaked pastry shells can be used. Prick with fork and microwave as directed.

• Other cooked frozen or canned seafood can be substituted for crab. Shrimp or a combination of shrimp and crab are good.

• With Combination Oven, omit microwaving in steps 3 and 4. In step 6 microwave-bake, uncovered, in preheated 400° oven 10 minutes. Then bake 4 to 5 minutes.

This tasty, colorful main dish is ideal for brunches any time of year. Much of the preparation can be done in advance with just a few minutes of heating required at serving time.

FIX-AHEAD SCRAMBLED EGGS

- 8 slices bacon
- 16 eggs
- 1 cup half & half cream
- ½ teaspoon salt
- ⅛ teaspoon pepper
- 3 tablespoons bacon drippings or margarine
- 1 can (10 ¾ oz.) condensed mushroom soup
- 1 pint (8 ozs.) sliced fresh mushrooms
- 1 tomato, chopped
- 1½ cups (6 ozs.) shredded Cheddar cheese

1. Layer bacon between paper towels in glass baking dish. Cover with paper towel.

2. MICROWAVE (high) 7 to 9 minutes or until crisp, rotating dish once. Drain bacon and set aside; reserve bacon drippings.

3. Beat eggs in 2-quart glass casserole. Beat in half & half, salt, pepper and bacon drippings. Cover with casserole lid.

4. MICROWAVE (high) 8 to 9 minutes or until just about set, stirring 2 or 3 times.

5. Spoon eggs into shallow 1½ or 2-quart glass baking dish. Spoon soup evenly over eggs. Top with mushrooms and tomato. Cover with waxed paper.

6. MICROWAVE (high) 5 minutes. Rotate dish. Sprinkle with cheese and crumbled bacon.

7. MICROWAVE (high), uncovered, 2 to 3 minutes or until eggs are heated and cheese melted.

8 to 10 Servings

TIP • To Make Ahead, prepare through step 5. If refrigerated, increase time in step 6 to 7 to 9 minutes, rotating dish once.

Tortilla Roll-Ups.

BLT-CHEESE SANDWICHES

  4 slices bacon
  4 slices bread, toasted
  1 medium tomato
     American or Cheddar cheese
     Mayonnaise or salad dressing
     Lettuce

1. Place a paper towel on glass plate. Arrange bacon slices in single layer on towel; top with another towel.

2. MICROWAVE (high) 2½ to 4 minutes or until bacon is crisp, rotating plate once. Set aside bacon.

3. While bread is toasting, cut tomato into 4 slices. Place slices on glass serving plate. Cut cheese into slices about the size of tomato slices. Place a piece of cheese on each tomato slice.

4. MICROWAVE (high), uncovered, 45 to 60 seconds or until cheese is melted rotating plate once.

5. Place a toast slice on 2 serving plates. Spread one side of each piece of toast with mayonnaise. Top each toast on plates with 2 slices tomato, 2 bacon strips and lettuce. Top with remaining slice of toast. Cut sandwiches in half.

About 2 Servings

SHRIMP-AVOCADO SANDWICHES

  2 slices bread, toasted
  ½ can (4-oz. size) broken shrimp, drained
  1 green onion, sliced
  2 tablespoons mayonnaise or salad dressing
  ½ teaspoon lemon juice
     Sliced avocado
  ½ tomato, chopped
  2 slices Cheddar cheese

1. Place bread on serving plate. Combine shrimp, onion, mayonnaise and lemon juice in small dish. Top bread with avocado slices. Divide shrimp mixture between sandwiches, spreading evenly. Top with chopped tomato and cheese slices.

2. MICROWAVE (high), uncovered, 45 to 60 seconds or until cheese starts to melt. Serve warm.

2 Sandwiches

TIPS • Half a 6½-oz. can drained tuna can be substituted for shrimp.

  • A hamburger bun or Kaiser roll, split and toasted can be substituted for bread slices.

These unique sandwiches are as nutritious as they are delicious.

TORTILLA ROLL-UPS

- 4 **flour tortillas (6-inch size)**
- 1 **package (3 oz.) cream cheese**
- 2 **tablespoons mayonnaise or salad dressing**
- 1 **teaspoon prepared mustard**
- ½ **teaspoon Beau Monde seasoning**
- 1 **package (2.5-oz.) dried corned beef**
- ½ **package (12-oz. size) sliced Mozzarella cheese**
- ½ **cup alfalfa sprouts**

1. Moisten both sides of tortillas with water. Set aside.

2. MICROWAVE (high) cream cheese in small glass mixing bowl ¼ to ½ minute or until softened. Stir until smooth. Stir in mayonnaise, mustard and seasoning. Spread on one side of each tortilla. Place about 3 slices beef on each tortilla; top with one half slice of cheese. Place a fourth of the sprouts in center of each tortilla. Roll up and place seam-side-down on glass tray or plate.

3. MICROWAVE (high), uncovered, 2 to 2½ minutes or until cheese is melted, rotating plate once.

4 Sandwiches
445 Calories Each

TIP • Sprouts can be omitted or other favorite sprouts can be substituted.

Tacos are enjoyable for any age. This recipe is simple to prepare and utilizes either leftover cooked poultry or canned chicken.

CHICKEN TACOS FOR TWO

- ½ **cup (half a 6½-oz. can) chopped cooked chicken**
- 1 **tablespoon chopped onion**
- ½ **cup (2 ozs.) shredded Cheddar cheese**
- ¼ **teaspoon chili powder**
- ¼ **teaspoon garlic salt**
- 4 **taco shells**
- ½ **cup shredded lettuce**
- 1 **small tomato, chopped**
  Taco sauce, if desired

1. Combine chicken, onion, cheese, chili powder and garlic salt in bowl; mix well.

Spoon ¼ of the mixture into each taco shell. Place filled shells on glass plate.

2. MICROWAVE (high), uncovered, 45 seconds to 1 minute or until cheese is melted. Top each with lettuce and tomato. Serve with taco sauce.

About 2 Servings (4 Tacos)

TIP • Leftover cooked chicken can be cubed and substituted for canned. Or, to quickly cook just enough chicken for this recipe, microwave a leg or thigh in a covered dish for about 2 minutes. Cool enough to handle before chopping.

French bread gives tuna sandwiches a new look and adds appeal for adults as well as kids.

HOT TUNA SANDWICHES

- 1 **can (9½ oz.) tuna, drained**
- ½ **cup chopped celery**
- ¼ **cup sliced green onions**
- 1 **cup (4 ozs.) shredded Swiss or Cheddar cheese**
- 3 **hard-cooked eggs, chopped**
- ⅓ **cup mayonnaise**
- ⅓ **cup sour cream**
- 2 **tablespoons chopped pimiento, drained**
- ½ **tablespoon lemon juice**
- 1 **small loaf French bread (about 12 inches long)**
  Parsley

1. Combine all ingredients except bread and parsley in small mixing bowl; mix well.

2. Cut French bread in half lengthwise; scoop out center of bread leaving a 1-inch shell. Place crust-side down on glass serving plate. Fill each half with tuna mixture and garnish with parsley.

3. MICROWAVE (high), uncovered, 2 to 2½ minutes or until warm, rotating plate once. Cut into 6 to 8 sections.

6 to 8 Sandwiches

TIPS • The bread that is removed can be used for breads crumbs.

• Individual sandwiches can be made by using French rolls. If you need less than 6 sandwiches, just fill the number of rolls desired and refrigerate remaining filling. Microwave smaller quantity 20 to 30 seconds for each sandwich.

Hot dogs become a special treat with a zesty combination of chili and cheese.

CHEDDAR CHILI DOGS

    1 **can (15 oz.) chili with beans**
    1 **small onion, chopped**
    1 **package (12 oz.) wieners**
    1 **package (16 oz.) wiener buns, split**
    1 **cup (4 ozs.) shredded Cheddar cheese**

1. Combine chili and onion in 1½-quart glass casserole. Cover with casserole lid.

2. MICROWAVE (high) 4 to 4½ minutes or until mixture boils, stirring once. Add wieners, turning to coat with chili. Cover.

3. MICROWAVE (high) 4 to 5 minutes or until wieners are hot, stirring once. Place wieners in buns, topping with chili. Sprinkle with cheese. Arrange on large glass serving plate.

4. MICROWAVE (high), uncovered, 1 to 1½ minutes or until cheese is melted, rotating plate once.

10 Sandwiches

TIP • For half a recipe, use a 1-quart glass casserole and microwave in step 2 for 3 minutes; step 3 for 2 to 3 minutes and step 4 for ½ to 1 minute.

If you like corned beef hash and eggs, you will enjoy this attractive variation.

CORNED BEEF HASH 'N EGGS

    1 **can (15 oz.) corned beef hash**
    1 **cup (4 ozs.) shredded Cheddar cheese**
    1 **package (3 oz.) cream cheese**
    3 **eggs**
    ¼ **teaspoon curry powder, if desired**
      Dash salt
      Snipped parsley

1. Spread corned beef hash into bottom and up sides of 1-quart glass casserole to form a crust. Sprinkle with Cheddar cheese.

2. MICROWAVE (high), uncovered, 3 to 3½ minutes or until cheese is melted, rotating dish once.

3. MICROWAVE (high) cream cheese in small mixing bowl 20 to 30 seconds or until softened. Blend until smooth. Beat in eggs,

one at a time, beating well after each. Blend in curry and salt. Pour into crust. Sprinkle with a little parsley.

4. MICROWAVE (high), uncovered, 5 to 6 minutes or until eggs are just about set in center. Let stand about 5 minutes before serving.

4 to 5 Servings

TIP • With Combination Oven, omit microwaving in step 2. In step 4, microwave-bake, uncovered, in preheated 425° oven 7 to 8 minutes; then bake 4 to 5 minutes.

These sandwiches combine zucchini, tomato and cheese for a tasty luncheon treat.

ZUCCHINI POCKETS

    3 **cups sliced, unpeeled zucchini**
    1 **small onion, sliced**
    1 **clove garlic, minced**
    1 **tablespoon butter or margarine**
    ¼ **teaspoon basil leaves**
    ¼ **teaspoon salt**
    1 **teaspoon cornstarch**
    1 **tomato, chopped**
    ¼ **cup Parmesan cheese**
    1 **package (3 oz.) cream cheese**
    3 **pocket bread rounds (6-inch size)**
    1 **cup (4 ozs.) shredded Mozzarella cheese**

1. Combine zucchini, onion, garlic, butter, basil and salt in 1-quart glass casserole. Cover with casserole lid.

2. MICROWAVE (high) 5 to 6 minutes or until tender-crisp, stirring once. Stir in cornstarch.

3. MICROWAVE (high), uncovered, 1 to 1½ minutes or until mixture boils, stirring once. Mix in tomato and Parmesan cheese. Set aside.

4. MICROWAVE (high) cream cheese in small glass dish ½ to ¾ minute or until softened. Cut pocket bread rounds vertically to form 6 pockets. Spread inside of each pocket with cheese. Spoon zucchini mixture into each pocket. Top zucchini with Mozzarella cheese. Arrange on glass serving plate.

5. MICROWAVE (high), uncovered, 1½ to 2 minutes or until cheese is melted and pockets are heated.

6 Sandwiches

This favorite uses zucchini, but can also be prepared with other favorite pizza toppings.

ZUCCHINI PIZZA

Crust:
- 1 **cup unsifted all-purpose flour**
- 2 **tablespoons yellow cornmeal**
- 1 **teaspoon baking powder**
- ½ **teaspoon salt**
- ⅓ **cup milk**
- 3 **tablespoons cooking oil**

Topping
- 3 **cups sliced, unpeeled zucchini**
- 1 **medium onion**
- ½ **lb. Italian sausage**
- ½ **can (6 oz. size) tomato paste**
- 2 **tablespoons catsup**
- ¾ **teaspoon oregano leaves**
- ¼ **teaspoon basil leaves**
- ¼ **teaspoon garlic salt**
- ¼ **cup Parmesan cheese**
- 1½ **cups (6 ozs.) Mozzarella cheese**

1. Combine zucchini and onion for Topping in 1-quart glass casserole. Cover with casserole lid.

2. MICROWAVE (high) 3½ to 4 minutes or until tender-crisp, stirring once. Set aside.

3. While zucchini is cooling, combine all crust ingredients. Mix until dough leaves sides of bowl and forms a ball. Knead 4 to 5 times. Shape into a ball.

4. Place ball of dough between squares of waxed paper. Roll to an 11-inch circle. Peel off top sheet of waxed paper. Place dough (on waxed paper) in microwave oven.

5. MICROWAVE (high), uncovered, 4 minutes. Invert dough onto rack or paperboard pizza pan; carefully peel off waxed paper.

6. MICROWAVE (high), uncovered, 1½ to 2 minutes or until dough is no longer doughy. Set aside.

7. Crumble sausage into 1-quart glass casserole.

8. MICROWAVE (high), uncovered, 2 to 2½ minutes or until no longer pink, stirring once; drain. Set aside.

9. Combine tomato paste, catsup, oregano, basil and garlic salt. Spread over crust. Sprinkle with Parmesan cheese. Drain zucchini. Arrange zucchini and onion slices evenly on crust. Top with cooked sausage and Mozzarella cheese.

10. MICROWAVE (high), uncovered, 5½ to 6½ minutes or until cheese is melted, rotating pizza once.

One 11-inch Pizza

Zucchini Pockets and Zucchini Pizza.

Pita bread makes a pocket for a tasty combination of avocado, chicken, tomato, sprouts and cheese.

CHICKEN-AVOCADO SANDWICHES

2 **lbs. chicken parts**
Salt
1 **ripe avocado, peeled and pitted**
½ **cup sour cream**
1 **tablespoon diced green chilies**
1 **tablespoon lemon juice**
¼ **teaspoon onion salt**
¼ **teaspoon celery salt**
Dash Tabasco sauce
4 **pocket bread rounds (6-inch size)**
1 **large tomato, chopped**
½ **package (4-oz. size) alfalfa sprouts**
½ **cup (2 ozs.) shredded Mozzarella cheese**

1. Place chicken skin-side-up on microwave meat rack or in hamburger cooker. Sprinkle lightly with salt. Cover with waxed paper.

2. MICROWAVE (medium-high — 70%) 16 to 18 minutes or until tender, rearranging pieces once. Uncover and cool.

3. Mash avocado with fork; mix in sour cream, chilies, lemon juice, onion salt, celery salt and Tabasco sauce. Cube cooled chicken; stir into avocado mixture.

4. Cut pocket bread rounds in half vertically; open each half to form a pocket. Arrange on glass serving plate. Spoon chicken mixture evenly into pockets. Top with tomato, sprouts and cheese.

5. MICROWAVE (high), uncovered, 1½ to 2 minutes or until warm, rotating plate once.

8 Sandwiches
275 Calories Each

TIPS • With Full Power, microwave 8 to 10 minutes in step 2.

• Sandwiches are also good served cold; just omit microwaving in step 5.

• About 2 cups cubed cooked chicken or turkey can be used.

These sandwiches are filled with mushrooms, cheese and sprouts which, when combined, make a nutritious substitute for meat.

MEATLESS POCKET SANDWICHES

3 **cups (12 ozs.) sliced fresh mushrooms**
2 **tablespoons butter or margarine**
¼ **teaspoon tarragon leaves**
½ **teaspoon salt**
1 **tablespoon flour**
½ **cup sour cream**
8 **mini pocket bread rounds (3-inch size)**
8 **slices Swiss cheese**
16 **cherry tomatoes, sliced**
½ **cup alfalfa or other sprouts**

1. Combine mushrooms, butter, tarragon and salt in 1-quart glass mix 'n pour bowl.

2. MICROWAVE (high), uncovered, 3½ to 4 minutes or until mushrooms are tender, stirring once. Stir in flour.

3. MICROWAVE (high), uncovered, ½ to 1 minute or until mixture boils. Stir in sour cream; set aside.

4. With kitchen shears, slit open one side of each pocket bread. Insert cheese slice (folding if necessary), a rounded spoonful of mushroom sauce, tomato slices and sprouts in each pocket. Place on large glass serving plate.

5. MICROWAVE (high), uncovered, 1½ to 2 minutes or until cheese is melted and sandwiches are heated, rotating plate once.

8 Sandwiches

TIPS • One tomato, sliced, can be substituted for cherry tomatoes.

• Four regular-sized pocket breads, halved vertically, can be substituted for mini-sized breads.

The Microwave Times

Soups & Salads

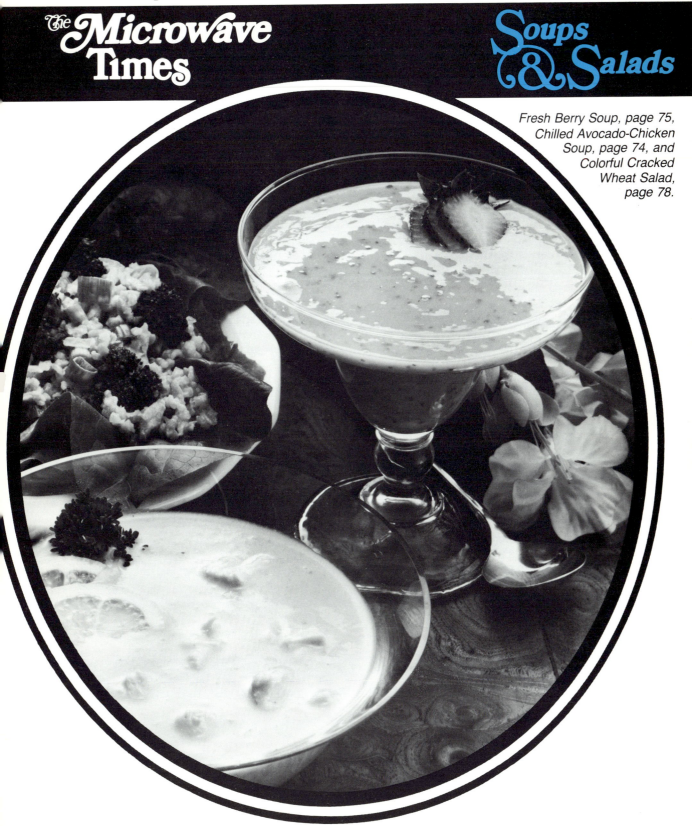

Fresh Berry Soup, page 75,
Chilled Avocado-Chicken
Soup, page 74, and
Colorful Cracked
Wheat Salad,
page 78.

Dry beans are always an economical bet and using a soup bone means additional savings. Other favorite dried beans can be used instead of pinto beans.

BEAN AND HAM SOUP

16 ozs. dry pinto beans
8 cups water
2 teaspoons salt
1 large ham shank (1 to 1½ lbs.)
1 large onion
1 bay leaf
1 can (6 oz.) tomato paste
½ teaspoon marjoram leaves
¼ teaspoon pepper

1. Sort and wash beans. Combine beans, water and salt in 4 or 5-quart glass casserole. Cover with casserole lid.

2. MICROWAVE (high) 18 to 20 minutes or until mixture boils.

3. Let stand covered 1 hour. Stir in remaining ingredients. Cover.

4. MICROWAVE (high) 1¼ to 1½ hours or until beans are tender, stirring once. Remove and discard bay leaf.

5. Remove ham shank from beans to cool. Place about 3 cups beans in food processor or blender. Process until smooth; return mixture to casserole. Remove meat from bone; chop and return to bean mixture. If necessary, cover and microwave 5 to 10 minutes or until heated through.

About 8 Servings

TIPS • This recipe freezes well.
• Northern or other favorite beans can be substituted for pinto beans.
• Leftover ham can be substituted for ham shank; add about 2 cups cubed ham in step 3.

This cold tomato soup, that was part of a low sodium section, has a delightful blend of chicken broth and vegetables. Since canned chicked broth is usually high in sodium, we've included directions for a homemade broth where herbs and spices are used for flavoring instead of salt.

GAZPACHO

1 lb. chicken parts (wings, backs, necks)
2 cups water
1 small onion, sliced
1 stalk celery with leaves, sliced
1 bay leaf
6 peppercorns
1 sprig parsley
3 fresh tomatoes
1 medium carrot
¼ green pepper
½ cucumber, seeds removed
1 teaspoon lemon juice
¼ teaspoon basil leaves
⅛ teaspoon garlic powder
4 lemon slices
4 tablespoons sour cream

1 .Combine chicken parts, water, onion, celery, bay leaf, peppercorns and parsley in 2-quart glass casserole. Cover with casserole lid.

2. MICROWAVE (high) 18 to 20 minutes or until chicken is cooked. (Set aside chicken to use as desired.) Reserve broth. Skim off fat or refrigerate until fat layer can be lifted off.

3. Coarsely dice tomatoes, carrot, green pepper and cucumber; place in blender or food processor container. Cover and process at medium speed until smooth. Add to chicken broth; stir in lemon juice, basil and garlic powder. Chill thoroughly. Garnish individual servings with lemon slices and sour cream.

4 Servings
97 Calories Each
40.5 mg. Sodium or 1.7 Points

TIP • A 16-oz. can tomatoes can be substituted for fresh, but the sodium content will be higher.

Easily prepared and economical too, this nutritious chowder is an ideal family-style soup.

TUNA-VEGETABLE CHOWDER

1½ cups water
 1 medium potato, diced
 2 tablespoons chopped onion
 ¼ cup diced carrot
 ¾ teaspoon salt
 ¼ teaspoon celery salt
   Dash pepper
 1 teaspoon chopped chives
 1 teaspoon Worcestershire sauce
 ⅔ cup fresh or frozen cut corn
 1 can (6½ to 7 oz.) tuna, drained
 1 cup half and half cream

1. Combine water, potato, onion, carrot, salt, celery salt, pepper, chives and Worcestershire sauce in 2-quart glass casserole. Cover with casserole lid.

2. MICROWAVE (high) 7 to 8 minutes or until vegetables are just about tender. Add corn. Cover.

3. MICROWAVE (high) 5 to 6 minutes or until corn is tender. Stir in tuna and cream. Cover.

4. MICROWAVE (high) 2 to 3 minutes or until heated through.

3 to 4 Servings

TIP • Soup can be thickened by blending 3 tablespoons flour with cream. Increase time in step 4 to 4 to 5 minutes or until mixture boils and thickens.

This Christmas Eve tradition can be enjoyed anytime with easy microwave preparation.

OYSTER STEW

 1 pint fresh oysters (16 ozs.), drained
 ¼ cup butter or margarine
 4 cups half & half or milk
 1 teaspoon salt
 ⅛ teaspoon pepper
   Dash nutmeg
 2 tablespoons snipped fresh parsley

1. Combine oysters and butter in 2-quart glass casserole. Cover with casserole lid.

2. MICROWAVE (high) 5 to 6 minutes or until oyster edges are curled, stirring once. Stir in half & half, salt, pepper and nutmeg. Cover.

3. MICROWAVE (high) 9 to 10 minutes or until steaming hot. Stir in parsley.

4 to 6 Servings

TIPS • With canned oysters, use two 8-oz. cans, undrained. Omit cooking in step 2 and reduce salt to ½ teaspoon.
 • Parsley flakes can be substituted for fresh; use 2 teaspoons.

This hearty, old-fashioned clam chowder is a New England favorite. You will find it is easily prepared in the microwave for use as a first course or as a meal in itself.

NEW ENGLAND CLAM CHOWDER

 3 slices bacon
 1 to 2 cans (6½ ozs. each) minced clams
 1 large potato, cubed (1 cup)
 ½ cup chopped celery
 1 small onion, chopped
 2 cups light cream
 3 tablespoons flour
 ¾ teaspoon salt
 ¼ teaspoon thyme leaves
 ⅛ teaspoon pepper
 1 teaspoon parsley flakes

1. Place bacon in single layer in 2-quart glass casserole. Cover with paper towel.

2. MICROWAVE (high) 3 to 4½ minutes or until bacon is crisp. Remove bacon and set aside.

3. Add liquid from clams to drippings along with potato, celery and onion. Cover with casserole lid.

4. MICROWAVE (high) 10 to 12 minutes or until vegetables are just about tender. Combine cream and flour until smooth. Stir into vegetable mixture. Stir in salt, thyme, pepper and parsley.

5. MICROWAVE (high), uncovered, 7 to 8 minutes or until mixture boils and thickens, stirring 2 or 3 times during last half of cooking time. Stir in clams.

6. MICROWAVE (high), uncovered, 1 to 2 minutes or until heated through. Crumble bacon and sprinkle over chowder.

4 to 6 Servings

TIP • If using fresh minced clams, use about 10 ozs. clams; add water to just cover clams in glass casserole dish. Cover and microwave 4 to 5 minutes or until clams are set. Use liquid and clams as directed for canned clams.

Fresh Mushroom Soup, Creamy Broccoli Soup and Velvety Cauliflower-Cheese Soup, page 73.

A gourmet's delight — cauliflower and zucchini in a rich cream soup. For an unusual and exciting flavor, we've added blue cheese. Delightful company fare.

VELVETY CAULIFLOWER-CHEESE SOUP

- 1½ cups sliced zucchini (1 medium)
- 1½ cups bite-sized cauliflower pieces
- 2 cups water
- 3 teaspoons (1 T.) instant chicken bouillon
- 1 cup whipping cream
- 2 egg yolks
- ¼ cup crumbled blue cheese (2 ozs.)

1. Combine zucchini, cauliflower, water and bouillon in 2-quart glass casserole. Cover with casserole lid.

2. MICROWAVE (high) 10 to 11 minutes or until vegetables are just about tender. Blend together whipping cream and egg yolks. Carefully stir into soup. Add cheese.

3. MICROWAVE (high), uncovered, 5 to 6 minutes or until mixture begins to thicken and bubble, stirring 3 or 4 times.

5 to 6 Servings

Fresh mushrooms provide the delicate flavor for this rich, creamy soup. Serve for special luncheons or as a meal starter for company.

FRESH MUSHROOM SOUP

- 2 cups (8 ozs.) fresh mushrooms, sliced or finely chopped
- 1 tablespoon finely chopped onion
- ¼ cup butter or margarine
- ¼ cup all-purpose flour
- 3 teaspoons (1 T.) instant beef bouillon
  Dash pepper
- 2 cups water
- 2 tablespoons dry white wine
- 1 cup half & half cream

1. Combine mushrooms, onion and butter in 1½-quart glass casserole.

2. MICROWAVE (high), uncovered, 3½ to 4 minutes or until mushrooms are just about tender, stirring once. Stir in flour, bouillon and pepper, mixing well. Gradually add water, stirring until smooth.

3. MICROWAVE (high), uncovered 7 to 8 minutes or until mixture boils and thickens, stirring 2 or 3 times. Stir in wine; then mix in cream.

4. MICROWAVE (high) 2 to 2½ minutes or until heated through.

4 to 5 Servings

Fresh or frozen broccoli can be used in this smooth, creamy soup. Try it as a luncheon dish or as a meal starter.

CREAMY BROCCOLI SOUP

- 1 lb. fresh broccoli, trimmed and cut into small pieces
- 1 small onion, chopped
- ¼ cup chopped celery
- 2 cups water
- 6 teaspoons (2 T.) instant chicken bouillon
- ⅛ teaspoon pepper
- ⅛ teaspoon garlic powder
- 2 cups half & half cream
- 3 tablespoons flour
- 1 teaspoon lemon juice
- 3 tablespoons Parmesan cheese

1. Combine broccoli, onion, celery, water, bouillon, pepper and garlic powder in 2-quart glass casserole. Cover with lid.

2. MICROWAVE (high) 15 to 17 minutes or until vegetables are tender. Transfer mixture to blender or food processor container. Process on medium speed until smooth. Return mixture to casserole.

3. Combine cream and flour until smooth. Stir into broccoli mixture.

4. .MICROWAVE (high), uncovered, 9 to 10 minutes or until mixture boils and thickens, stirring 2 or 3 times. Stir in lemon juice and Parmesan cheese. If desired, garnish with lemon slices.

About 6 Servings

TIP • A 10-oz. package frozen cut broccoli can be substituted for fresh. Microwave broccoli in package about 5 minutes or until thawed before combining with other ingredients in step 1.

This smooth, creamy soup with a light cheese flavor can incorporate a variety of garden vegetables. It is equally good hot or chilled.

CHEESY BROCCOLI SOUP

- **2 cups fresh broccoli pieces**
- **1 medium onion, quartered**
- **1 can (14½ oz.) chicken broth**
- **½ teaspoon Beau Monde seasoning, if desired**
- **1 cup milk**
- **2 tablespoons flour**
- **Dash pepper**
- **¼ cup pasteurized process cheese spread (cheese whiz)**

1. Combine broccoli, onion, half of chicken broth and the seasoning in 2-quart glass mix 'n pour bowl. Cover with plastic wrap.

2. MICROWAVE (high) 8 to 9 minutes or until broccoli is tender. Let stand 5 minutes. Pour mixture into blender or food processor container. Cover and process at medium speed until smooth. Return mixture to mix 'n pour bowl. Combine milk and flour until smooth. Blend into hot vegetable mixture. Add pepper.

3. MICROWAVE (high), uncovered 3 to 4 minutes or until mixture boils and thickens, stirring twice. Stir in cheese spread until blended. Mix in remaining chicken broth. Cover and refrigerate until chilled.

4 to 5 Servings

TIP • Other favorite vegetables such as cabbage, carrots, zucchini or cauliflower can be substituted for the broccoli. Or, use a combination of 2 or 3 vegetables.

A rich cheese soup like this one can be a meal in itself. Just add bread or rolls and a salad.

CHEESE SOUP

- **1 cup diced carrot**
- **1 small onion, chopped**
- **6 tablespoons butter or margarine**
- **½ cup unsifted all-purpose flour**
- **½ teaspoon dry mustard**
- **2 tablespoons instant chicken bouillon**
- **4 cups milk**
- **4 ozs. processed cheese spread**
- **2 cups (8 ozs.) shredded Cheddar cheese**
- **¼ cup beer or white wine, if desired**

1. Combine carrot, onion and butter in 2-quart glass mix 'n pour bowl. Cover with plastic wrap.

2. MICROWAVE (high), 6 to 7 minutes or until carrot is just about tender. Blend in flour, mustard and bouillon. Stir in milk.

3. MICROWAVE (high), uncovered, 14 to 16 minutes or until mixture boils, stirring several times during the last half of cooking time. Crumble processed cheese and add to soup along with Cheddar cheese. Stir until blended. Stir in wine or beer.

4. MICROWAVE (high), uncovered, 2 to 3 minutes or until heated through.

About 5 Servings

A creamy chilled soup to serve with fruit and rolls. Or, try small bowls before a favorite meal.

CHILLED AVOCADO-CHICKEN SOUP

- **1 medium onion, chopped**
- **½ cup chopped celery**
- **1 whole chicken breast (about 16 ozs.)**
- **1 can (10¾ oz.) condensed chicken broth**
- **½ cup water**
- **1 tablespoon flour**
- **½ teaspoon salt**
- **½ teaspoon curry powder**
- **1 avocado, peeled and chopped**
- **½ cup half & half cream**

1. Combine onion and celery in 2-quart glass mix 'n pour bowl. Cut chicken breast in half; place on vegetables, skin-side-up. Cover with waxed paper.

2. MICROWAVE (high) 9 to 10 minutes or until chicken is done, rotating dish once. Remove chicken and set aside. Add chicken broth to vegetables. Combine water, flour, salt and curry powder. Blend into chicken broth.

3. MICROWAVE (high), uncovered, 4½ to 5 minutes or until mixture boils, stirring once. Cool.

4. Combine broth mixture and avocado in blender or food processor container. Cover and process at medium speed until smooth. Return to mix 'n pour bowl. Blend in half & half. Dice chicken and add to soup. Cover and refrigerate until chilled. If desired, garnish with parsley and lemon slices.

About 4 Servings

A rich, cheesy flavor from a minimal amount of cheese makes this soup acceptable for many special diets. Our staff liked it as well as any cheese soup they'd tasted.

BEER-CHEESE SOUP

½ cup finely chopped celery
½ cup finely chopped carrot
3 green onions, sliced
1 clove garlic, minced
2 tablespoons water
2 cans (14½ ozs. each) chicken broth
⅓ cup cornstarch
⅔ cup (6 ozs.) beer
1 jar (8 oz.) pasteurized process cheese spread
1 cup popped popcorn

1. Combine celery, carrot, onions, garlic and water in 1½-quart casserole. Cover with casserole lid.

2. MICROWAVE (high) 5 to 6 minutes or until vegetables are tender, stirring once. Add 1½ cans of chicken broth. Cover.

3. MICROWAVE (high) 8 to 9 minutes or until steaming hot. Combine cornstarch with remaining ½ can broth. Stir into hot soup, mixing until blended.

4. MICROWAVE (high), uncovered, 4 to 5 minutes or until mixture boils, stirring once or twice. Stir in beer and cheese spread.

5. MICROWAVE (high), uncovered, 2 to 3 minutes or until heated through. Top each serving with popcorn.

6 Servings
222 Calories Each

Choose a favorite berry for this delightful fruit soup. Serve as a fruit dessert with meals or as an afternoon snack. Children will love it, too.

FRESH BERRY SOUP

4 cups fresh strawberries, raspberries, blueberries or boysenberries
2 cups water
½ cup sugar
2 tablespoons quick-cooking tapioca
1 carton (8 oz.) fruit flavored yogurt (flavor to go with berries)

1. Wash and hull berries. Reserve a few berries for garnish. Place remaining berries in blender or food processor container. Cover and process at medium speed until smooth; transfer to 2-quart glass mix 'n pour bowl. Stir in water, sugar and tapioca.

2. MICROWAVE (high), uncovered, 9 to 10 minutes or until mixture boils, stirring once.

Cool slightly. Using wire whip, mix in yogurt until smooth. Cool. Cover and refrigerate until chilled. Garnish with whole or sliced fruit.

4 to 5 Servings

Make your own gelatin salads with unflavored gelatin and pureed fresh fruit or juices. Here, watermelon adds a delightful fruity flavor in combination with berries and bananas.

BERRY-MELON GELATIN SALAD

½ cup water
2 envelopes unflavored gelatin
¼ cup sugar
About 4 cups cubed watermelon
1 can (8 oz.) crushed pineapple, drained
2 bananas, sliced
1 to 2 cups berries (raspberries, blueberries, sliced boysenberries or sliced strawberries)

1. Combine water and gelatin in 2-cup glass measure. Stir in sugar.

2. MICROWAVE (high) 1½ to 2 minutes or until gelatin is dissolved. Set aside.

3. Process watermelon in blender or food processor until pureed. Measure 3 cups of puree. Stir in gelatin mixture, pineapple, bananas and berries. Pour into 2-quart serving dish or mold. Refrigerate until set.

About 6 Servings

A light yogurt dressing coats favorite fresh fruits—a year around favorite.

FROSTED FRUIT SALAD

1 can (20 oz.) pineapple tidbits or chunks
3 tablespoons sugar
1 tablespoon cornstarch
1 egg
1 carton (8 oz.) plain yogurt
10 to 12 cups cut-up fruit (apples, oranges, bananas, grapes, berries)

1. Drain pineapple juice into 1-quart glass mix 'n pour bowl; add water to make 1 cup juice. Add sugar, cornstarch and egg. Beat with rotary beater until smooth.

2. MICROWAVE (high), uncovered, 3 to 3½ minutes or until mixture begins to bubble, stirring occasionally during last half of cooking time. Cool. Stir in yogurt. Store covered in refrigerator until ready to use.

3. Combine fruits, including pineapple, in large bowl. Add dressing; mix lightly to coat evenly. Refrigerate until served.

10 to 12 Servings

Wedges of orange surround chicken salad. A generous serving for one or enough to share with a friend.

FRUITED CHICKEN SALAD

   1 **whole chicken breast (about 16 ozs.)**
   2 **tablespoons sliced almonds**
   2 **tablespoons mayonnaise or salad dressing**
   1 **teaspoon lemon juice**
   ½ **teaspoon honey**
   ⅛ **teaspoon salt**
   ⅛ **teaspoon curry powder**
   ½ **cup seedless green grapes, halved**
   1 **or 2 oranges**

1. Place chicken skin-side-up on mini meat rack. Cover with waxed paper, tucking edges under plate.

2. MICROWAVE (high) 6 to 7 minutes or until tender, rotating rack once. Uncover and cool. Place almonds in glass custard cup.

3. MICROWAVE (high), uncovered 2 to 2½ minutes or until lightly toasted, stirring 2 or 3 times. Set aside.

4. Remove cooled chicken from bone and cube. Place in small mixing bowl. Stir in mayonnaise, lemon juice, honey, salt and curry powder. Stir in grapes. Chill.

5. Slice off a thin layer from one end of orange so it will sit flat. Cut almost through orange to form 8 wedges. Place orange on serving plate, separating wedges to form cup shape. Spoon chicken mixture into center of orange. Garnish with toasted almonds.

About 1 Serving
740 Calories

TIP • If serving 2 people, divide chicken mixture in half and fill 2 orange cups.

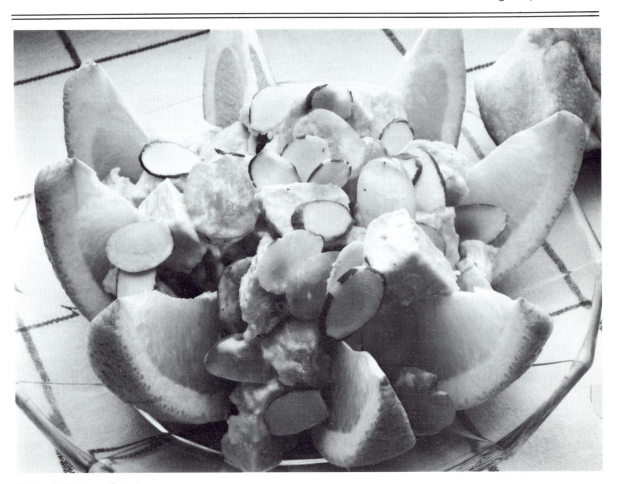

Fruited Chicken Salad.

Cauliflower and broccoli are partially cooked for a tender-crisp addition to a marinated salad mixture. The vinegar is added just prior to serving since it often bleaches green vegetables.

MARINATED GARDEN SALAD

- ½ medium head cauliflower
- 1 lb. fresh broccoli
- ½ cup salad oil
- ½ teaspoon salt
- ½ teaspoon oregano leaves
- ⅛ teaspoon pepper
- 1 clove garlic, minced
- 6 green onions, sliced
- 6 to 8 radishes, sliced
- 1 medium cucumber, thinly sliced
- ¼ cup plain or tarragon-flavored wine vinegar

1. Cut cauliflower and broccoli into bite-sized pieces. Place in 2-quart glass casserole. Add 2 tablespoons water. Cover with casserole lid.

2. MICROWAVE (high) 5 to 6 minutes or until tender-crisp. Drain and cool slightly. Combine oil, salt, oregano, pepper and garlic. Add to vegetables; mix lightly. Cover and refrigerate overnight.

3. Just before serving, add onions, radishes, cucumber and vinegar; toss lightly. Serve in salad bowl or on salad greens.

5 to 6 Servings

Marinated Garden Salad.

This versatile salad dressing goes well on any combination of fresh garden greens. See "Tips" for delicious variations.

FAST 'N EASY SALAD

- 2 slices bacon
- 12 ozs. fresh spinach
- ¼ medium head lettuce (about 2 cups)
- 6 green onions, sliced
- 3 hard-cooked eggs, chopped

Dressing:
- ¼ cup mayonnaise or salad dressing
- 2 tablespoons sugar
- 2 tablespoons vinegar

1. Place bacon in single layer in glass baking dish. Cover with paper towel.

2. MICROWAVE (high) 3 to 4 minutes or until crisp. Set aside.

3. Wash spinach and lettuce; drain well. Tear into bite-sized pieces. Crumble bacon; add to greens along with onions and eggs.

4. Combine mayonnaise, sugar and vinegar in 1-cup glass measure.

5. MICROWAVE (high), uncovered, 1½ to 2 minutes or until mixture boils, stirring once. Pour over salad; toss lightly.

About 6 Servings
170 Calories Each

TIPS • For Mexican salad, toss dressing with ripe olives, avocado slices and salad greens.

• For Chinese salad, toss dressing with toasted almonds, mandarin oranges and salad greens.

• For Italian salad, toss dressing with croutons, Parmesan cheese and salad greens.

Warm spicy meat and crisp lettuce combine with garden fresh vegetables and crunchy chips for a delectable main dish salad.

MEXICAN TOSSED SALAD

- 1 lb. ground beef
- 1 can (16 oz.) kidney beans, drained
- 1 can (8 oz.) tomato sauce
- ½ envelope (3 tablespoons) dry onion soup mix
- 1 teaspoon chili powder
- 1 medium head lettuce, torn into pieces
- 2 medium tomatoes, chopped
- 1 avocado, peeled, pitted and chopped
- 1 cup (4 ozs.) shredded Cheddar cheese
- ½ cup taco sauce
- 1 cup coarsely crushed taco chips

1. Crumble ground beef into 1-quart glass casserole.

2. MICROWAVE (high), uncovered, 5 to 6 minutes or until no longer pink, stirring once. Stir in beans, tomato sauce, onion soup mix and chili powder. Cover with casserole lid.

3. MICROWAVE (high) 5 to 6 minutes or until heated through, stirring once. Set aside.

4. Combine lettuce, tomatoes, avocado, cheese and taco sauce in large salad bowl. Toss lightly. Add warm meat mixture; toss lightly. Sprinkle with chips. Serve immediately.

5 to 6 Servings

TIP • Since the salad is best when freshly prepared, add the warm meat to only that portion needed. Leftover greens and meat can be stored separately for use the following day. Just warm the meat in the microwave before adding to the greens.

A colorful marinated vegetable salad featuring fresh beans and corn. It is ideal for patio dinners or summer picnic.

BEAN AND CORN SALAD

- 2 cups cut fresh green beans
- 1 cup cut fresh yellow wax beans
- ¼ cup water
- 1 cup fresh cut corn
- ¼ cup cooking oil
- ¼ cup vinegar
- ¼ cup sugar
- 1 teaspoon garlic salt
- ½ teaspoon celery seed
  Dash pepper
- 1 Bermuda onion, sliced

1. Combine beans and water in 1-quart glass casserole. Cover with casserole lid.

2. MICROWAVE (high) 5 minutes; stir. Then MICROWAVE (medium — 50%) 8 to 10 minutes or until beans are just about tender, stirring once. Add corn. Cover.

3. MICROWAVE (high) 4 to 5 minutes or until vegetables are tender, stirring once. Set aside.

4. Combine oil, vinegar, sugar, garlic salt, celery seed and pepper in 1-cup glass measure.

5. MICROWAVE (high), uncovered, 1 to 1½ minutes or until heated. Stir to dissolve sugar. Pour over vegetables. Toss lightly to mix. Add onion. Cover and refrigerate until served.

About 5 Servings

TIP • With Full Power in step 2, microwave 5 minutes and let stand 3 minutes. Stir and repeat once. Add corn and continue as directed.

Bulgur has a nutty rice-like texture that combines well with fresh vegetables for a chilled salad.

COLORFUL CRACKED WHEAT SALAD

- ½ cup cracked wheat bulgur
- 1 cup water
- ½ teaspoon salt
- 1 cup shredded carrot
- 2 cups small broccoli pieces
- 4 green onions, sliced
- ½ cup chopped celery
- ½ cup mayonnaise or salad dressing
- 1 tablespoon sugar
- 1 tablespoon tarragon vinegar
- ¼ teaspoon Dijon or prepared mustard

1. Combine wheat, water and salt in 1-quart glass mix 'n pour bowl or casserole.

2. MICROWAVE (high), uncovered, 7½ to 8 minutes or until most of water is absorbed. Add carrot and broccoli pieces. Cover with plastic wrap.

3. MICROWAVE (high) 4 to 4½ minutes or until vegetables are just about tender, stirring once. Let stand covered 5 minutes. Uncover and cool.

4. Add remaining ingredients; mix lightly. cover and refrigerate until served.

About 4 Servings

TIP • Vary this interesting salad by substituting other favorite vegetables and/or adding cooked ham, chicken or tuna with mayonnaise.

Vegetables

Sunny Vegetable Combo, page 80, Sherried Carrots, page 81, and Colorful Stuffed Baked Potatoes, page 88.

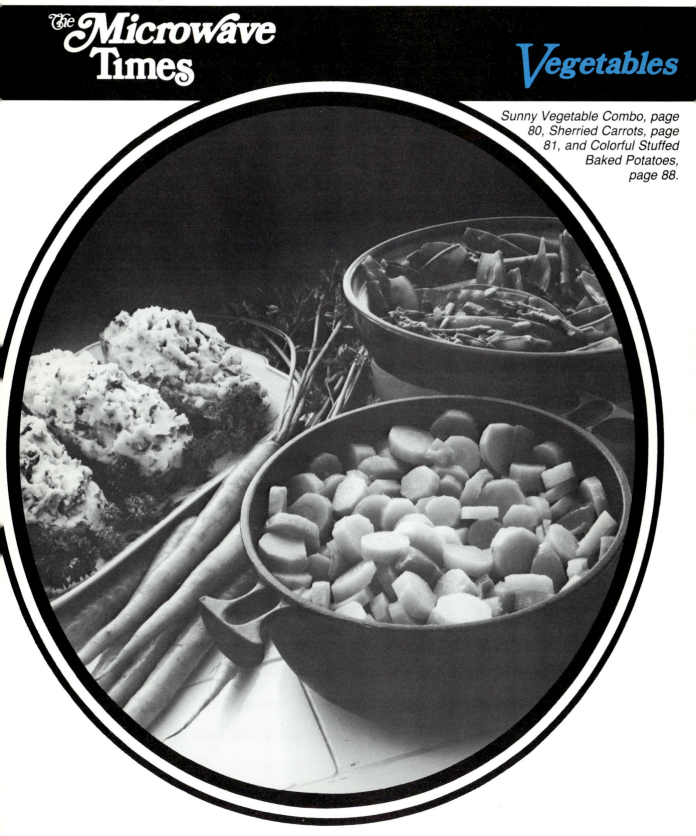

Highlight fresh vegetable combinations from your garden with sunflower seeds. Here, two of the early green vegetables are combined for a tasty, nutritious accompaniment for favorite barbecued meats.

SUNNY VEGETABLE COMBO

- **8 ozs. fresh pea pods (about 2 cups)**
- **8 ozs. fresh asparagus (about 2 cups pieces)**
- **3 tablespoons butter or margarine**
- **1 teaspoon cornstarch**
- **2 tablespoons toasted sunflower seeds or almonds**

1. Remove stems from pea pods; wash and place in 1-quart glass casserole. Wash asparagus, break into 1-inch pieces, discarding tough portion of stalk. Add to pea pods along with butter. Cover with casserole lid.

2. MICROWAVE (high) 5 to 6 minutes or until just about tender. Add cornstarch; mix until blended. Cover.

3. MICROWAVE (high) 1 to 1½ minutes or until vegetables are desired doneness. Sprinkle with sunflower seeds.

4 to 5 Servings

TIPS • A 6-oz. package frozen pea pods and 10-oz. package cut asparagus can be substituted for fresh. Increase time in step 2 to 8 to 9 minutes.

• If using one frozen vegetable and the other fresh, partially thaw the frozen vegetable in warm water before adding to casserole. Cook as directed for fresh vegetables.

White wine and sour cream add a special touch to broccoli for company.

BROCCOLI IN SOUR CREAM SAUCE

- **1 bunch fresh broccoli (about 12 ozs.)**
- **1 tablespoon water**
- **1 can (4 oz.) mushroom stems and pieces, drained**
- **2 green onions, sliced**
- **½ cup sour cream**
- **1 tablespoon white wine**
- **¼ teaspoon salt**
- **Dash Pepper**

1. Wash and drain broccoli; cut top 4-inches off and discard remainder. Cut into small spears. Place in 1-quart glass casserole; add water. Cover with casserole lid.

2. MICROWAVE (high) 6 to 7 minutes or until tender-crisp. Drain; stir in mushrooms and green onions. Combine sour cream, wine, salt and pepper. Spoon over broccoli; cover.

3. MICROWAVE (high) 1 to 1½ minutes or until heated through.

4 to 5 Servings

TIP • Two packages (10 ozs. each) frozen broccoli spears can be substituted for fresh. Omit water.

Here is an easy to season broccoli recipe which cooks to a perfect tender-crispness in the microwave.

HERB-BUTTER BROCCOLI

- **1 bunch fresh broccoli (about 12 ozs.)**
- **1 tablespoon water**
- **2 tablespoons butter or margarine**
- **¼ teaspoon garlic salt**
- **⅓ cup salad croutons, if desired**

1. Wash and drain broccoli. Cut top 4-inches off and discard remainder. Cut into small spears. Place in 1-quart glass casserole; add water. Cover with casserole lid.

2. MICROWAVE (high) 6 to 7 minutes or until tender-crisp, rotating dish once. Allow to stand covered 5 minutes; drain. Add butter and garlic salt. Cover.

3. MICROWAVE (high) ½ to 1 minute or until butter is melted. Stir to coat broccoli with butter. Sprinkle with croutons.

About 4 Servings

Seasoned butter adds a finishing touch to frozen Brussels sprouts.

BRUSSELS SPROUTS WITH SEASONED BUTTER

- **1 package (10 oz.) frozen Brussels sprouts**
- **2 tablespoons butter or margarine**
- **½ teaspoon lemon juice**
- **¼ teaspoon celery salt**
- **¼ teaspoon chopped chives**

1. MICROWAVE (high) Brussels sprouts in covered 1-quart glass casserole 7 to 8 minutes or until tender. Drain.

2. Combine butter, lemon juice, celery salt and chives in 1-cup glass measure.

3. MICROWAVE (high), uncovered, 1 to 1½ minutes or until bubbly. Drizzle over Brussels sprouts.

About 4 Servings

This cabbage dish makes a welcome accompaniment for many meals. The cabbage is cooked until just about tender and then combined with a sweet-sour sauce.

PENNSYLVANIA DUTCH CABBAGE

- **4 slices bacon**
- **6 cups shredded cabbage (about 1 small head)**
- **¼ cup water**
- **1 small onion, chopped**
- **½ cup water**
- **¼ cup vinegar**
- **2 tablespoons flour**
- **2 tablespoons brown sugar**
- **¾ teaspoon salt**
- **⅛ teaspoon pepper**

1. Arrange bacon evenly in 2-quart glass casserole. Cover with paper towel.

2. MICROWAVE (high) 4 to 5 minutes or until crisp. Remove bacon and set aside. Discard all but 2 tablespoons drippings.

3. Add cabbage, ¼ cup water, and the onion drippings. Cover with casserole lid.

4. MICROWAVE (high) 9 to 10 minutes or until just about tender, stirring once. Combine ½ cup water, the vinegar, flour, brown sugar, salt and pepper; stir into cabbage. Cover with casserole lid.

5. MICROWAVE (high) 1½ to 2 minutes or until mixture boils and thickens, stirring once. Crumble bacon and sprinkle over cabbage.

5 to 6 Servings

Fresh carrots are welcome and available any time and this recipe enhances the garden-sweet flavor with a buttery sherry sauce.

SHERRIED CARROTS

- **3 cups sliced carrots (about 10 medium)**
- **¼ cup water**
- **¼ cup chopped green pepper**
- **2 tablespoons butter or margarine**
- **1 tablespoon dry sherry**
- **½ teaspoon cornstarch**
- **¼ teaspoon salt**

1. Combine carrots and water in 1-quart glass casserole. Cover with casserole lid.

2. MICROWAVE (high) 4 minutes. Stir in green pepper. Cover.

3. MICROWAVE (medium — 50%) 6 to 8 minutes or until carrots are tender, stirring once. Drain.

4. Stir in remaining ingredients, mixing until butter is melted.

5. MICROWAVE (high), uncovered, ¾ to 1 minute or until sauce is bubbly.

4 to 5 Servings

TIPS • Scraped whole baby carrots can be substituted for slices. Increase amount to about 4 cups and cook as directed.

• With Combination Oven, microwave in steps 2 and 3 for 11 to 13 minutes or until just about tender. Microwave in step 5 for 1 to 2 minutes.

Vegetables are more attractive and may even taste better when served in an attractive combination.

MINI VEGETABLE PLATE

- **¾ cup bite-sized cauliflower pieces**
- **¾ cup bite-sized broccoli pieces**
- **½ tablespoon butter or margarine**
- **Salt and pepper**

1. Wash cauliflower and broccoli. Trim off stalk portions. Cut into bite-sized pieces.

2. Arrange cauliflower and broccoli on small glass serving plate, either alternating vegetables on plate or grouping vegetables in sections. Cover with plastic wrap.

3. MICROWAVE (high) 2 to 2½ minutes or until vegetables are tender. (Test doneness by piercing through plastic wrap with a sharp knife.) Lift one corner of plastic wrap and carefully pour off any liquid, protecting hands with hot pads. Cut butter into small pieces; place on vegetables. Season with salt and pepper.

About 2 Servings

TIP • Other favorite vegetable seasonings can be used. Or, spoon 1 to 2 tablespoons pasteurized process cheese spread over cooked vegetables.

An easy vegetable dish to prepare in your microwave.

CHEESY VEGETABLE BAKE

- 2 **packages (20 ozs. each) frozen broccoli cuts with cauliflower**
- ½ **cup chopped celery**
- 1 **jar (8 oz.) pasteurized process cheese spread**
- 1 **can (10¾ oz.) condensed cream of celery soup**
- 1 **jar (2 oz.) diced pimiento, undrained**
- 1 **can (3½ oz.) French fried onions**

1. Combine frozen vegetables and celery in 12 x 8-inch glass baking dish. Cover with plastic wrap.

2. MICROWAVE (high) 12 to 13 minutes or until vegetables are just about thawed, stirring once. Drain by lifting the plastic wrap from one corner and holding the dish and vegetables in place with a towel-covered hand. Remove plastic wrap.

3. Combine cheese spread, soup and piniento in small mixing bowl. Mix well. Pour over vegetables.

4. MICROWAVE (high), uncovered, 7 to 8 minutes or until vegetables are almost tender, rotating dish once. Sprinkle with onions.

5. MICROWAVE (high), uncovered, 2 to 3 minutes or until vegetables are tender.

8 to 10 Servings

TIPS • Vegetables can be prepared ahead through step 3. If refrigerated, increase time in step 4 to 10 to 12 minutes.
• Recipe can be halved. Use an 8-inch square glass baking dish and microwave in step 2 for 6 to 7 minutes, step 4 for 4 to 4½ minutes and in step 5 for 1 to 1½ minutes.

Cauliflower in Cheese Sauce.

Here is a quick cheese sauce that does not require precooking. Use it with other favorite vegetables.

CAULIFLOWER IN CHEESE SAUCE

- 1 **small head cauliflower**
- 2 **tablespoons water**
- 1 **jar (8 oz.) pasteurized process cheese spread**
- ½ **can (10¾-oz. size) condensed cream of celery soup**
- 1 **green onion, sliced**

1. Cut cauliflower into flowerettes; wash and drain. Place in 1½-quart glass casserole. Add water; cover with casserole lid.

2. MICROWAVE (high) 6 to 7 minutes or until cauliflower is just about tender.

3. Combine cheese spread, soup and onion in small mixing bowl; stir well. Spoon over cauliflower. Cover cauliflower and replace lid loosely.

4. MICROWAVE (high) 1½ to 2½ minutes or until heated through.

3 to 4 Servings

TIP • Half a large head of cauliflower can be used instead of 1 small head.

Frozen vegetables in bags are easy to portion into small-sized servings.

BACON 'N VEGIES

- ½ **strip bacon**
- ½ **cup frozen mixed vegetables**
- 1 **tablespoon milk**
- ¼ **teaspoon flour**
  Salt

1. Place bacon in 10-oz. (about 1 cup) glass serving dish. Cover with paper towel.

2. MICROWAVE (high) ½ to 1 minute or until crisp. Set aside bacon. If desired, discard part of drippings. Add vegetables, milk and flour to drippings. Stir until well mixed. Cover with lid or plastic wrap.

3. MICROWAVE (high) 2½ to 3 minutes or until vegetables are just about tender, stirring once. Let stand a few minutes. Sprinkle with salt and garnish with crumbled bacon.

1 Serving

TIP • Other favorite frozen vegetables can be substituted for the frozen mixed vegetables.

A tangy sauce gives cauliflower an Italian touch.

ITALIAN-STYLE CAULIFLOWER

1 **medium head cauliflower**
2 **tablespoons water**
1 **clove garlic**
¼ **cup cooking oil**
1 **tablespoon lemon juice**
1 **teaspoon sugar**
1 **teaspoon prepared mustard**
½ **teaspoon salt**
¼ **teaspoon paprika**
3 **green olives, sliced**
1 **tablespoon drained capers, if desired**

1. Separate cauliflower into flowerettes. Combine cauliflower and water in 1½-quart glass casserole. Place garlic on top of cauliflower. Cover with casserole lid.

2. MICROWAVE (high) 8 to 9 minutes or until cauliflower is tender. Remove garlic and discard; drain.

3. Combine remaining ingredients; pour over cauliflower. Toss lightly.

5 to 6 Servings

TIP • Cauliflower can also be cooked and served as whole head. Cut out core and combine with water in deep bowl or casserole. Cover with plastic wrap. Microwave 10 to 11 minutes; let stand 5 minutes. Remove to serving plate. Spoon seasonings over cauliflower.

Corn and green beans combine for an attractive and flavorful combination.

CORN AND BEAN DUO

2 **cups cut fresh green beans**
½ **cup water**
2 **cups cut fresh corn (2 to 3 ears)**
½ **cup half and half cream**
2 **teaspoons flour**
1 **teaspoon chopped chives**
¾ **teaspoon salt**
2 **tablespoons Parmesan cheese**

1. Combine beans and water in 1-quart glass casserole. Cover with casserole lid.

2. MICROWAVE (high) 5½ to 6 minutes or until mixture boils. Then, MICROWAVE (low — 30%) 9 to 10 minutes or until beans are just about tender. Drain.

3. Add corn, cream, flour, chives and salt; mix well. Cover.

4. MICROWAVE (high) 4½ to 5 minutes or until sauce thickens and corn is tender. Stir in Parmesan cheese.

5 to 6 Servings

TIP • When fresh vegetables are not available, combine cooked frozen or canned beans and corn with this sauce.

Celery makes an interesting vegetable dish that goes well with poultry.

CELERY CASSEROLE

4 **cups sliced celery**
2 **tablespoons water**
½ **cup dry bread crumbs**
¼ **cup slivered almonds**
2 **tablespoons butter or margarine**
1 **can (5 oz.) sliced water chestnuts, drained**
1 **can (10¾ oz.) condensed cream of chicken soup**
¼ **cup chopped pimiento**

1 Combine celery and water in 1-quart glass casserole. Cover with casserole lid.

2. MICROWAVE (high) 8 to 10 minutes or until tender, stirring once. Let stand covered.

3. Combine bread crumbs, almonds and butter in 9-inch glass pie plate.

4. MICROWAVE (high), uncovered, 5 to 6 minutes or until toasted, stirring 4 or 5 times. Set aside.

5. Stir water chestnuts, soup and pimiento into celery. Top with toasted crumbs.

6. MICROWAVE (high), uncovered, 4 to 5 minutes or until heated through, rotating dish once.

About 8 Servings
130 Calories Each

TIP • With Combination Oven, microwave in step 2 for 12 to 15 minutes. Omit step 4 and 6. Microwave-bake in preheated 375° oven for 8 to 12 minutes.

Onion slices make interesting and flavorful garnishes for meat platters. Serve these with barbecued steaks or meat patties.

CRUMB-TOPPED ONION SLICES

2 tablespoons butter or margarine
1 tablespoon brown sugar
2 medium onions, peeled
3 tablespoons dry bread crumbs
2 tablespoons Parmesan cheese
¼ teaspoon basil leaves
¼ teaspoon paprika

1. Combine butter and brown sugar in 8-inch round glass baking dish.

2. MICROWAVE (high) 1½ to 2 minutes or until bubbly, stirring twice. Cut onions crosswise into ½-inch slices. Place cut-side-down in butter. Cover with waxed paper.

3. MICROWAVE (high) 2 minutes. Turn onion slices over. Cover.

4. MICROWAVE (high) 1½ to 2 minutes or until just about tender.

5. Combine crumbs, cheese, basil and paprika. Stir in 1 tablespoon liquid from onions. Spoon onto onion slices. Cover with paper towel.

6. MICROWAVE (high) 1½ to 2 minutes or until heated through.

8 to 10 Slices

TIP • When using fresh basil leaves, increase quantity to 1 teaspoon.

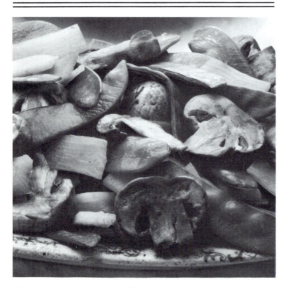

Far East Vegetable Combo.

Enjoy peas fresh from the garden with a mildly seasoned cream sauce.

FRESH PEAS IN CREAM SAUCE

3 cups fresh peas
⅓ cup light cream or evaporated milk
½ teaspoon cornstarch
½ teaspoon sugar
½ teaspoon salt
⅛ teaspoon thyme leaves or ground nutmeg

1. Combine all ingredients in 1-quart glass casserole. Cover with casserole lid.

2. MICROWAVE (high) 7 to 8 minutes or until peas are tender, stirring once.

5 to 6 Servings

TIPS • If using frozen peas, increase time to 8 to 9 minutes.
• When using fresh thyme, increase to ½ teaspoon.

Snow peas are a natural addition to any meal. Here, they are teamed with mushrooms and bamboo shoots for an Oriental ensemble.

FAR EAST VEGETABLE COMBO

1 package (6 oz.) frozen pea pods
8 ozs. fresh mushrooms, sliced (about 2 cups)
1 teaspoon instant chicken bouillon
2 teaspoons soy sauce
2 teaspoons cornstarch
2 tablespoons water
1 can (8½ oz.) bamboo shoots, drained

1. Combine pea pods, mushrooms, bouillon and soy sauce in 1-quart glass casserole. Cover with casserole lid.

2. MICROWAVE (high) 5 to 6 minutes or until almost tender, stirring once. Dissolve cornstarch in water; stir into vegetables. Add bamboo shoots; cover.

3. MICROWAVE (high) 2 to 3 minutes or until sauce is slightly thickened, stirring once or twice.

About 6 Servings
35 Calories Each

TIP • Two cups fresh pea pods can be substituted for frozen. Decrease time in step 2 to 4 to 5 minutes.

Bacon and cream cheese add flavor to these potatoes. Make extras and freeze for reheating later.

TWICE BAKED POTATOES

  2 **large potatoes**
  1 **slice bacon**
  2 **tablespoons cream cheese (half a 3-oz. pkg.)**
  1 **green onion, sliced**
  ¼ **teaspoon salt**
  ¼ **to ⅓ cup milk**
    Paprika

1. MICROWAVE (high) potatoes 6 to 7 minutes or until just about tender, turning potatoes over once or twice. Let stand until cool enough to handle.

2. Place bacon between layers of paper toweling on glass plate.

3. MICROWAVE (high) 1 to 1½ minutes or until crisp. Set aside.

4. Cut potatoes in half lengthwise; scoop out insides into mixing bowl leaving about ¼ inch potato in shell. Mash potato well. Cut cheese into pieces; add to hot potato and mix well. Blend in onion, salt and milk until of desired consistency; beat well.

5. Spoon potato mixture into shells. Crumble bacon over potato. Sprinkle with paprika.

6. MICROWAVE (high), uncovered, 1½ to 2 minutes or until heated through.

About 2 Servings

TIP • These potatoes freeze well. To heat one frozen half, just microwave (high) 2 to 2½ minutes. To heat two frozen halves, microwave 2½ to 3½ minutes.

One of our readers sent in this recipe which is very simple, yet has exceptional flavor.

ONION SOUP POTATOES

  4 **medium potatoes**
  1 **envelope (.33 oz.) dry onion soup mix**
  ½ **cup butter or margarine**

1. Scrub potatoes; slice ¼-inch thick into 1½-quart glass casserole. Add onion soup mix and stir lightly. Cut butter into pieces; place on potatoes. Cover with casserole lid.

2. MICROWAVE (high) 9 to 11 minutes or until potatoes are just about tender, stirring once. Let stand covered about 5 minutes before serving.

4 to 5 Servings
260 Calories Each

TIP • Potatoes can be peeled if desired.

Yogurt can be used with potatoes like sour cream. Here it is combined with cooked, sliced potatoes. The addition of mayonnaise mellows the tangy yogurt flavor.

CREAMY YOGURT POTATOES

  4 **cups sliced, raw potatoes (about 4 medium)**
  1 **small onion, sliced**
  ¼ **cup water**
  ¾ **cup plain yogurt**
  1 **tablespoon chopped chives**
  1 **teaspoon salt**
  ⅛ **teaspoon pepper**
  ¼ **cup mayonnaise or salad dressing**

1. Combine potatoes, onion and water in 1-quart glass casserole. Cover with casserole lid.

2. MICROWAVE (high) 8 to 10 minutes or until tender, stirring once or twice. Let stand 5 minutes. Stir in remaining ingredients; cover.

3. MICROWAVE (high) 1 to 2 minutes or until heated through.

4 to 5 Servings

TIPS • Potatoes can be cooked up to 1 hour ahead. Add yogurt and remaining ingredients just before serving. Increase heating time in step 3 to 4 to 6 minutes.

• This is a good recipe for fresh new red potatoes, too. Select small, tender potatoes and scrub skins, but do not peel.

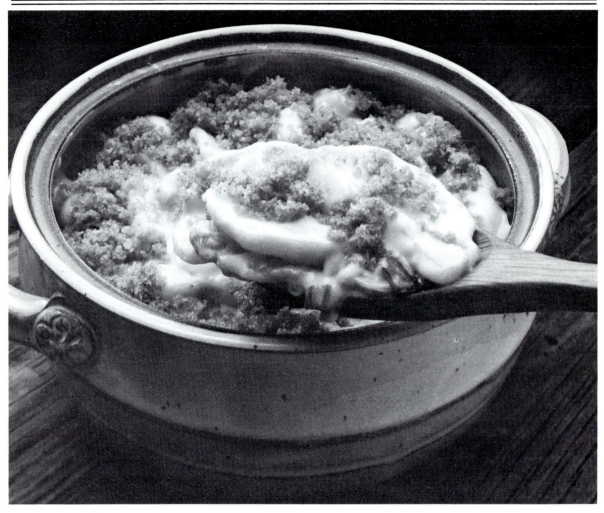

Potato Casserole.

This recipe is a favorite from our Micro Adapting regular feature. Try it the next time you serve barbecued or roasted meats.

POTATO CASSEROLE

  4 large potatoes, peeled and sliced (about 4 cups)
 ¼ cup water
 ¼ cup butter or margarine
 ½ can (10¾-oz. size) condensed cream of chicken soup
 ⅓ cup shredded Cheddar cheese
 ½ cup sour cream
 2 green onions, sliced
 1 tablespoon butter or margarine
 ¼ cup cornflake crumbs
 ¼ teaspoon paprika

1. Combine potatoes and water in 1-quart glass casserole. Cover with casserole lid.

2. MICROWAVE (high) 9 to 10 minutes or until potatoes are just about tender, stirring once. Let stand covered.

3. Combine ¼ cup butter and the soup in 2-cup glass measure.

4. MICROWAVE (high), uncovered, 1½ to 2 minutes or until hot and bubbly. Stir until smooth. Blend in cheese, sour cream and onions; stir into potatoes. Cover.

5. MICROWAVE (high) 3½ to 4 minutes or until heated through. Let stand covered.

6. MICROWAVE (high) 1 tablespoon butter in glass custard cup 30 to 45 seconds or until melted. Mix in cornflake crumbs and paprika. Sprinkle on potatoes just before serving.

4 to 5 Servings

Sliced potatoes and onions are lightly seasoned and cooked in a small amount of cream.

OTHER POTATOES

3 to 4 medium potatoes, peeled and sliced
1 medium onion, sliced
¾ teaspoon seasoned or regular salt
1 teaspoon parsley flakes
1 tablespoon butter or margarine
½ cup half and half cream

1. Rinse sliced potatoes; place in 1-quart glass casserole. Add onion, salt and parsley; mix lightly. Dot with butter. Add half of cream (¼ cup). Cover with casserole lid.

2. MICROWAVE (high) 5 minutes. Add remaining cream; stir lightly.

3. MICROWAVE (high) 5 to 7 minutes or until tender.

About 5 Servings

A touch of lemon combined with creamy butter and a cheese topping make this a simple, yet especially flavorful dish.

LEMON-BUTTER POTATOES

4 medium potatoes, peeled
¼ cup butter or margarine
½ teaspoon grated lemon peel
1 tablespoon lemon juice
1 teaspoon salt
1 teaspoon chopped chives
¼ cup whipping cream
½ cup (2 ozs.) shredded Cheddar cheese
Paprika

1. Slice potatoes into 1-quart glass casserole. Add butter. Cover with casserole lid.

2. MICROWAVE (high) 7 to 8 minutes or until just about tender, stirring once. Add lemon peel and juice, salt and chives; mix lightly. Pour cream over potatoes. Sprinkle with cheese and paprika.

3. MICROWAVE (high), uncovered, 2 to 3 minutes or until cheese is melted and potatoes are tender.

TIP • Frozen hash brown potatoes also work well in this recipe. Use a 12-oz. package. Place frozen potatoes in casserole and prepare as directed.

Here's another favorite from a subscriber.

PARIS POTATOES

5 cups potatoes, peeled and cut into ½-inch cubes
4 green onions, sliced
1 cup creamed cottage cheese
½ cup sour cream
½ teaspoon garlic salt
¼ teaspoon salt
Dash pepper
¾ to 1 cup shredded Cheddar cheese

1. Place potatoes in 1½-quart glass casserole. Add onions. Cover with casserole lid.

2. MICROWAVE (high) 10 to 11 minutes or until potatoes are tender-crisp, stirring once Let stand covered.

3. Combine cottage cheese, sour cream, garlic salt, salt and pepper. Stir carefully into potatoes. Cover.

4. MICROWAVE (high) 7 to 8 minutes or until potatoes are tender, stirring once. Sprinkle with cheese.

5. MICROWAVE (high), uncovered, 1 to 1½ minutes or until cheese is melted. Let stand a few minutes before serving.

6 to 8 Servings

These quick potato wedges taste a little like French Fries. They're so easy, you'll want to enjoy them often.

CHEESY MICRO-FRIES

3 medium potatoes
3 tablespoons butter or margarine
¼ cup Parmesan cheese
½ teaspoon garlic salt
½ teaspoon paprika

1. MICROWAVE (high) butter in 8-inch round glass or plastic baking dish ½ to 1 minute or until melted.

2. Scrub potatoes. Cut each lengthwise into eight wedges. Dip wedges into butter to coat; arrange peel-side-down in baking pan. Combine cheese, garlic salt and paprika. Sprinkle evenly over potatoes. Cover with paper towel.

3. MICROWAVE (high) 10 to 11 minutes or until potatoes are just about tender, rotating dish once or twice. Let stand a few minutes before serving.

3 to 4 Servings

If you are looking for additional ways to incorporate spinach into your menu plans, we think you'll find this idea a favorite. It adds a delightful color and unique appearance to stuffed baked potatoes, but maintains a delicate flavor.

COLORFUL STUFFED BAKED POTATOES

- **4 medium to large potatoes**
- **4 cups fresh spinach leaves (about 5 ozs.)**
- **½ teaspoon salt**
- **3 tablespoons butter or margarine**
- **½ cup sour cream**
- **⅓ to ½ cup milk**
- **¾ cup shredded Cheddar cheese**

1. MICROWAVE (high) potatoes 12 to 14 minutes or until just about tender, turning potatoes over once. Let stand 5 minutes.

2. Place washed spinach leaves in 1-quart glass casserole. Cover with casserole lid.

3. MICROWAVE (high) 3 to 4 minutes or until limp. Drain. Chop finely and set aside.

4. Cut potatoes in half lengthwise; scoop out insides into mixing bowl, leaving about ¼ inch potato in shell. Mash potato well. Mix in salt and butter until melted. Beat in sour cream and enough milk to make a light, fluffy consistency. Stir in chopped spinach and cheese.

5. Fill potato shells; place shells on glass serving plate.

6. MICROWAVE (high), uncovered, 4 to 5 minutes or until heated through, rotating plate once.

About 8 Servings

TIPS • The cooked spinach can be added to the milk and easily chopped in a blender or food processor.

• Half a 10-oz. package frozen chopped spinach can be substituted for fresh. Wrap half the box in foil (so it will remain frozen) and microwave package 4 to 5 minutes or until thawed. Drain and stir thawed spinach into potatoes in step 4. Wrap frozen portion and return to freezer.

• Potatoes can be prepared ahead through step 5. To serve, microwave 6 to 7 minutes or until heated through.

Sliced potatoes in a creamy sour cream sauce make a perfect accompaniment for sauceless meats or poultry.

POTATOES ROMANOFF

- **⅓ cup water**
- **2 tablespoons instant chicken bouillon**
- **6 cups thinly sliced potatoes**
- **1 small onion**
- **¾ cup light cream or milk**
- **1 tablespoon flour**
- **½ teaspoon salt**
- **½ teaspoon garlic salt**
- **¼ teaspoon dill weed, if desired**
- **2 tablespoons butter or margarine**
- **¾ cup sour cream**
- **½ teaspoon prepared mustard**
- **½ cup (2 ozs.) shredded Cheddar cheese**

1. Combine water, bouillon, potatoes and onion in 2-quart glass casserole. Cover with casserole lid.

2. MICROWAVE (high) 11 to 12 minutes or until potatoes are tender, stirring once. Combine cream, flour, salt, garlic salt and dill weed. Stir into potatoes. Add butter.

3. MICROWAVE (high), uncovered, 3 to 4 minutes or until sauce boils and thickens, stirring twice. Stir in sour cream and mustard. Sprinkle with cheese.

4. MICROWAVE (high), uncovered, 2 to 3 minutes or until heated through.

5 to 6 Servings

These unpeeled potatoes are quartered and then dipped in a cheesy, seasoned butter before quick microwave cooking.

ZIPPY BUTTERED POTATOES

- **4 medium potatoes**
- **3 tablespoons butter or margarine**
- **½ teaspoon garlic salt**
- **½ teaspoon paprika**
- **2 tablespoons Parmesan cheese**

1. Scrub potatoes.

2. MICROWAVE (high) butter in 8-inch square glass baking dish ½ to 1 minute or until melted. Blend in garlic salt, paprika and cheese.

3. Quarter potatoes lengthwise; dip cut edges in butter mixture. Arrange cut-side-down in dish. Cover with paper towel.

4. MICROWAVE (high) 10 to 12 minutes or until potatoes are tender, rearranging once or twice.

5 to 6 Servings

Canned or fresh sweet potatoes already cooked make this side dish quick and easy. Orange juice and a hint of nutmeg add the interesting flavor.

QUICK ORANGE SWEET POTATOES

- ¼ **cup butter or margarine**
- ¼ **cup packed brown sugar**
- ¼ **cup orange juice**
- 1 **cup miniature marshmallows**
- ¼ **teaspoon nutmeg**
- 1 **can (16 oz.) vacuum-packed sweet potatoes**
- 2 **tablespoons chopped nuts, if desired**

1. MICROWAVE (high) butter in 1½-quart glass casserole ½ to 1 minute or until melted.

2. Stir in brown sugar, orange juice, marshmallows and nutmeg. Add sweet potatoes; mash with fork while mixing with other ingredients. Top with nuts. Cover with paper towel.

3. MICROWAVE (high) 6 to 7 minutes or until heated through (150°), rotating dish once.

4 to 6 Servings

TIP • If desired, 4 medium sweet potatoes or yams, cooked and peeled can be substituted for canned sweet potatoes. If necessary, increase orange juice for desired consistency.

Yams are seasoned with brown sugar and butter and served in attractive boats like twice-baked potatoes.

YAM BOATS

- 3 **medium yams**
- ¼ **cup butter or margarine**
- 1 **teaspoon salt**
- ¼ **cup packed brown sugar**
- ½ **cup half & half cream**
- ¼ **cup chopped pecans**

1. MICROWAVE (high) yams 13 to 15 minutes or until tender, turning yams over and rearranging once or twice. Cool enough to handle.

2. Cut yams in half lengthwise. Scoop out potato mixture into bowl, leaving ¼ inch shell. Cut butter into pieces; add to yam mixture along with salt, brown sugar and half of cream. Beat until smooth. Continue beating in enough cream until of desired consistency.

3. Spoon mixture into shells. Place on glass serving plate. Sprinkle with pecans.

4. MICROWAVE (high), uncovered, 2 to 3 minutes or until heated through.

6 Boats

TIP • Yams can be prepared ahead through step 3, except for adding pecans. Then, just sprinkle with pecans and heat as directed in step 4. If they have been refrigerated, increase time in step 4 to 3 to 4 minutes.

Although this was developed as a low calorie, low sodium recipe, it is a favorite of many. Serve it with broiled meat, fish or poultry for a healthful entree.

SPAGHETTI SQUASH PASTA

- 1 **medium (2 lb.) spaghetti squash**
- 1 **cup chopped fresh mushrooms**
- 1 **clove garlic, minced**
- 2 **tablespoons chopped onion**
- ¼ **cup water**
- ½ **can (6-oz. size) tomato paste**
- ½ **teaspoon Italian seasoning**
- ¾ **cup water**
-   **Parmesan cheese, if desired**

1. Prick squash several times with fork.

2. MICROWAVE (high) whole squash 12 to 14 minutes or until just about tender, turning squash over once. Set aside.

3. Combine mushrooms, garlic, onion and water in 1-quart glass casserole. Cover with casserole lid.

4. MICROWAVE (high) 3 to 4 minutes or until tender.

5. Stir in tomato paste, seasoning and water until blended. Cover.

6. MICROWAVE (high) 2 to 3 minutes or until bubbly.

7. Cut squash in half; remove seeds. Using a fork, unwind spaghetti-like strands onto plate. Top with sauce. Sprinkle with Parmesan cheese.

2 Servings
Calories: 65
Cholesterol: 7 mg.
Sodium: 300 mg.

TIP • There is a low-salt tomato paste available if you need even less sodium.

Mounds of sausage dressing fill acorns for a meal-in-one.

SAUSAGE-STUFFED ACORNS

- **2 acorn squash**
- **½ teaspoon salt**
- **1 small onion, chopped**
- **½ cup chopped celery**
- **1 tablespoon water**
- **½ lb. lean ground beef**
- **½ lb. sausage**
- **1 egg**
- **1 cup herb-seasoned bread cubes**
- **¼ cup water**
- **¼ teaspoon poultry seasoning**
- **4 tablespoons chili sauce or catsup**

1. MICROWAVE (high) whole squash 14 to 15 minutes or until just about tender, turning squash over once or twice. Let stand 10 minutes.

2. Cut squash in half; scoop out seeds. Place halves cut-side-up on large glass plate. Sprinkle with salt.

3. Combine onion, celery and 1 tablespoon water in glass mixing bowl. Cover with plastic wrap.

4. MICROWAVE (high) 2 to 3 minutes or until vegetables are tender. Combine vegetables, beef, sausage, egg, bread cubes, ¼ cup water and poultry seasoning; mix well. Spoon into acorn halves, mounding mixture as necessary. Cover with waxed paper.

5. MICROWAVE (high) 11 to 12 minutes or until meat is set and squash is tender, rotating plate once. Top each squash half with 1 tablespoon chili sauce.

About 4 Servings

Herbs add flavor but not calories to naturally nutritious vegetables.

VEGETABLE SAUTE

- **4 green onions, sliced**
- **2 medium tomatoes, coarsely chopped**
- **1 clove garlic, minced**
- **1 teaspoon salt**
- **1 teaspoon cornstarch**
- **1 teaspoon basil leaves**
- **1 teaspoon dried parsley**
- **⅛ teaspoon pepper**
- **3 cups chopped zucchini (2 small)**

1. Combine green onions, tomatoes, garlic, salt, cornstarch, basil, parsley and pepper in 1-quart glass casserole; mix well. Stir in zucchini. Cover with casserole lid.

2. MICROWAVE (high), uncovered, 5 to 6 minutes or until tender, stirring once.

About 8 Servings
20 Calories Each

The tartness of apple and richness of cheese add a deliciously different topping to acorn squash halves.

CHEESE 'N APPLE ACORNS

- **1 acorn squash**
- **½ teaspoon salt**
- **1 medium cooking apple, peeled and sliced**
- **1 tablespoon butter or margarine**
- **2 tablespoons pasteurized processed cheese spread (Cheese Whiz)**

Topping:
- **1 teaspoon butter or margarine**
- **2 tablespoons dry bread crumbs**
- **Dash nutmeg**

1. Prick acorn squash several times with fork.

2. MICROWAVE (high) whole acorn squash 5 to 6 minutes or until partially cooked, turning squash over halfway through cooking time. Let stand 5 minutes.

3. Cut squash in half; scoop out seeds. Place halves cut-side-up on glass serving plate. Sprinkle each half with salt. Fill cavities with apple slices. Add butter to each. Cover with waxed paper.

4. MICROWAVE (high) 5 to 6 minutes or until apples and squash are tender. Set aside.

5. MICROWAVE (high) butter for Topping ½ to 1 minute or until melted. Stir in bread crumbs and nutmeg. Spoon cheese spread onto apples. Top with crumbs.

6. MICROWAVE (high), uncovered, 1 to 1½ minutes or until cheese is softened. Let stand several minutes before serving.

About 2 Servings

TIP • For 2 acorn squash, double ingredient quantities and increase microwave time as follows: step 2 — 9 to 10 minutes; step 4 — 8 to 9 minutes; step 5 — the same; step 6 — 1½ to 2 minutes.

Fresh zucchini seasoned with garlic butter and highlighted with cherry tomatoes makes a winning combination for any meal.

ZUCCHINI SPECIAL

4	cups sliced zucchini
3	tablespoons butter or margarine
1	teaspoon cornstarch
½	teaspoon garlic salt
⅛	teaspoon thyme leaves
12	cherry tomatoes

1. Combine zucchini and butter in 1-quart glass casserole. Cover with casserole lid.

2. MICROWAVE (high) 5 to 5½ minutes or until just about tender, stirring once. Stir in cornstarch. Add garlic salt, thyme and tomatoes; stir lightly.

3. MICROWAVE (high), uncovered, 1 to 1½ minutes or until heated through.

5 to 6 Servings

Lentils are a type of bean, but cook more quickly than most dry beans. This recipe is rich in protein so can be used as a meatless main dish or as a hearty vegetable.

SPANISH LENTILS

1¼	cups (8 ozs.) lentils
1	medium onion, chopped
3	cups water
1	can (16 oz.) tomatoes, undrained
1	can (12 oz.) vacuum-packed corn, undrained
½	cup chopped green pepper
¼	cup catsup
1	teaspoon salt
1	teaspoon sugar
1	teaspoon chili powder
⅛	teaspoon garlic powder
⅛	teaspoon pepper

1. Wash and drain lentils. Combine lentils, onion and water in 3-quart glass casserole. Cover with casserole lid.

2. MICROWAVE (high) 30 to 35 minutes or until lentils are just about tender. Stir in remaining ingredients. Cover.

3. MICROWAVE (high) 20 to 25 minutes or until lentils are tender and most of liquid is absorbed.

About 6 Servings

Cheese 'N Apple Acorns.

Begin with packaged spinach soufflé to create this flavorful tomato dish.

SOUFFLE-TOPPED TOMATOES

  4 **slices bacon**
  1 **package (12 oz.) frozen spinach soufflé**
  ½ **cup (2 ozs.) shredded Cheddar cheese**
  8 **tomato slices**

1. Arrange bacon slices evenly in 8-inch square glass baking dish or bacon rack. Cover with paper towel.

2. MICROWAVE (high) 4 to 4½ minutes or until bacon is crisp, rotating dish once. Crumble bacon into small pieces; set aside.

3. Remove soufflé from foil container; place in 1-quart glass casserole. Cover with casserole lid.

4. MICROWAVE (high) 4 to 5 minutes or until thawed, stirring once with fork to break up pieces. Lightly mix in bacon and cheese. Cover.

5. MICROWAVE (high) 2 to 3 minutes or until soufflé has started to set, stirring once.

6. Arrange tomato slices on glass serving plate. Spoon soufflé mixture onto each tomato slice.

7. MICROWAVE (high), uncovered, 1½ to 2 minutes or until soufflé is set, rotating plate once.

About 8 Servings

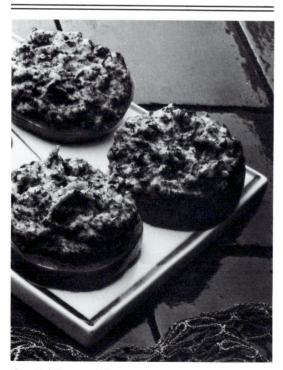

Soufflé-Topped Tomatoes.

No longer is it necessary to use the oven when you wish to serve baked beans. Remember to soak the beans overnight.

HEARTY BAKED BEANS

  2   **cups (16 ozs.) pea or navy beans**
  6   **cups water**
  ½   **teaspoon salt**
  ⅓   **cup packed brown sugar**
  ⅓   **cup dark molasses**
  ⅓   **cup catsup**
  1   **medium onion, chopped**
  1   **teaspoon dry mustard**
  8   **slices (about 4 ozs.) bacon, cut up**
  2½ **cups (about 1 lb.) cubed, cooked ham**

1. Combine beans and water in unsoaked simmer pot. Cover with simmer pot lid. Let stand at room temperature overnight.

2. Add salt to beans. Cover.

3. MICROWAVE (high) 15 to 17 minutes or until mixture boils. Then, MICROWAVE (medium — 50%) 55 to 60 minutes or until beans are just about tender.

4. Stir in brown sugar, molasses, catsup, onion, mustard, bacon and ham until evenly mixed. Cover.

5. MICROWAVE (medium — 50%) 50 to 60 minutes or until beans are tender. If mixture becomes too dry, mix in a little more water.

8 to 10 Servings

TIPS • If it is not convenient to start the beans the night before, bring the beans and water to boil. Then, allow to stand at room temperature, covered, 1 hour before continuing with the cooking in step 3. It will require 8 to 10 minutes to again bring the mixture to boil.

• A 3-quart glass casserole can be substituted for simmer pot. Prepare as directed, stirring once or twice in step 5.

The Microwave Times

Breads

Rye Bread, page 102,
Quick Caramel Rolls,
page 101, and
Oatmeal Batter
Rolls, page
100.

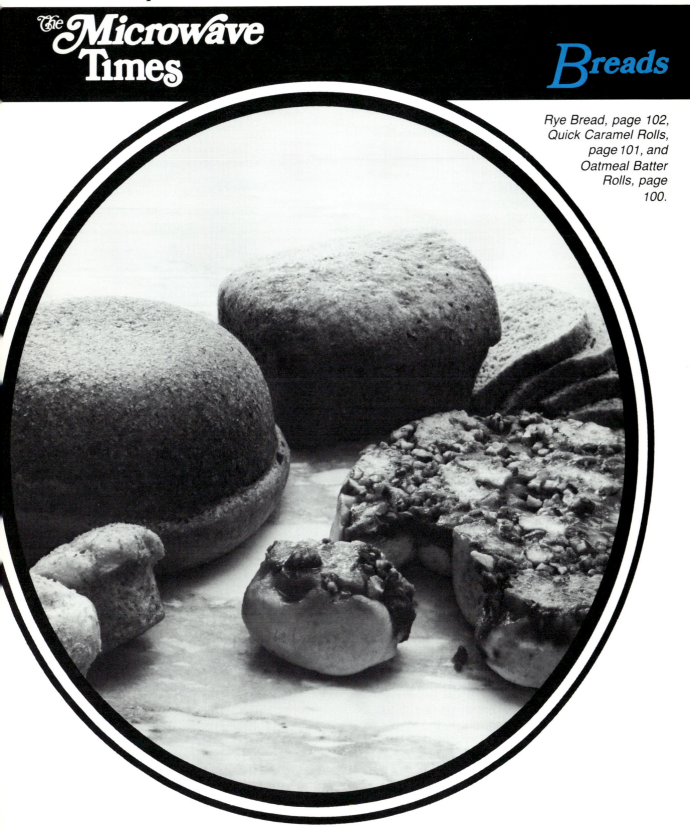

This muffin batter has a yeast flavor and aroma. There are several "Tips" for varying the recipe each time you make it. Cook just enough for yourself or treat your family or friends to warm, freshly cooked muffins.

VERSATILE STORE AND BAKE MUFFINS

1 **egg, slightly beaten**
½ **cup milk**
¼ **cup sugar**
¼ **cup cooking oil**
1 **teaspoon active dry yeast**
½ **cup unsifted all-purpose flour**
½ **cup whole wheat flour**
1 **teaspoon baking powder**
¼ **teaspoon salt**

1. Combine egg, milk, sugar, oil and yeast in mixing bowl. Stir in flours, baking powder and salt until smooth.

2. Spoon into paper-lined muffin cups, filling half full. Store any remaining batter for 3 to 5 days in tightly covered container in refrigerator.

3. MICROWAVE (high), uncovered:
    1 muffin -25   to 35 seconds
    2 muffins -40   to 50 seconds
    3 muffins - 1   to 1¼ minutes
    4 muffins - 1½ to 2   minutes
    5 muffins - 2   to 2½ minutes

About 10 Muffins

TIPS • Caramel Upside-Down Muffins: (omit paper liners) For each muffin, combine the following in a glass custard cup: 2 teaspoons brown sugar, 1 teaspoon butter or margarine, 1 teaspoon honey and 1 teaspoon chopped nuts. Microwave (high) each cup for 20 to 30 seconds or until bubbly. Stir to combine. Spoon about 2 tablespoons batter into each cup. Increase microwave time about 15 seconds. After cooking, allow muffin to stand 2 minutes. Loosen sides from cup and invert onto serving plate.

• Cinnamon-Coated Muffins: Prepare and cook muffins in paper-lined muffin cups. Melt butter (about 1 tablespoon for each 3 muffins) in small glass dish by microwaving about 30 seconds. Dip tops of muffins in butter; then coat with a mixture of cinnamon and sugar. (Use about 1 tablespoon sugar and ¼ teaspoon cinnamon for 3 muffins.)

• Jam-Topped Muffins: spoon batter into paper-lined cups, filling cups about half full. Top each with 1 teaspoon of favorite jam. Microwave as directed.

• Streusel Muffins: Fill paper-lined cups about half full with batter. For 5 muffins, combine 1 tablespooon brown sugar, ½ tablespoon butter or margarine, 2 teaspoons flour and ¼ teaspoon cinnamon until crumbly, mixing with fork. Stir in 1 tablespoon chopped nuts, if desired. Spoon about 1 teaspoon of mixture onto batter for each muffin. Microwave as directed.

The moist, mild flavor of these muffins compliments spicy casseroles and stews.

CORN MUFFINS

3 **tablespoons butter or margarine**
3 **tablespoons sugar**
2 **eggs**
1 **cup buttermilk or sour milk**
1 **cup unsifted all-purpose flour**
¾ **cup yellow cornmeal**
1 **teaspoon baking powder**
½ **teaspoon salt**
¼ **teaspoon soda**

1. MICROWAVE (high) butter in glass mixing bowl ½ to 1 minute or until melted.

2. Blend in sugar; beat in eggs. Stir in buttermilk and remaining ingredients just until smooth.

3. Line microwave muffin pan or glass custard cups with paper liners. Spoon batter into cups, filling ⅔ full.

4. MICROWAVE (high) 6 muffins at a time, uncovered, 2 to 2½ minutes, or until no longer doughy, rotating pan once. Repeat with remaining batter, microwaving last 2 muffins about 1 minute.

12 to 14 Muffins

A flavorful butter to serve with favorite coffee cake, muffins, pancakes or rolls.

HONEY-ALMOND BUTTER

⅓ **cup butter or margarine**
3 **tablespoons honey**
¼ **teaspoon almond extract**

1. MICROWAVE (high) butter in glass bowl ¼ to ½ minute or until softened. Beat until creamy. Gradually beat in honey and almond extract. Spoon into serving bowl.

2. Store in refrigerator or at room temperature.

About ½ Cup Butter

Rolled wheat adds fiber, nutrients and a nutty flavor to these muffins.

BLUEBERRY MUFFINS

- ¾ **cup buttermilk**
- ¾ **cup rolled whole wheat**
- ¼ **cup cooking oil**
- ⅓ **cup packed brown sugar**
- 1 **egg**
- ¾ **cup unsifted all-purpose flour**
- ½ **teaspoon baking powder**
- ½ **teaspoon salt**
- ½ **teaspoon cinnamon**
- ¼ **teaspoon soda**
- ⅔ **cup fresh or frozen blueberries**

1. Combine buttermilk and whole wheat in mixing bowl; mix well. Stir in oil, brown sugar and egg. Add flour, baking powder, salt, cinnamon and soda; mix just until moistened. Stir in blueberries.

2. Spoon batter into paper-lined microwave muffin pan or custard cups, filling cups half full.

3. MICROWAVE (high) 6 muffins at a time, uncovered, 1¾ to 2¼ minutes (2 to 2½ if blueberries are frozen) or until no longer doughy, rotating pan once.

About 15 Muffins

TIPS • For 3 muffins, microwave 1 to 1½ minutes (1¼ to 1¾ for frozen blueberries.)
 • Chopped cranberries can be substituted for blueberries.

These muffins are richer and more cake-like than traditional muffins and cook well in the microwave. They can be seved as muffins or cupcakes and will be popular with all ages.

ZUCCHINI SPICE MUFFINS

- 1 **egg**
- ½ **cup packed brown sugar**
- ⅓ **cup cooking oil**
- ½ **teaspoon vanilla**
- ¾ **cup unsifted all-purpose flour**
- 1 **teaspoon cinnamon**
- ¼ **teaspoon salt**
- ¼ **teaspoon soda**
- ⅛ **teaspoon baking powder**
- ⅔ **cup shredded zucchini squash**
- ¼ **cup shredded coconut**

1. Beat egg; blend in brown sugar, oil and vanilla until smooth. Add remaining

ingredients; stir until moistened.

2. Line 10 microwave muffin cups or glass custard cups with paper liners. Spoon batter into cups, filling ⅔ full.

3. MICROWAVE (high) 6 muffins at a time, uncovered, 2 to 2½ minutes or until no longer doughy, rotating pan once. Repeat with remaining batter, microwaving 4 muffins 1½ to 2 minutes.

10 Muffins

These light, flavorful muffins will go perfectly on many cookout tables. The addition of whole wheat flour adds color and flavor and also helps control the leavening quantity in the biscuit mix.

BEER MUFFINS

- 1 **cup buttermilk biscuit mix**
- ½ **cup whole wheat flour**
- 1 **tablespoon sugar**
- ¾ **cup beer**
- 1 **egg**
- 2 **tablespoons cooking oil**

1. Combine biscuit mix, whole wheat flour and sugar in mixing bowl. Add beer, egg and oil. Stir until smooth.

2. Spoon mixture into paper-lined microwave muffin cups, filling cups ⅔ full.

3. MICROWAVE (high), uncovered, 6 muffins at a time, 2 to 2½ minutes or until no longer doughy, rotating pan once. Repeat with remaining batter.

About 12 Muffins

TIPS • For Cheese Muffins, place a ¼-inch cube of cheese in the center of each muffin cup before cooking. If desired, add ½ teaspoon poppy seed to batter or sprinkle muffin batter with poppy seed before cooking.
 • For Rye Muffins, substitute rye flour for whole wheat and add ¼ teaspoon caraway seed.

An ever-popular favorite that cooks nicely in the microwave.

BANANA-NUT BREAD

½ **cup cooking oil**
¾ **cup packed brown sugar**
2 **eggs**
¼ **cup milk or orange juice**
1 **cup mashed ripe banana (2 to 3 medium bananas)**
1¾ **cups unsifted all-purpose flour**
½ **teaspoon baking powder**
½ **teaspoon soda**
¾ **teaspoon salt**
½ **cup chopped nuts**
1 **to 2 tablespoons graham cracker crumbs**

1. Blend together oil and brown sugar in large mixing bowl. Add eggs, one at a time, beating well after each. Stir in milk and banana. Add remaining ingredients except graham cracker crumbs. Stir until thoroughly mixed.

2. Grease bottom and sides of 8 x 4-inch or 9 x 5-inch (1½-quart) plastic or glass loaf dish. Sprinkle with graham cracker crumbs; shake out excess crumbs. Pour batter into dish, spreading evenly.

3. MICROWAVE (medium — 50%), uncovered, 10 minutes, rotating dish once or twice. Rotate dish. Then, MICROWAVE (high) 3 to 4 minutes or until surface is no longer doughy, rotating dish once. Let cool 10 minutes. Turn bread out of dish and cool completely. Wrap tightly and store in refrigerator at least several hours before slicing and serving.

1 Loaf

TIPS • Batter can also be cooked in a 2-quart glass casserole. Grease casserole and sprinkle with graham cracker crumbs. Place a glass in center with open end up. Pour batter around glass. (If glass is lightweight, fill with cornmeal or rice to add weight.) Cook as directed in step 3.
• For Full Power directions, see Cinnamon-Apple Bread recipe "Tips".
• For Combination Oven directions, see Cinnamon-Apple Bread recipe "Tips".

A moist, spicy bread that's popular anytime, but particularly in the fall.

WHOLE WHEAT-PUMPKIN BREAD

½ **cup cooking oil**
¾ **cup packed brown sugar**
2 **eggs**
2 **tablespoons orange juice or milk**
1 **cup canned or mashed, cooked pumpkin**
1 **cup whole wheat flour***
¾ **cup unsifted all-purpose flour**
½ **teaspoon baking powder**
½ **teaspoon soda**
¾ **teaspoon salt**
½ **teaspoon cinnamon**
½ **teaspoon nutmeg**
1 **cup raisins or ½ cup chopped nuts**
1 **to 2 tablespoons graham cracker crumbs**

1. Blend together oil and brown sugar in large mixing bowl. Add eggs, one at time, beating well after each. Stir in orange juice and pumpkin. Add remaining ingredients except graham cracker crumbs. Stir until thoroughly mixed.

2. Grease bottom and sides of 8 x 4-inch or 9 x 5-inch (1½-quart) plastic or glass loaf dish. Sprinkle with graham cracker crumbs; shake out excess crumbs. Pour batter into dish, spreading evenly.

3. MICROWAVE (medium — 50%), uncovered, 10 minutes, rotating dish once or twice. Rotate dish. Then, MICROWAVE (high) 3 to 4 minutes or until surface is no longer doughy, rotating dish once. Let cool 10 minutes. Turn bread out of dish and cool completely. Wrap tightly and store in refrigerator at least several hours before slicing and serving.

1 Loaf

TIPS • For Full Power directions, see Tips of Cinnamon-Apple Bread recipe.
• For Combination Oven, increase juice to ¼ cup. See Tips of Cinnamon-Apple Bread recipe for cooking directions.
• *All-purpose flour can be substituted for whole wheat flour.

Cinnamon and apples combine for a nut bread that has been very popular in classes.

CINNAMON-APPLE BREAD

½ cup cooking oil
¾ cup sugar
2 eggs
1 teaspoon vanilla
¼ cup milk
2 cups shredded apple* (about 3 medium)
1¾ cups unsifted all-purpose flour
½ teaspoon baking powder
½ teaspoon soda
¾ teaspoon salt
1½ teaspoons cinnamon
½ cup chopped nuts
1 to 2 tablespoons graham cracker crumbs

1. Blend together oil and sugar in large mixing bowl. Add eggs, one at a time, beating well after each. Stir in vanilla, milk and apple. Add remaining ingredients except graham cracker crumbs. Stir until thoroughly mixed.

2. Grease bottom and sides of 8 x 4 or 9 x 5-inch (1½-quart) plastic or glass loaf dish. Sprinkle with graham cracker crumbs; shake out excess crumbs. Pour batter into dish, spreading evenly.

3. MICROWAVE (medium — 50%), uncovered, 10 minutes, rotating dish once or twice. Rotate dish. Then, MICROWAVE (high) 3 to 4 minutes or until surface is no longer doughy, rotating dish once. Let cool 10 minutes. Turn bread out of dish and cool completely. Wrap tightly and store in refrigerator at least several hours before slicing and serving.

1 Loaf

TIPS • *The peel can be left on the apple or removed.

• With Full Power, place 4-cup glass measure filled with 4 cups water in microwave during cooking. Microwave (high) 10 to 11 minutes, rotating dish 2 or 3 times.

• With Combination Oven in step 3, bake in preheated 375° oven 15 minutes. Then, microwave-bake 7 to 9 minutes.

Cinnamon-Apple Bread.

A traditional German coffee cake that cooks well in the microwave. Serve as a brunch or coffee time bread or as a dessert.

APPLE KUCHEN

- ¼ **cup milk**
- 1 **tablespoon sugar**
- 1 **tablespoon butter or margarine**
- ¼ **cup warm water**
- 1 **package active dry yeast**
- 1 **teaspoon salt**
- ⅛ **teaspoon nutmeg**
- 1 **egg**
- 1½ **cups unsifted all-purpose flour**
- 2 **medium cooking apples, peeled and sliced (about 2 cups)**
- 1 **tablespoon butter or margarine**
- ½ **cup sugar**
- 1 **teaspoon cinnamon**
- ¼ **cup half & half cream**
- 1 **egg yolk**

1. Combine milk, 1 tablespoon sugar and 1 tablespoon butter in 2-quart glass mix 'n pour bowl.

2. MICROWAVE (high), uncovered, 30 to 45 seconds or until heated. Set aside.

3. Combine water and yeast; let stand a few minutes to soften yeast. Add salt and nutmeg to warm milk; beat in egg. Stir in yeast. Gradually add flour, beating well after each addition. Cover loosely with plastic wrap.

4. MICROWAVE (warm — 10%) 2 to 3 minutes or until dough feels warm, but not hot, rotating dish once. Let stand 15 to 25 minutes or until dough is doubled in size.

5. Grease bottom and sides of 8-inch round glass or plastic baking dish. Coat bottom and sides of dish with toasted wheat germ or cornflake crumbs. Spoon dough into dish to cover most of bottom. Arrange apples on dough, pressing as necessary to spread dough over bottom of dish.

6. MICROWAVE (high) 1 tablespoon butter in small glass dish 15 to 20 seconds or until melted. Mix in ½ cup sugar and the cinnamon. Spoon over apples. Cover loosely with plastic wrap.

7. MICROWAVE (warm — 10%) 1½ to 2 minutes or until dough is warm, but not hot, rotating dish once. Let stand 15 to 25 minutes or until dough is doubled in size. Remove plastic wrap. Cover with paper towel.

8. MICROWAVE (medium — 50%) 4½ to 5 minutes or until bread is just about cooked, rotating dish once or twice. Blend together cream and egg yolk. Pour evenly over coffee cake. Cover with waxed paper.

9. MICROWAVE (medium — 50%) 1½ to 2 minutes or until cream mixture is just about set, rotating dish once. Let stand about 10 minutes before cutting into wedges for serving.

8 to 10 Servings

This quick and easy coffee cake takes just minutes to make in the microwave.

BLUEBERRY COFFEE CAKE

- 1 **cup fresh or frozen blueberries**
- ⅓ **cup butter or margarine**
- ½ **cup sugar**
- ½ **cup packed brown sugar**
- 1 **egg**
- ½ **teaspoon vanilla**
- ¾ **cup milk**
- 1¾ **cups unsifted all-purpose flour**
- 1½ **teaspoons baking powder**
- ¼ **teaspoon salt**
- 1 **tablespoon sugar**
- ½ **teaspoon cinnamon**

1. Wash fresh blueberries; place frozen berries in glass bowl. Set aside.

2. MICROWAVE (high) butter in glass mixing bowl ¼ to ½ minute or until softened. Beat until creamy. Blend in sugars; beat in egg. Stir in vanilla and milk. Add flour, baking powder and salt; mix just until smooth.

3. Grease bottom only of 8-inch round glass or plastic baking dish. Spread half of batter evenly in dish. Sprinkle with blueberries (if still frozen, microwave about ½ minute to partially thaw). Spoon remaining batter over blueberries; carefully spread to cover. Combine sugar and cinnamon; sprinkle over coffee cake.

4. MICROWAVE (medium — 50%), uncovered, 12 minutes, rotating dish once or twice. Then, MICROWAVE (high) 4 to 5 minutes or until no longer doughy. Serve warm with Honey-Almond Butter, page 94.

8 to 10 Servings

TIPS • With Full Power in step 4, microwave 7 to 8 minutes, rotating dish 3 or 4 times.

• With combination oven in step 4, bake in preheated 400° oven for 15 minutes. Then, microwave-bake 3 to 5 minutes or until toothpick inserted in center comes out clean.

Apple Kuchen.

A delicious moist bread that can be made into either a loaf or rolls.

OATMEAL BATTER BREAD OR ROLLS

1¼ **cups water**
¾ **cup quick rolled oats**
¼ **cup butter or margarine**
¼ **cup molasses or honey**
1½ **teaspoons salt**
¼ **cup warm water**
1 **package active dry yeast**
1 **egg**
2¾ **to 3 cups unsifted all-purpose flour**

1. MICROWAVE (high) water in 2-quart glass mix 'n pour bowl 3½ to 4 minutes or until boiling. Stir in oats, butter, molasses and salt. Cool to lukewarm.

2. Combine yeast with ¼ cup warm water. Let stand a few minutes to soften yeast.

3. Add 1 cup flour and egg to warm oatmeal mixture; beat well. Stir in softened yeast. Gradually stir in remaining 1¾ to 2 cups flour to form a stiff batter. Cover loosely with plastic wrap.

4. MICROWAVE (warm — 10%) 4 to 6 minutes or until mixture feels warm but not hot, rotating dish once. Let stand 15 to 20 minutes.

5. MICROWAVE (warm — 10%) 3 to 5 minutes or until mixture feels warm but not hot, rotating dish once. Let stand 10 to 15 minutes or until dough is doubled in size.

6. Stir down batter. Grease 2-quart glass casserole. Sprinkle with toasted wheat germ or cornflake crumbs, coating bottom and sides of dish. Turn batter into casserole; sprinkle surface with crumbs.

7. MICROWAVE (warm — 10%), uncovered, 6 to 8 minutes or until mixture feels warm but not hot, rotating dish once. Let stand 15 to 20 minutes or until doubled (at top of dish). Cover with paper towel.

8. MICROWAVE (medium — 50%) 10 to 11 minutes or until surface springs back when touched lightly, rotating dish once or twice. Cool 5 minutes; turn out of dish. Cool completely.

1 Loaf

TIPS • For Rolls, in step 6 spoon batter into 18 greased, crumb-coated microwave muffin cups or 5-oz. glass custard cups, filling ⅔ full. Sprinkle tops with crumbs. Microwave (warm — 10%), uncovered, 6 cups at a time, 4 to 5 minutes. Let stand 15 to 25 minutes, or until doubled in size. To cook rolls, cover with paper towel and microwave (medium — 50%), 6 cups at a time, 3 to 3½ minutes or until surface springs back when touched lightly.

• Dough can be baked, uncovered, after step 7 at 375° for 35 to 40 minutes.

• With Combination Oven, microwave in step 1 for 4 to 5 minutes. In step 4, microwave (defrost) 3 to 4 minutes, in step 5 for 2 to 2½ minutes and in step 7 for 3 to 4 minutes. In step 8, bake uncovered in preheated 375° oven for 15 minutes. Then, microwave-bake for 4 to 6 minutes or until loaf sounds hollow when tapped.

Oatmeal Batter Rolls.

Use your very low microwave setting to help thaw and proof two loaves of frozen bread dough in about 1 hour. Then, either bake the bread conventionally or cook it in the microwave. Be careful not to let bread rise too high before microwaving or it will collapse after cooking.

FROZEN BREAD DOUGH

1. Generously grease two 8 x 4-inch plastic or glass loaf pans. Sprinkle each with toasted wheat germ or cornflake crumbs, coating bottom and sides of dishes. Shake out excess crumbs.

2. Place a frozen loaf of dough in each pan. Grease top of loaf. Cover loosely with plastic wrap. Place both pans in microwave oven.

3. MICROWAVE (warm — 10%) 13 to 15 minutes or until dough feels warm, but not hot, rotating pans once. Let stand 20 minutes.

4. MICROWAVE (warm — 10%) 3 to 5 minutes or until dough feels warm. Let stand 15 to 30 minutes or until dough is doubled in size (about 1 inch below top of pan). Do not allow to rise too much. Remove plastic covering. Sprinkle surface with additional wheat germ or cornflake crumbs. Cover each loaf with paper towel. Place one loaf in the microwave oven.

5. MICROWAVE (medium — 50%) one loaf at a time 7 to 8 minutes or until surface springs back when touched lightly, rotating dish 2 or 3 times. Repeat with other loaf. Cool 5 minutes. Remove from pan; cool completely.

2 Loaves

TIPS • If you wish to bake the bread conventionally, allow the dough to rise to top of pan. Then bake both loaves at once, uncovered, as directed on frozen dough package. (Crumbs can be omitted.)
• For one loaf, microwave in step 3 for 8 to 10 minutes and in step 4 for 2 to 3 minutes. Cook as directed in step 5.
• With Combination Oven, microwave (defrost) in step 3 for 7 to 8 minutes and in step 4 for 2 to 2½ minutes. In step 5, bake both loaves uncovered in preheated 375° oven 15 minutes. Then, microwave-bake 3 to 5 minutes or until loaves sound hollow when tapped.

Start with frozen roll dough and have hot caramel rolls on the table in about 30 minutes.

QUICK CARAMEL ROLLS

¼ **cup butter or margarine**
½ **cup packed brown sugar**
½ **package (about 3-oz. size) regular vanilla pudding mix (not instant)**
⅓ **cup chopped nuts**
12 **frozen dough rolls**

1. Combine butter and brown sugar in 2-cup glass measure.

2. MICROWAVE (high), uncovered, 1½ to 2 minutes or until bubbly, stirring once. Stir in pudding mix (about 4 tablespoons).

3. Grease bottom and sides of 8 or 9-inch round glass or plastic baking dish. Sprinkle bottom with nuts. Arrange frozen dough evenly in dish. Slowly pour butter mixture over rolls. Cover with plastic wrap.

4. MICROWAVE (warm — 10%) 7 to 8 minutes or until dough is thawed and feels warm but not hot, rotating dish once. Let stand covered 15 to 20 minutes or until doubled in size. Remove plastic wrap; cover dough with paper towel.

5. MICROWAVE (medium — 50%) 6½ to 7 minutes or until dough springs back when touched lightly, rotating dish once. Let stand 5 minutes. Invert onto serving plate. Serve warm.

12 Rolls

TIPS • For a double recipe, microwave in step 2 for 2 to 2½ minutes. In step 4, microwave both dishes at once 18 to 20 minutes, rearranging dishes twice. Microwave rolls in step 5, one pan at a time, as directed.
• After thawing and proofing in step 4, rolls can be baked uncovered in 350° oven for 15 to 20 minutes.
• With Combination Oven, microwave in step 2 for 3 to 3½ minutes and microwave (defrost) in step 4 for 4 to 4½ minutes. In step 5, bake uncovered in preheated 400° oven 10 minutes. Then, microwave-bake 2 to 3 minutes.

A mild rye bread with a delicious European taste and texture. Very good either baked or microwaved.

RYE BREAD

  1 **cup water**
1½ **cups rye flour**
 ⅓ **cup molasses or packed brown sugar**
  2 **tablespoons butter or margarine**
  1 **teaspoon salt**
 ¼ **cup warm water**
  1 **package active dry yeast**
2½ **to 2¾ cups unsifted all-purpose flour**

1. MICROWAVE (high) water in 1-cup glass measure 2 to 2½ minutes or until boiling.

2. Combine rye flour, molasses, butter and salt in large mixing bowl; stir in boiling water. Cool to lukewarm.

3. Combine yeast with ¼ cup warm water. Let stand a few minutes to soften yeast.

4. Beat 1 cup all-purpose flour into rye mixture. Stir in softened yeast. Gradually stir in remaining 1½ to 1¾ cups all-purpose flour to form a stiff dough.

5. Turn dough onto floured surface. Knead 5 to 7 minutes or until smooth, adding additional flour as necessary. Place dough in greased 2-quart glass mix 'n pour bowl, turning dough to grease top. Cover loosely with plastic wrap.

6. MICROWAVE (warm — 10%) 8 to 10 minutes or until dough feels warm, but not hot, rotating dish once. Let stand 15 minutes.

7. MICROWAVE (warm — 10%) 3 to 5 minutes or until dough feels warm but not hot, rotating dish once. Let stand 10 to 15 minutes or until dough is doubled in size.

8. Punch down dough. Knead a few times until smooth and free of air bubbles. Grease 1½-quart glass casserole. Sprinkle with toasted wheat germ or cornflake crumbs, coating bottom and sides of dish. Place dough in dish, smooth side up. Grease top of dough. Cover loosely with plastic wrap.

9. MICROWAVE (warm — 10%) 6 to 8 minutes or until dough is warm, but not hot, rotating dish once. Let stand 15 to 20 minutes or until dough is doubled in size. Remove plastic wrap. Cover with paper towel.

10. MICROWAVE (medium — 50%) 9 to 10 minutes or until surface springs back when touched lightly, rotating dish once or twice. Cool 5 minutes; turn out of dish. Cool completely.

1 Loaf

TIPS • A 9-inch glass pie pan can be substituted for casserole.
• Dough can be baked, uncovered, after step 9 at 375° for 30 to 35 minutes.
• For a double quantity, microwave in step 1 for 3½ to 4 minutes, step 6 for 13 to 15 minutes, step 7 for 4 to 5 minutes. Form 2 loaves and microwave in step 9 for 8 to 10 minutes. Microwave loaves one at a time as directed in step 10.
• With Combination Oven, microwave in step 1 for 3½ to 4 minutes. In step 6, microwave (defrost) 3 to 4 minutes, step 7 for 2 to 2½ minutes and in step 9 for 3 to 4 minutes. In step 10, bake uncovered in preheated 375° oven 15 minutes. Then, microwave-bake 3 to 5 minutes or until loaf sounds hollow when tapped.

Use the microwave to quickly heat French bread.

CHEESY FRENCH BREAD

 ½ **loaf French bread (about 12 inches)**
 ¼ **cup butter or margarine**
 ¾ **teaspoon garlic salt**
  2 **tablespoons Parmesan cheese**
  1 **tablespoon snipped parsley**

1. Cut loaf of bread in half lengthwise.

2. MICROWAVE (high) butter and garlic salt in small glass dish 30 to 60 seconds or until melted. Brush both sides of bread with butter mixture. Sprinkle with cheese and parsley. Place two halves together. Place on paper napkin or paper towels. Cut into pieces if desired.

3. Place bread on waxed paper in microwave oven.

4. MICROWAVE (high), uncovered, 1 to 1½ minutes or until warm.

About 4 Servings

Favorite Recipes from

The Microwave Times

Chapter 8

Desserts & Pies

Rhubarb Creme, page 117.

Fruit, rice, gelatin and whipped topping combine for a favorite dessert.

GLORIFIED RICE

   1 **cup uncooked long-grain rice**
   2 **cups water**
   1 **teaspoon salt**
   2 **cups water**
   1 **package (3 oz.) raspberry-flavored gelatin**
   1 **can (15¼ oz.) crushed pineapple, undrained**
   1 **package (10 oz.) frozen sweetened sliced strawberries**
   2 **cups whipped topping**

1. Combine rice, 2 cups water and salt in 2-quart glass casserole. Cover with casserole lid.

2. MICROWAVE (high) 6 to 7 minutes or until boiling. Let stand 10 minutes. Add 2 cups water; cover.

3. MICROWAVE (high) 8 to 10 minutes or until mixture boils. Stir in gelatin until dissolved. Add pineapple and strawberries; stir until strawberies are partially thawed. Refrigerate until mixture mounds.

4. Fold in whipped topping. Spoon into serving bowl or individual dishes.

10 to 12 Servings

Pudding mix and crushed pineapple team to make this simple, yet special tasting dessert.

PINEAPPLE CREAM PUDDING

1⅓ **cups milk**
   1 **package (3 oz.) vanilla pudding and pie filling mix**
   1 **can (8 oz.) crushed pineapple, undrained**
   ½ **cup plain yogurt or sour cream**

1. Measure milk in 4-cup glass measure. Stir in pudding mix and pineapple.

2. MICROWAVE (high), uncovered, 5½ to 6½ minutes or until mixture starts to bubble, stirring once or twice during last half of cooking time. Cool. Stir in yogurt. Spoon into serving dishes.

5 to 6 Servings

This recipe, based on Danish tradition, has a pudding-type rather than custard-like base, making it especially easy.

INSTANT RICE PUDDING

   3 **cups milk**
1¾ **cups quick-cooking rice**
   ⅔ **cup sugar**
   2 **tablespoons cornstarch**
   1 **teaspoon salt**
   2 **tablespoons butter or margarine**
   1 **teaspoon vanilla**
   1 **cup whipping cream, whipped**
   ¼ **cup finely chopped almonds**
   1 **whole blanched almond**

1. Combine milk, rice, sugar, cornstarch and salt in 2-quart glass mix 'n pour bowl.

2. MICROWAVE (high), uncovered, 9 to 10 minutes or until mixture boils and thickens, stirring twice. Stir in butter and vanilla. Cool.

3. Fold whipped cream, chopped almonds and whole almond into cooled pudding mixture. Spoon into 1-quart serving dish or into individual serving dishes.

4 to 6 Servings

If you've not already discovered how easy puddings are to cook in the microwave, this is a good recipe from which to learn. Just remember to stir occasionally once the mixture starts to thicken.

CUSTARD PUDDING

   ⅔ **cup sugar**
2½ **tablespoons cornstarch**
   1 **tablespoon flour**
   ½ **teaspoon salt**
   3 **cups milk**
   3 **egg yolks, beaten**
   1 **tablespoon butter or margarine**
   1 **teaspoon vanilla**

1. Combine sugar, cornstarch, flour and salt in 2-quart glass mix 'n pour bowl. Slowly stir in milk.

2. MICROWAVE (high), uncovered, 8 to 9 minutes or until mixture comes to a full boil, stirring 2 or 3 times. Blend a small amount of hot mixture into egg yolks; return to hot mixture, blending well.

3. MICROWAVE (high), uncovered, ¾ to 1 minute or until bubbly around edge, stirring once or twice. Stir in butter and vanilla. Serve warm or cold.

6 to 8 Servings

Here's a quick last-minute February dessert that is delicious served warm from the oven any time of year.

CHERRY BREAD PUDDING

- 1 **can (21 oz.) prepared cherry pie filling**
- 4 **slices bread, cubed**
- ¼ **cup butter or margarine**
- 1 **tablespoon lemon juice**
- 1 **cup milk**
- 3 **eggs**
- ½ **cup sugar**
- ½ **teaspoon almond extract**
  Cinnamon

1. Spread pie filling evenly in shallow 1½-quart glass casserole. Top with bread cubes.

2. MICROWAVE (high) butter in 4-cup glass measure 45 to 60 seconds or until melted. Drizzle evenly over bread; sprinkle with lemon juice.

3. Combine milk, eggs, sugar and almond extract in 4-cup measure; beat well. Pour slowly over bread. Press bread cubes into milk to coat evenly. Sprinkle with cinnamon.

4. MICROWAVE (medium — 50%) 17 to 19 minutes or until bread mixture is just about set in center, rotating dish once or twice. Serve warm or cold.

6 to 8 Servings

TIPS • With Full Power, set casserole in another baking dish. Add about 1 cup warm water to dish. Microwave (high) 16 to 18 minutes.
  • Other fruit pie fillings can be used.
  • With Combination Oven, microwave-bake, uncovered, in preheated 400° oven 15 to 17 minutes in step 4.

A cake mix and pie filling make this simple and tasty cobbler desert.

QUICK CHERRY DESSERT

- 1 **can (21 oz.) prepared cherry pie filling**
- 1 **can (15 oz.) applesauce**
- 1 **package (9 oz.) yellow cake mix**
- ½ **teaspoon cinnamon**
- ½ **cup chopped nuts or flaked coconut**
- ½ **cup butter or margarine**

1. Combine pie filling and applesauce in 8-inch round plastic or glass baking dish; mix well and spread evenly in dish.

2. Sprinkle with dry cake mix, then with cinnamon and nuts.

3. MICROWAVE (high) butter in 2-cup glass measure ½ to 1 minute or until melted. Drizzle over cake mix mixture.

4. MICROWAVE (high), uncovered, 12 to 13 minutes or until bubbly throughout, rotating dish 2 or 3 times.

6 to 8 Servings

TIP • Other favorite pie fillings can be used. Blueberry, strawberry and peach go well with applesauce.

A festive fruit combination to serve warm or chilled.

HOT FRUIT COMPOTE

- 2 **packages (10 ozs. each) frozen sweetened raspberries**
- 2 **tablespoons cornstarch**
- 2 **teaspoons grated orange peel**
- 1 **teaspoon mint flakes or 1 tablespoon chopped fresh mint leaves**
- 1 **can (16 oz.) peach slices, drained**
- 1 **can (16 oz.) pear slices, drained**
- 2 **cups fresh green grapes**

1. Remove 1 metal end (cover) from each package of raspberries. Place frozen packages in microwave.

2. MICROWAVE (high), uncovered, 3½ to 4 minutes or until just about thawed. Drain juices into 1½ to 2-quart glass serving dish. Stir in cornstarch, orange peel and mint flakes. Mix well.

3. MICROWAVE (high), uncovered, 3 to 3½ minutes or until mixture boils and thickens, stirring once or twice. Stir in peaches, pears, grapes and raspberries.

4. MICROWAVE (high), uncovered, 2 to 3 minutes or until warmed. Serve warm or chilled, garnished with fresh mint leaves.

8 to 10 Servings

TIPS • When fresh grapes are not available, substitute drained canned.
  • Strawberries can be substituted for raspberries.

Almond Float.

Colorful fresh fruits float with diamonds of almond-orange pudding in this light and refreshing dessert.

ALMOND FLOAT

- ⅔ **cup cold water**
- ½ **cup milk**
- 1 **envelope unflavored gelatin**
- 2 **tablespoons sugar**
- ½ **teaspoon almond extract**
- 1 **can (11 oz.) mandarin oranges, drained**
- ¼ **cup sugar**
- 1 **cup water**
- 1 **can (8 oz.) pineapple chunks, drained**
- ½ **pint (1 cup) fresh strawberries, halved**
- 1 **kiwi fruit, peeled and sliced**

1. Combine ⅔ cup water and the milk in 2-cup glass measure. Add gelatin and let stand about 5 minutes to soften. Add 2 tablespoons sugar and the almond extract.

2. MICROWAVE (high), uncovered, 1½ to 2 minutes or until steaming hot, stirring once. Pour into 8 x 4 or 9 x 5-inch loaf pan. Stir in half the mandarin oranges; chill until set (about 2 hours).

3. Combine ¼ cup sugar and 1 cup water in 2-cup glass measure.

4. MICROWAVE (high), uncovered, 2 to 3 minutes or until mixture boils, stirring twice. Chill.

5. To serve, combine remaining orange segments, pineapple and strawberries in 2 to 3-quart glass serving bowl. Cut gelatin mixture into 1-inch diamond shapes. Arrange on top of fruit. Pour syrup over mixture. Garnish with kiwi slices. Refrigerate until served.

About 6 Servings
130 Calories Each

TIP • Other fruits such as lychees, seedless grapes or cut melon can be substituted.

This recipe, named after Johnny Appleseed, is popular across the country. The microwaved version may become one of your favorites.

APPLE JONATHAN

- 6 **cups peeled, sliced cooking apples (about 6 medium)**
- ½ **cup maple syrup or packed brown sugar**
- ¼ **cup butter or margarine**
- ½ **cup packed brown sugar**
- 1 **egg**
- ¼ **cup all-purpose flour**
- ½ **cup whole wheat flour**
- 1 **teaspoon baking powder**
- ½ **teaspoon salt**
- ¼ **teaspoon cinnamon**
- ½ **cup milk**
  Nutmeg

1. Combine apples and syrup in 8-inch square glass baking dish. Stir until well coated. Cover with plastic wrap.

2. MICROWAVE (high) 4 minutes. Stir apples and set aside covered.

3. MICROWAVE (high) butter in glass mixing bowl ¼ to ½ minute or until softened. Blend in brown sugar; beat in egg. Add flours, baking powder, salt, cinnamon and milk; stir until smooth. Spoon onto apple slices. Sprinkle with nutmeg.

4. MICROWAVE (high), uncovered, 8 to 9 minutes or until no longer doughy, rotating dish 2 or 3 times.

6 to 8 Servings

TIPS • To cook with lower power in step 4, microwave (medium-high — 70%) 10 to 12 minutes, rotating dish once.

• With Combination Oven, microwave-bake at 400° for 12 to 13 minutes.

This makes a quick family dessert that can be enjoyed by some on special diets.

SIMPLE APPLE DESSERT

- 4 **medium cooking apples**
- ¼ **cup all-purpose flour**
- 2 **tablespoons sugar**
- ½ **teaspoon cinnamon**
- 3 **tablespoons butter or margarine**

1. Peel, core and slice apples into shallow 1-quart glass casserole or 9-inch glass pie plate. Combine flour, sugar and cinnamon. Sprinkle over apples. Cut butter into thin pieces. Place evenly over flour mixture.

2. MICROWAVE (high), uncovered, 5½ to 6½ minutes or until apples are tender, rotating dish once. Serve warm or cold.

6 Servings
129 Calories Each

TIP • With Combination Oven, microwave-bake in preheated 425° oven for 10 to 12 minutes.

Here is an easy and economical way to enjoy your abundant apple harvest.

CRUMB-TOPPED BAKED APPLES

- 2 **tablespoons flour**
- 2 **tablespoons brown sugar**
- 1 **tablespon butter or margarine**
- 2 **tablespoons flaked coconut**
- 2 **tablespoons chopped nuts**
- ½ **teaspoon cinnamon**
- 3 **medium cooking apples**

1. Combine flour, brown sugar and butter in small glass mixing bowl.

2. MICROWAVE (high) ¼ to ½ minute or until butter is softened. Mix with fork until crumbly. Stir in coconut, nuts and cinnamon. Set aside.

3. Cut apples in half lengthwise; remove core, but do not peel. Arrange cut-side-up in 8-inch round glass baking dish. Spoon topping evenly into center of apples. Cover with waxed paper or casserole cover.

4. MICROWAVE (high) 5½ to 6½ minutes or until apples are tender, rotating dish once. Serve warm or cold.

About 6 Servings

Select an apple that retains its shape (like Winesap, Rome Beauty or Yellow Delicious) for these sauteed apple slices. This dessert makes a light, but special finale to any meal.

HONEY-GLAZED APPLE SLICES

- 6 **medium apples, peeled**
- ¼ **cup butter or margarine**
- ¼ **cup honey**
- 2 **teaspoons cornstarch**
- 2 **tablespoons cream sherry, if desired**
- 1 **teaspoon lemon juice**
- ¼ **teaspoon cinnamon**
- ½ **cup whipping cream**
- 1 **teaspoon lemon juice**
- ½ **teaspoon vanilla**

1. Quarter and core apples. Cut each quarter into 3 slices. Place in 8 or 9-inch round shallow glass dish. Add butter.

2. MICROWAVE (high), uncovered, 5 to 6 minutes or until steaming hot, stirring once. Combine honey, cornstarch, sherry, lemon juice and cinnamon. Pour over apples. Stir lightly to mix.

3. MICROWAVE (high), uncovered, 5 to 6 minutes or until apples are glazed and tender, stirring 2 or 3 times. Cool.

4. Combine cream, lemon juice and vanilla. Chill until served.

5. Serve apple slices topped with cream.

5 to 6 Servings

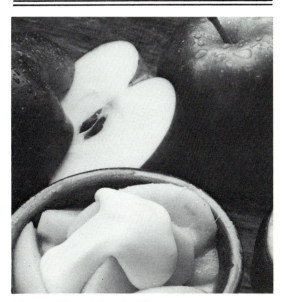

Honey-Glazed Apple Slices.

Cranberries and apples team for an easy dessert that will be enjoyed year around.

CRAN-APPLE CRISP

- 2 cups raw cranberries
- 4 cups sliced, peeled apples (4 med.)
- ¾ cup sugar

Topping:
- ½ cup butter or margarine
- ½ cup packed brown sugar
- ½ cup unsifted all-purpose flour
- 1 cup old-fashioned or quick-cooking rolled oats
- ½ teaspoon cinnamon

1. Combine cranberries, apples and sugar in 8 or 9-inch glass baking dish; mix lightly and spread evenly in dish. Set aside.

2. MICROWAVE (high) butter in glass mixing bowl ¼ to ½ minute or until softened. Blend in brown sugar; mix in flour, oats and cinnamon until crumbly. Crumble over cranberries and apples.

3. MICROWAVE (high), uncovered, 10 to 11 minutes or until fruits are tender, rotating dish once. Serve warm with ice cream or whipped cream.

About 8 Servings

TIP • This dessert freezes well.

Several readers requested help in adapting this recipe. The broiler was necessary to retain the slightly crisp crust and moist interior.

APPLE-NUT TORTE

- 4 eggs
- 1 cup sugar
- ¾ cup unsifted all-purpose flour
- 1 teaspoon baking powder
- ½ teaspoon salt
- 2 cups chopped peeled apple
- 1 cup chopped nuts
- Whipped cream

1. Beat eggs at high speed until frothy, about 1 minute. Gradually add sugar, beating at high speed until mixture forms soft mounds, about 5 minutes. Fold in flour, baking powder and salt. Fold in apples and nuts.

2. Grease bottom only of 12 x 8-inch glass baking dish. Spoon batter into dish; spread evenly. Cover with waxed paper.

3. MICROWAVE (high) 7 to 9 minutes or until center is set, rotating dish once or twice. Meanwhile, preheat broiler.

4. BROIL about 3 inches from heat 1½ to 3 minutes or until golden brown. Serve warm or cold with whipped cream.

About 15 Servings

TIP • One of the recipes omitted the nuts and added 1 teaspoon almond extract.

Apple-Nut Torte.

This fresh pineapple variation with a butter-rum sauce makes a flavorful topping for ice cream, pudding, yogurt or Bavarian creme.

FRESH PINEAPPLE TOPPING

- 1 fresh pineapple
- 3 tablespoons butter or margarine
- ¼ cup packed brown sugar
- 1 to 2 tablespoons rum

1. Cut pineapple in half lengthwise, cutting through top. Using a grapefruit knife, carefully remove pulp by cutting around inside of pineapple, leaving about ½ inch around edge. Cut pulp into bite-sized pieces; discard core. Spoon pineapple back into shells. Set aside.

2. Combine butter and brown sugar in 1-cup glass measure.

3. MICROWAVE (high), uncovered, 1½ to 2 minutes or until bubbly. Stir in rum. Spoon butter mixture over pineapple. Serve immediately or, if desired, microwave (high) 1 to 1½ minutes to warm pineapple.

About 6 Servings

TIP • Toasted coconut makes a delectable topping. To toast in microwave, place ⅓ cup coconut in glass pie plate. Microwave 3 to 4 minutes or until lightly browned, stirring every minute. Sprinkle over pineapple just before serving to retain crunchy texture.

Pears are plentiful throughout the Fall months and can be used in many simple desserts such as this "crisp."

COCONUT CRUNCH PEARS

- 5 cups peeled, sliced pears (5 medium)
- 2 tablespoons flour
- 1 tablespoon lemon juice
- ¼ cup butter or margarine
- ½ cup packed brown sugar
- ⅓ cup unsifted all-purpose flour
- ½ cup flaked coconut
- ½ cup chopped nuts
- ½ teaspoon cinnamon

1. Combine pears, 2 tablespoons flour and the lemon juice in 8 or 9-inch round glass baking dish; mix lightly and spread evenly in dish. Set aside.

2. MICROWAVE (high) butter in glass mixing bowl 20 to 30 seconds or until softened. Mix in brown sugar, flour, coconut, nuts and cinnamon until crumbly. Spoon over pears.

3. MICROWAVE (high), uncovered, 9 to 10 minutes or until pear are tender, rotating dish once.

5 to 6 Servings

Fresh Pineapple Topping.

Cheesy Pears.

A beautiful dessert that is ideal for a brunch or other light meal. It takes very little preparation time and can be made ahead.

STRAWBERRY CREME MELON

>   1 **package (8 oz.) cream cheese**
> 1/3 **cup sugar**
>   1 **egg**
>   1 **teaspoon vanilla**
>   1 **honeydew melon**
> 1/2 **cup sliced fresh strawberries**

1. MICROWAVE (high) cream cheese in 2-cup glass measure 1 to 1¼ minutes or until softened, stirring once. Blend in sugar; beat in egg.

2. MICROWAVE (high), uncovered, 1½ to 2 minutes or until thickened, stirring every ½ minute. Stir in vanilla. Cool.

3. Cut melon in half; remove seeds. Peel each half.

4. Spread cream cheese mixture in each melon half. Cover with plastic wrap. Refrigerate at least 3 hours or until ready to serve. Cut into wedges just before serving; garnish with fresh strawberries, if desired.

About 8 Servings

TIP • Muskmelon or cantaloupe can be substituted for honeydew melon.

This simple dessert would be a good starter when learning to use the microwave. It's simple, yet has a special flavor that will be welcome at almost any meal.

CHEESY PEARS

>   1 **can (29 oz.) pear halves, drained**
>   1 **package (3 oz.) cream cheese**
>   2 **teaspoons sugar**
> 1/2 **teaspoon vanilla**
>   **Apricot or other favorite preserves**

1. Arrange pear halves, cut-side-up, on glass serving plate or shallow dish.

2. MICROWAVE (high) cream cheese in glass bowl ¼ to ½ minute or until softened. Stir until creamy. Blend in sugar and vanilla.

3. Spoon mixture evenly into pear halves. Top each with a small amount of preserves.

4. MICROWAVE (high), uncovered, ¾ to 1 minute or until pears are warm, rotating plate once.

About 6 Servings

Orange gives this versatile sauce a special flavor. Serve warm sauce over cake, pudding or ice cream, or serve it in dessert cups. Try stirring chilled sauce into plain yogurt for another treat.

TANGY RHUBARB SAUCE

- 4 cups sliced rhubarb (16 ozs.)
- 1 cup sugar
- 1 teaspoon grated orange peel
- ¼ cup orange juice
- ½ tablespoon quick-cooking tapioca

1. Combine all ingredients in 1½-quart glass casserole. Cover with casserole lid.

2. MICROWAVE (high) 10 to 12 minutes or until mixture boils and rhubarb is tender, stirring twice. Serve warm or cold.

About 3 Cups Sauce

TIP • If using frozen rhubarb, increase the cooking time to 14 to 16 minutes.

A gourmet finale that's so quick and easy you can prepare it in less than 5 minutes. For added fun, see "Tips" for a flaming dessert.

BANANAS FOSTER

- 2 tablespoons butter or margarine
- ⅓ cup packed brown sugar
- 1 firm banana, sliced
- 1 tablespoon brandy
- 2 scoops vanilla ice cream

1. Combine butter and brown sugar in 2-cup glass casserole.

2. MICROWAVE (high), uncovered, 1 to 1½ minutes or until slightly thickened, stirring twice. Add banana and brandy.

3. MICROWAVE (high), uncovered, 1 to 1½ minutes or until heated through. Place scoops of ice cream in serving dishes; top with banana mixture. Serve immediately.

About 2 Servings
400 Calories Each

TIPS • For best results, use firm ice cream.
• For flaming dessert, microwave (high) 1 tablespoon brandy in 1-cup glass measure, ¼ to ½ minute or until heated. Ignite and pour over bananas just before serving. (Pour flaming mixture from side of cup to avoid burning hand.)

When your sweet tooth can no longer be ignored, try this chocolate treat with added nutritional value.

CHOCO BANANA ON A STICK

- 8 ozs. chocolate coating
- ½ cup peanut butter
- 4 bananas
- 8 popsicle sticks
- ½ cup finely chopped peanuts, coconut or granola (if desired)

1. Cut chocolate into pieces; place in 4-cup glass measure.

2. MICROWAVE (medium — 50%), uncovered, 2 to 3 minutes or until melted, stirring twice. Stir until smooth. Stir in peanut butter.

3. Cut bananas in half vertically and place a popsicle stick in each cut end. Dip bananas, one at a time into chocolate, using a spoon to coat banana completely. Lift from chocolate, allowing excess to drip off. Roll in chopped nuts if desired. Place on waxed paper covered cookie sheet. Place in freezer until frozen. Remove from freezer when frozen and wrap individually in foil.

8 Snacks
325 Calories Each

TIPS • Bananas can be cut into thick slices, dipped in chocolate and rolled in nuts for finger snacks.
• Pour any leftover chocolate mixture into candy cups or spoon onto waxed paper. Allow to stand until set.

Choco Banana On A Stick.

A creamy chocolate cheesecake is topped off with cherry pie filling. It's sure to be a favorite year around.

CHERRY CHOCOLATE CHEESECAKE

Crust:
- 2 tablespoons butter or margarine
- 1¾ cups pecan or almond shortbread cookie crumbs (about 12 cookies)

Filling:
- 2 packages (8 ozs. each) cream cheese
- ⅔ cup sugar
- 2 eggs
- 1 teaspoon almond extract
- ⅓ cup semi-sweet chocolate pieces
- 1 can (21 oz.) prepared cherry pie filling
- Whipped cream, if desired

1. MICROWAVE (high) butter in 9-inch glass pie plate ½ to 1 minute or until melted. Mix in cookie crumbs; press mixture evenly into bottom and up sides of dish.

2. MICROWAVE (high), uncovered, 1½ to 2 minutes or until heated through, rotating dish once. Set aside.

3. MICROWAVE (high) cream cheese in 2-quart glass mix 'n pour bowl 1 to 1½ minutes or until softened. Blend until smooth. Beat in sugar. Add eggs, one at a time, beating well after each. Blend in extract.

4. MICROWAVE (high), uncovered, 3½ to 4 minutes or until thickened, stirring 2 or 3 times. Beat until smooth. Stir in chocolate pieces until melted. Pour into crust; spread evenly.

5. MICROWAVE (high), uncovered, 1 to 1½ minutes or until edges just begin to bubble. Cool.

6. Spoon cherry pie filling carefully onto chocolate layer. Refrigerate until well chilled, about 6 hours. If desired, serve with whipped cream.

About 8 Servings

TIPS • A graham cracker crust can be substituted for cookie crust. Substitute graham cracker crumbs for cookies and add 2 tablespoons sugar.
• Other favorite pie fillings can be used. Strawberry or apricot would be good.

Strawberries and whipped cream between layers of pound cake give this dessert a festive look.

STRAWBERRY RIBBON CAKE

- 1 package (10¾ oz.) frozen pound cake
- 1 cup water
- 1 package (3 oz.) strawberry-flavored gelatin
- 1 package (10 oz.) frozen sweetened sliced strawberries
- 1 tablespoon orange-flavored brandy, if desired
- 1 cup thawed frozen whipped topping

1. Remove cake from foil container. Cut horizontally through cake forming two layers. Place layers cut-side-up on tray. Using a fork, make holes in each layer. Set aside.

2. MICROWAVE (high) water in 2-cup glass measure 2 to 3 minutes or until boiling. Stir in gelatin. Set aside.

3. MICROWAVE (high) strawberries in package 1 to 1½ minutes or until juice starts to thaw. Measure ½ cup gelatin mixture; stir juice from strawberries into this portion. Blend in brandy. Pour over cake layers letting liquid soak into cake. Refrigerate layers.

4. Place strawberries in a small mixing bowl; break apart with fork. Stir in remaining gelatin. Refrigerate until slightly thickened.

5. Beat thickened gelatin until light. Fold in whipped topping. Refrigerate until spreadable. Spread half of mixture on one cake layer. Top with other cake layer. Spread with remaining cream mixture. Refrigerate until served.

About 8 Servings

Strawberry Ribbon Cake.

Crushed berries and whipped cream combine for a refreshing dessert for a luncheon or dinner.

STRAWBERRY CREAM DESSERT

  2 **tablespoons butter or margarine**
  ½ **cup graham cracker crumbs**
  1 **tablespoon sugar**
  ⅓ **cup water**
  1 **envelope (1 tablespoon) unflavored gelatin**
  2 **eggs**
  ½ **cup sugar**
  2 **tablespoons Grand Marnier**
  1 **pint (2 cups) fresh strawberries, crushed**
  1 **cup (½ pt.) whipping cream, whipped**

1. MICROWAVE (high) butter in 8 or 9-inch round glass baking dish 30 to 60 seconds or until melted. Mix in crumbs and 1 tablespoon sugar. Press evenly into bottom of dish.

2. MICROWAVE (high), uncovered, 1 to 1¼ minutes or until heated through, rotating dish once. Set aside.

3. Add gelatin to water in 1-cup glass measure. Let stand a few minutes to soften.

4. MICROWAVE (high), uncovered, 45 to 60 seconds or until gelatin is dissolved. Cool 15 minutes.

5. Beat eggs until frothy. Gradually beat in ½ cup sugar until mixture is light. Fold in Grand Marnier, crushed strawberries and gelatin mixture. Fold in whipped cream.

6. Pour into crust, spreading evenly. Refrigerate 3 to 4 hours or until set. If desired, garnish each serving with additional whipped cream and a strawberry.

6 to 8 Servings

TIPS • When fresh strawberries are not available, substitute frozen unsweetened berries. Thaw before adding to gelatin mixture. Or, use other fruits, such as raspberries, boysenberries, blueberries or peaches.

• For a Double Recipe, prepare crumb mixture in glass mixing bowl. Microwave butter in step 1 as directed. Then, microwave crumb mixture in bowl 1¼ to 1½ minutes, stirring once. Press warm crumbs into 9-inch springform pan. Microwave in step 4 for 1¼ to 1½ minutes. Pour completed gelatin mixture onto crumbs. Refrigerate 4 to 5 hours. Loosen from edge of pan with knife. Remove sides of pan for ease in serving.

• Other orange-flavored liqueurs or ¼ teaspoon grated orange peel can be substituted for Grand Marnier.

This two-layer strawberry dessert is highlighted by a crunchy base that is stirred as it cooks in the baking dish.

STRAWBERRY CRUNCH

  ½ **cup butter or margarine**
  1 **cup unsifted all-purpose flour**
  ¼ **cup packed brown sugar**
  ½ **cup chopped walnuts**
1⅔ **cups water**
  1 **package (3 oz.) strawberry-flavored gelatin**
  1 **pint (2 cups) fresh strawberries, halved**
  1 **carton (4 oz.) frozen whipped topping, thawed**

1. MICROWAVE (high) butter in 8-inch square glass baking dish 1 to 1½ minutes or until melted. Mix in flour, brown sugar and walnuts until thoroughly blended.

2. MICROWAVE (high), uncovered, 5 to 6 minutes or until mixture has a dry appearance and is lightly toasted, stirring 2 or 3 times. Set aside ½ cup crumbs. Press remaining crumbs with fork into bottom of dish.

3. MICROWAVE (high) water in 4-cup glass measure 4 to 4½ minutes or until boiling. Stir in gelatin until dissolved. Refrigerate until slightly thickened.

4. Set aside ½ cup gelatin. Stir strawberries into remaining gelatin. Pour mixture into crust. Fold the remaining ½ cup gelatin into the whipped topping. Spoon onto strawberries. Sprinkle with reserved crumbs. Refrigerate 3 hours or until served. Serve cut into squares.

About 9 Servings

TIPS • If desired, raspberries, blueberries or peaches can be substituted for strawberries. Use a complimentary flavor of gelatin with each of these fruits.

• Whipped cream can be substituted for whipped topping. Beat 1 cup whipping cream until thickened; fold in the ½ cup gelatin and proceed as directed.

A creamy, chilled dessert to complete a hearty meal. Pictured on cover.

RASPBERRY DELIGHT

   1 **cup sugar**
   ⅔ **cup water**
   1 **envelope (1 tablespoon) unflavored gelatin**
   1 **tablespoon light corn syrup**
   3 **egg whites**
   ¼ **teaspoon cream of tartar**
   1 **package (12 oz.) lightly sweetened raspberries, thawed**
   2 **tablespoons Grand Marnier or Amaretto, if desired**
   1 **cup (½ pt.) whipping cream, whipped**

1. Combine sugar, water, gelatin and corn syrup in 2-quart glass mix 'n pour bowl. Mix well and let stand a few minutes to soften gelatin.

2. MICROWAVE (high) 3½ to 4 minutes or until mixture boils. Stir to dissolve sugar. Then, continue MICROWAVING (high) 6 minutes.

3. Beat egg whites with cream of tartar at high speed in large mixing bowl until mixture forms stiff peaks. Gradually add syrup mixture, continuing to beat at high speed until well combined. Fold in raspberries and Grand Marnier. Refrigerate until mixture begins to thicken.

4. Fold in whipped cream. Pour into 4-cup serving bowl or into 5 or 6 individual serving dishes. Refrigerate several hours until set. If desired, garnish with additional whipped cream and raspberries.

                    5 to 6 Servings

TIPS • Fresh raspberries can be substituted for the frozen. Use about 2 cups, sweetened with 2 tablespoons sugar.
   • Frozen raspberries can be thawed by microwaving 1½ to 1¾ minutes, rearranging once.

This delicate pink soufflé adds a light touch after a hearty meal.

PINK SQUIRREL SOUFFLE

   1¾ **cups milk**
   2 **envelopes (2 tablespoons) unflavored gelatin**
   ⅓ **cup sugar**
   4 **eggs, separated**
   1 **package (8 oz.) cream cheese**
   3 **tablespoons creme de noya (almond)**
   2 **tablespoons white creme de cacao**
   4 **to 5 drops red food coloring**
   ½ **cup sugar**
   1 **cup whipping cream, whipped**
   ½ **cup slivered almonds**
   2 **tablespoons sugar**
   1 **teaspoon water**

1. Combine milk and gelatin in 4-cup glass measure. Let stand 2 to 3 minutes or until softened. Add ⅓ cup sugar.

2. MICROWAVE (high), uncovered, 4 to 4½ minutes or until steaming hot. Beat egg yolks slightly. Beat in a small amount of hot milk; return mixture to 4-cup glass measure, mixing well.

3. MICROWAVE (high), uncovered, 1 to 1½ minutes or until mixture begins to thicken slightly, stirring 2 or 3 times. Cut cream cheese into small pieces. Add to hot milk mixture; let stand a few minutes or until softened. Beat with wire whip until smooth. Blend in creme de noya, creme de cacao and red food coloring. Refrigerate until mixture mounds, 2 to 3 hours.

4. Beat egg whites in 2-quart glass mix 'n pour bowl until frothy. Gradually add ½ cup sugar, beating until mixture forms stiff peaks. Fold in chilled gelatin mixture and whipped cream just until blended.

5. Lightly grease a 1-inch band around inside edge of 1½-quart soufflé dish. Cut a 3-inch strip of waxed paper and place inside dish against greased area to form a collar. Pour soufflé mixture into dish. Refrigerate at least 6 hours.

6. Combine almonds, sugar and water in buttered 9-inch glass pie plate.

7. MICROWAVE (high), uncovered, 4 to 4½ minutes or until toasted, stirring 3 or 4 times. Cool.

8. Carefully remove collar from soufflé just before serving. Spoon nuts around top.

                    10 to 12 Servings

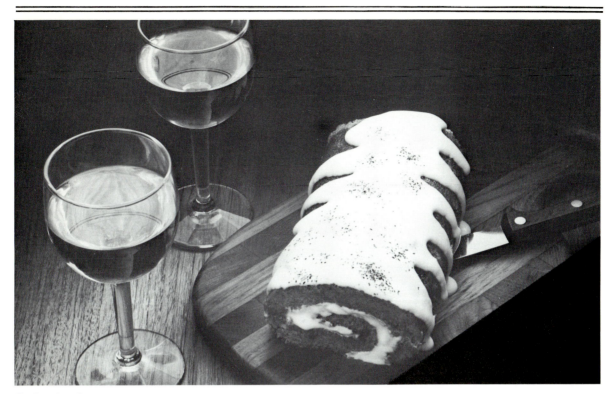

Delightful Carrot Roll.

The traditional flavors of carrot cake rolled up in an interesting dessert.

DELIGHTFUL CARROT ROLL

- 2 eggs
- ½ cup sugar
- ⅓ cup cooking oil
- 1 cup shredded carrot
- 1 teaspoon vanilla
- ¾ cup unsifted all-purpose flour
- 1 teaspoon cinnamon
- ½ teaspoon baking powder
- ½ teaspoon soda
- ½ teaspoon salt

Filling:
- 1 package (3 oz.) cream cheese
- ¼ cup unsifted powdered sugar
- ½ teaspoon vanilla
- ½ cup whipping cream, whipped

1. Beat eggs at high speed until frothy, about 1 minute. Add sugar gradually, continuing to beat until mixture forms soft mounds, about 2 minutes. Blend in oil, carrot and vanilla at low speed. Add flour, cinnamon, baking powder, soda and salt; mix at low speed just until blended.

2. Line bottom of 12 x 8-inch glass baking dish with waxed paper. Pour batter into dish; spread evenly.

3. MICROWAVE (high), uncovered, 5 to 6 minutes or until no longer doughy, rotating dish once or twice. Let stand in oven 5 minutes. Invert onto a piece of plastic wrap; carefully peel off waxed paper. Roll up warm cake, starting with narrow end. Cool completely.

4. MICROWAVE (high) cream cheese in glass bowl 30 to 40 seconds or until softened. Mix until creamy; blend in powdered sugar and vanilla. Beat cream until thickened; fold into cream cheese mixture. Unroll cake; spread cream cheese mixture on cake. Reroll and place seam-side-down on serving plate. Cover tightly and refrigerate until served. Cut into slices for serving.

8 to 10 Servings

TIPS • Frozen whipped topping can be substituted for the whipped cream in the filling. Blend 1 tablespoon milk into cream cheese mixture before folding in 1 cup thawed whipped topping.

• With Combination Oven in step 3, bake in preheated 350° oven for 10 minutes. Then, microwave-bake 2 to 3 minutes.

Chocolate tart shells are filled with a smooth marshmallow mixture and then topped off appropriately with bright red cherries. Very simple to make, yet looks like you spent hours!

CHOCOLATE CHERRY TARTS

   1 **bar (8 oz.) milk chocolate candy**
  ¼ **cup butter or margarine**
 30 **large marshmallows**
  ⅓ **cup milk**
  ½ **cup sour cream**
  ½ **teaspoon almond extract**
  ½ **cup whipping cream, whipped,**
     or 1 cup whipped topping
  1 **can (21 oz.) prepared cherry pie filling**

1. Break chocolate into pieces and place in 2-cup glass measure. Add butter.

2. MICROWAVE (high), uncovered, 1¼ to 1½ minutes or until softened, stirring once. Stir until smooth.

3. Line 12 muffin or custard cups with paper liners. Divide chocolate mixture evenly among the cups. Spread chocolate evenly over bottom and up sides of paper liners, using back of spoon. Refrigerate to set.

4. Combine marshmallows and milk in 1-quart glass mix 'n pour bowl.

5. MICROWAVE (high), uncovered, 1¼ to 1½ minutes or until marshmallows are puffed. Stir until smooth. Refrigerate until partially set, about 45 minutes.

6. Fold sour cream, almond extract and whipped cream into marshmallow mixture. Spoon mixture into chocolate cups, filling about ¾ full. With back of spoon, make slight indentation in mixture. Refrigerate until set, 3 to 4 hours.

7. Remove tarts from cups, lifting with tip of knife if necessary. Peel off paper and place cups on serving plate. Refrigerate until served.

8. Just before serving, spoon pie filling into each cup. If desired, garnish with a little whipped cream.

12 Tarts

TIPS • Make tarts ahead through step 7 and refrigerate in covered pan. Complete just before serving.

  • The tarts freeze well for up to 2 weeks. Leave papers on during freezing. Allow to stand in refrigerator about 2 hours before filling with cherries and serving.

Cherry Bread Pudding, page 105, Pink Squirrel Soufflé, page 114, and Chocolate Cherry Tarts.

An outstanding ice cream dessert! It may make more servings than needed for a meal, but your family will not object to leftovers.

CARAMEL-FUDGE SUNDAE DESSERT

Caramel Sauce:
- ⅓ cup evaporated milk
- 24 caramels, unwrapped (about 7 ozs.)

Fudge Sauce:
- 2 squares (1 oz. each) unsweetened chocolate
- ½ cup sugar
- ⅔ cup evaporated milk
- 1 tablespoon butter or margarine
- 1 teaspoon vanilla

Dessert:
- ¼ cup butter or margarine
- 2 cups (20 cookies) crushed creme-filled chocolate cookies
- ½ gallon vanilla ice cream
- 1 cup dry roasted peanuts

1. Prepare Caramel Sauce by combining ⅓ cup evaporated milk and the caramels in 2-cup glass measure.

2. MICROWAVE (high), uncovered, 2 to 2½ minutes or until caramels are completely melted, stirring once or twice. Stir until smooth. Set aside to cool.

3. Prepare Fudge Sauce by combining chocolate, sugar, ⅔ cup evaporated milk and 1 tablespoon butter in 1-quart glass mix 'n pour bowl.

4. MICROWAVE (high), uncovered, 3 to 4 minutes or until mixture boils and has a thickened sauce-like consistency, stirring once. Stir in vanilla. Set aside to cool.

5. MICROWAVE (high) ¼ cup butter in 12 x 8-inch glass baking dish 45 to 60 seconds or until melted. Mix in cookie crumbs. Press evenly into bottom of baking dish.

6. When sauces are completely cooled, spoon ice cream onto cookie crust, spreading evenly. With back of spoon make lengthwise grooves in ice cream. Pour cooled caramel sauce in every other groove. Then pour fudge sauce in alternating grooves. Sprinkle with peanuts. Cover and freeze several hours or until served.

15 to 18 Servings

TIP • If desired, 12-oz. jars of prepared caramel and fudge ice cream toppings can be used.

This pink molded dessert is light and airy, making it a perfect finale for a hearty meal.

RHUBARB CREME

- 3 cups sliced rhubarb
- ½ cup sugar
- 1 cup water
- 1 package (3 oz.) strawberry-flavored gelatin
- ½ cup sugar
- 3 tablespoons flour
- 1 envelope (1 tablespoon) unflavored gelatin
- 1 cup milk
- 1 teaspoon vanilla
- 2 cups (1 pt.) whipping cream

1. Combine rhubarb, ½ cup sugar and ½ cup water in 4-cup glass measure.

2. MICROWAVE (high), uncovered, 6 to 7 minutes or until rhubarb is tender, stirring twice. Stir in strawberry gelatin until dissolved. Blend in remaining ½ cup water. Refrigerate until thickened, about 3 hours.

3. Combine ½ cup sugar, flour, gelatin and milk in 2-quart glass mix 'n pour bowl; mix well.

4. MICROWAVE (high), uncovered, 3 to 4 minutes or until mixture boils and thickens, stirring twice. Stir in vanilla. Cool to lukewarm.

5. Beat cream until thickened. Fold into milk mixture. Fold in partially set gelatin mixture. Spoon into 2-quart (8 cup) mold. Refrigerate overnight; unmold.

8 to 10 Servings

TIP • If desired, place gelatin in a crumb crust-lined 8-inch square pan. Refrigerate until set; serve cut into squares.

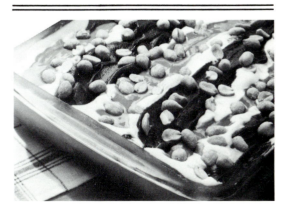

Caramel-Fudge Sundae Dessert.

These ice cream cookies are not just for kids. Mint ice cream enhanced by vanilla wafers and chocolate make them irresistible for kids of all ages.

ICE CREAM SANDWICHES

- ⅓ **cup chopped roasted peanuts**
- 1 **cup (½ pt.) mint-flavored ice cream**
- 18 **vanilla wafers**
- 2 **squares (2.5 ozs.) chocolate bark coating**

1. Place peanuts in shallow custard cup or plate. Spoon a slightly rounded tablespoon ice cream onto peanuts; form into a ball with fingers while coating with nuts. Place ball on bottom side of a wafer. Place another wafer on top, bottom side down, and press gently to flatten ice cream to edges. Repeat with remaining peanuts, ice cream and wafers. Freeze at least 1 hour to harden.

2. Place chocolate in glass custard cup.

3. MICROWAVE (high), uncovered, 1½ to 2 minutes or until softened, stirring once. Stir until smooth. Coat edges of ice cream sandwiches with chocolate, covering ice cream filling. Place on waxed paper-lined plate; freeze at least 1 hour. Store frozen in plastic bag.

9 Sandwiches

TIPS • It is important to roll ice cream sandwiches quickly through chocolate so ice cream does not melt.

• For ease in coating cookies, make sure ice cream extends to edge of cookie.

Ice Cream Sandwiches.

Three popular citrus fruits are combined to make this tangy, refreshing sorbet. It will be a favorite during summer days as well as a light, cool finish for hearty meals all year around.

SUNSHINE SORBET

- 1 **cup water**
- 1 **cup sugar**
- 1 **teaspoon grated orange peel**
- 1 **large white or pink grapefruit**
- 1 **large orange**
- 1 **can (6 oz.) frozen orange juice concentrate**
- ¼ **cup fresh lemon juice**
- 2 **tablespoons whipping cream**

1. Combine water and sugar in 4-cup glass measure.

2. MICROWAVE (high) 4 to 5 minutes or until mixture boils. Stir and cool. Refrigerate until chilled.

3. Add orange peel to chilled syrup. Peel and section grapefruit and orange, removing all white membrane (pith) and seeds. Place fruit sections in blender or food processor container. Process until puréed. Combine purée, orange juice concentrate, lemon juice and fruit syrup in 2-quart ice cream freezer.

4. Add ice and salt to freezer as directed by manufacturer and freeze until mixture begins to thicken. Add cream. Continue mixing and freezing until desired consistency. Store in covered container in freezer.

About 1½ Quarts

TIP • If you don't have an ice cream freezer, combine fruit mixture and pour into metal pan or ice cube trays and freeze until just about set. Spoon into food processor or blender container, or mixing bowl. Blend or beat until smooth and fluffy. Beat in whipping cream until blended. Pour into metal container and freeze until firm. Spoon into covered container for storage.

Lower in calories than ice cream, frozen yogurt is a popular alternative. And, now you can make it yourself, using your microwave oven.

FROZEN YOGURT

- 1 **envelope unflavored gelatin**
- ½ **cup milk**
- 2 **eggs**
- 2 **cups plain yogurt**
- ½ **cup fruit-flavored jelly (strawberry, raspberry or cherry)**
- 2 **tablespoons sugar**
- 2 **tablespoons light corn syrup**
- 1 **tablespoon lemon juice**
- 2 **teaspoons vanilla**
- ⅛ **teaspoon salt**

1. Combine gelatin and milk in 1-cup glass measure. Let stand 5 minutes or until gelatin is softened.

2. MICROWAVE (high), uncovered, 1 to 1½ minutes or until gelatin is dissolved. Cool 5 minutes.

3. Beat eggs until light and lemon colored, about 5 minutes. Beat in yogurt, jelly, sugar, corn syrup, lemon juice, vanilla and salt. Blend in milk mixture.

4. Cover with plastic wrap and freeze until ½ inch around side of bowl is frozen (about 2 hours). Remove from freezer. Beat with mixer about 1 minute, scraping sides of bowl. Return to freezer and repeat freezing and beating. Store in tightly covered container.

About 1 Quart
125 Calories/½ Cup

TIPS • If using ice cream maker, omit step 4 and pour mixture into ice cream freezer. Freeze as directed by manufacturer.
  • Jam can be used in place of jelly, but it is best to select a type without large seeds.

An easy ice cream dessert to make on short notice. You may even want to keep an extra in the freezer for unexpected entertaining.

GRANOLA ICE CREAM PIE

- ¼ **cup butter or margarine**
- ¼ **cup packed brown sugar**
- 1½ **cups granola**
- 1 **quart vanilla ice cream**
- 2 **cups fresh fruit, lightly sweetened**

1. Combine butter and brown sugar in 9-inch glass pie plate.

2. MICROWAVE (high), uncovered, 1½ to 2 minutes or until bubbly, stirring once. If granola is chunky, crush slightly. Add granola to sugar mixture; mix until evenly coated. Set aside ⅓ cup of mixture. Press remaining mixture into bottom and up sides of pie plate.

3. MICROWAVE (high), uncovered, 1½ to 2 minutes or until heated through, rotating plate once. Cool.

4. Spoon ice cream into cooled crust. Sprinkle with reserved granola mixture. Cover and freeze until served. Top individual servings with sweetened fruit.

9-inch Pie

TIP • Other favorite ice cream toppings can also be served on the pie. Chocolate or caramel sauce or prepared fruit pie fillings are very good.

Offer fruits, cake cubes and bite-sized cookies for dipping in this yummy chocolate sauce.

CHOCOLATE-BRICKLE FONDUE

- 1 **cup (6 ozs.) semi-sweet chocolate pieces**
- ¾ **cup (4 ozs.) almond brickle chips**
- 1 **can (14 oz.) sweetened condensed milk**
- 2 **teaspoons instant coffee or 1 teaspoon vanilla**
- ¼ **cup milk**

Dippers:
  Fresh pear wedges
  Banana slices
  Fresh whole strawberries
  Angel food cake cubes
  Vanilla wafers or butter cookies

1. Combine chocolate pieces, brickle chips, condensed milk, coffee and milk in 1-quart glass fondue pot or casserole.

2. MICROWAVE (high), uncovered, 3 to 3½ minutes or until melted, stirring once or twice. Stir until smooth. Set over warming candle and pass tray of dippers for dipping in the chocolate.

8 to 10 Servings

TIPS • Leftover sauce can be thinned with a little water and served warm over ice cream.
  • For half a recipe, microwave 2 to 2½ minutes.

Dessert fondues are fun and relaxing to serve for both family and friends.

CHEESECAKE FONDUE

- **1 package (8 oz.) cream cheese**
- **⅓ cup sugar**
- **1 egg**
- **1 teaspoon vanilla**

Dippers:
- **Assorted fruits**
- **Angel food cake cubes**
- **Sugar cookies or wafers**

1. MICROWAVE (high) cream cheese in 2 to 3-cup glass serving dish 1 to 1¼ minutes or until softened, stirring once. Blend in sugar; beat in egg.

2. MICROWAVE (high), uncovered, 1½ to 2 minutes or until thickened, stirring every ½ minute. Stir in vanilla.

3. Arrange fruits, cake cubes and cookies on large tray with sauce. Have guests dip the items in the sauce.

6 to 8 Servings

Cocoa adds the flavor to this velvety smooth and tempting chocolate topping sent in by a reader.

FUDGE SAUCE

- **¾ cup sugar**
- **3 tablespoons unsweetened cocoa**
- **Dash salt**
- **2 tablespoons water**
- **1 can (6 oz.) evaporated milk (¾ cup)**
- **2 tablespoons butter or margarine**
- **1 teaspoon vanilla**

1. Combine sugar, cocoa and salt in 2-quart glass mix 'n pour bowl. Add water; stir until cocoa is moistened. Stir in milk and butter.

2. MICROWAVE (high), uncovered, 3½ to 4 minutes or until mixture boils hard, stirring once. Stir and then MICROWAVE (high) 4 to 5 minutes or until sauce begins to thicken, stirring as necessary to prevent boilovers. Stir in vanilla. Serve warm or cold.

1 Cup Sauce

Cheesecake Fondue with fruits for dipping.

This elegant pie features a melt-in-your-mouth chocolate filling with a refreshing strawberry topping.

STRAWBERRY-CHOCOLATE PIE

9 - inch baked pastry shell
½ cup butter or margarine
1 package (3 oz.) cream cheese
¾ cup sugar
1 square (1 oz.) unsweetened chocolate
1 teaspoon vanilla
1 egg
1½ pints (3 cups) fresh strawberries
⅓ cup sugar
1½ tablespoons cornstarch

1. Prepare pastry shell in 9-inch glass pie plate by microwaving (high) 4 to 5 minutes or until crust is flaky, rotating plate 2 or 3 times. Set aside.

2. Place butter and cream cheese in glass mixing bowl.

3. MICROWAVE (high), uncovered, 20 to 30 seconds or until softened. Beat with electric mixer until light and fluffy. Gradually add ¾ cup sugar, beating until well blended.

4. MICROWAVE (high) chocolate in small glass dish 2 to 2½ minutes or until melted, stirring once. Beat chocolate into butter mixture. Beat in vanilla. Add egg and beat at high speed about 3 minutes or until light and fluffy. Spread evenly in cooled pie shell. Refrigerate about 2 hours.

5. While pie is chilling, wash and hull strawberries. Set aside 2 cups berries. Process remainder in blender or food processor until smooth. Place in 4-cup glass measure. Add water to make 1 cup. Blend in ⅓ cup sugar and the cornstarch until smooth.

6. MICROWAVE (high), uncovered, 2 to 3 minutes or until mixture boils and thickens, stirring twice. Cool to lukewarm.

7. Slice reserved berries and arrange on chocolate mixture. Spoon glaze mixture over berries, coating evenly. Refrigerate several hours or until served.

9-inch Pie

TIPS • Premelted chocolate can be substituted for chocolate that requires melting.
• Raspberries can be substituted for strawberries.

This custard filling with its mild rhubarb flavor, is a favorite of many who may not care for the tartness often associated with rhubarb.

RHUBARB CREAM PIE

9 - inch baked pastry shell

Filling:
1 package (3 oz.) cream cheese
3 cups sliced rhubarb
1 cup sugar
3 tablespoons flour
3 eggs, well beaten
¼ teaspoon nutmeg, if desired
Whipped cream or topping

1. Prepare pastry shell in 9-inch glass pie plate by microwaving (high) 4 to 5 minutes or until crust is flaky, rotating plate 2 or 3 times.

2. MICROWAVE (high) cream cheese in small glass dish 30 to 45 seconds or until softened, stirring once. Spread evenly over crust; set aside.

3. Combine rhubarb, sugar and flour in 1-quart glass mix 'n pour bowl.

4. MICROWAVE (high), uncovered, 4 to 5 minutes or until mixture boils and thickens, stirring once or twice. Beat eggs; slowly mix eggs into hot rhubarb, mixing well. Pour mixture into crust, spreading evenly.

5. MICROWAVE (high), uncovered, 1½ to 2 minutes or until filling is just about set, rotating once. Refrigerate. Top with whipped cream just before serving.

9-inch Pie

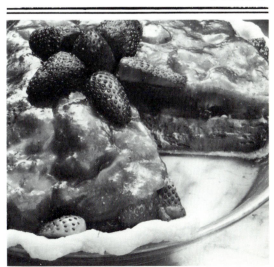

Strawberry-Chocolate Pie.

Sour cream adds a special creaminess and flavor to this crumb-topped pie.

SOUR CREAM-APPLE PIE

     9-inch baked pastry shell
     4 cups peeled, sliced cooking apples
     ⅔ to ¾ cup sugar
     1 tablespoon flour
     ½ teaspoon cinnamon
     ½ cup sour cream

Topping:
     ¾ cup unsifted all-purpose flour
     ⅓ cup packed brown sugar
     ½ teaspoon cinnamon
     ¼ cup butter or margarine

1. Prepare pastry shell in 9-inch glass pie plate by microwaving (high) 4 to 5 minutes or until crust is flaky, rotating plate 2 or 3 times.

2. Combine apples, sugar, flour, cinnamon and sour cream; set aside.

3. Combine flour, brown sugar and cinnamon for Topping. Cut in butter until crumbly.

4. Spoon apples evenly into pastry shell. Top with crumb mixture, covering apples completely.

5. MICROWAVE (high), uncovered, 7½ to 8½ minutes or until apples are tender, rotating plate once.

6. Place pie under Broiler or Browning Element for a few minutes to brown topping. Serve pie warm or cold, plain or with ice cream.

9-inch Pie

Key Lime Chiffon Pie.

TIP • With Combination Oven, use an unbaked pastry shell. Microwave-bake in preheated 450° oven for 9 to 11 minutes or until browned and apples are tender. Omit browning in step 6.

There are a variety of recipes for Key Lime Pie, but our favorite is this gelatin-based variation.

KEY LIME CHIFFON PIE

     ¼ cup butter or margarine
     1 cup graham cracker crumbs (about 15 squares)
     2 tablespoons sugar

Filling:
     ½ cup water
     1 envelope (1 T.) unflavored gelatin
     ⅔ cup sugar
     1 teaspoon grated lime peel
     ½ cup lime juice
     3 to 4 drops green food coloring
     2 eggs, separated
     3 tablespoons sugar
     1 cup (½ pt.) whipping cream

1. MICROWAVE (high) butter in 9-inch glass pie plate ½ to 1 minute or until melted. Stir in crumbs and sugar until combined. Press mixture into bottom and up side of pie plate.

2. MICROWAVE (high), uncovered, 1½ to 2½ minutes or until heated through, rotating plate once or twice.

3. Combine water and gelatin in 4-cup glass measure. Let stand a few minutes to soften gelatin. Stir in ⅔ cup sugar, the lime peel and juice, food coloring and egg yolks; beat until blended.

4. MICROWAVE (high), uncovered, 3 to 4 minutes or until mixture begins to bubble around edge, stirring 2 or 3 times. Cool until slightly thickened.

5. Beat whites until frothy. Gradually add 3 tablespoons sugar and beat until mixture forms soft peaks. Beat cream until thickened in large bowl. Fold cooled lime mixture into cream. Fold in egg whites. Pour into cooled pie shell. Refrigerate until set, about 3 hours. If desired, serve with additional whipped cream and garnish with lime slices.

9-inch Pie

This refreshing, light pie is the perfect dessert for a summer evening.

REFRESHING CITRUS PIE

   9-inch baked pastry shell
   1 cup sugar
   ¼ cup cornstarch
   1¾ cups water
   2 eggs, separated
   1½ teaspoons fresh grated orange peel
   1 teaspoon fresh grated lemon peel
   ¼ cup orange juice
   ¼ cup lemon juice
   1 tablespoon butter or margarine
   ¼ cup sugar
   Sweetened whipped cream

1. Prepare pastry shell in 9-inch glass pie plate by microwaving (high) 4 to 5 minutes or until crust is flaky, rotating plate 2 or 3 times. Set aside.

2. Combine 1 cup sugar and cornstarch in 2-quart glass mix 'n pour bowl; gradually stir in water until smooth.

3. MICROWAVE (high), uncovered, 5½ to 6½ minutes or until mixture boils thoroughly, stirring twice. Beat egg yolks slightly; stir in small amount of hot mixture. Then return to hot mixture, blending well.

4. MICROWAVE (high), uncovered, 1 to 1½ minutes or until bubbly, stirring once. Stir in peels, juices and butter. Refrigerate until barely warm.

5. Beat egg whites until soft peaks form; gradually add ¼ cup sugar, beating until mixture forms stiff peaks. Fold into pudding mixture. Spoon into pastry shell. Refrigerate 3 to 4 hours or until well chilled. Serve with whipped cream if desired.

9-inch Pie

Refreshing Citrus Pie.

A chocolate coconut crust holds a creamy smooth filling.

COCONUT CREAM PIE

- 1 square (1 oz.) semi-sweet chocolate
- ¼ cup butter or margarine
- 2 cups flaked coconut

Filling:
- ½ cup sugar
- ¼ cup cornstarch
- ½ teaspoon salt
- 2 cups milk
- 2 eggs
- ½ teaspoon almond extract
- 2 tablespoons butter or margarine
- 2 tablespoons rum or ½ teaspoon rum flavoring

Topping:
- 1 cup (½ pint) whipping cream
- 2 tablespoons sugar
- ½ teaspoon vanilla

1. Combine chocolate and butter in 1-quart glass mix 'n pour bowl.

2. MICROWAVE (high), uncovered, 1 to 1½ minutes or until melted, stirring once. Stir in coconut.

3. MICROWAVE (high), uncovered, 2 to 2½ minutes or until bubbly, stirring once. Cool 15 minutes. Set aside ½ cup of coconut mixture. Spoon remainder into 9-inch pie pan; press evenly into bottom and up sides. Set aside.

4. Combine sugar, cornstarch and salt in 1-quart glass mix 'n pour bowl. Stir in milk; mix well.

5. MICROWAVE (high), uncovered, 7 to 7½ minutes or until mixture boils and thickens, stirring twice. Beat eggs; pour small amount of hot milk mixture into eggs, stirring constantly. Return egg mixture to remaining hot milk mixture, blending well.

6. MICROWAVE (high), uncovered, ½ to 1 minute or until mixture bubbles around edge, stirring once. Stir in butter and rum. Cool 15 minutes. Carefully pour into coconut crust. Refrigerate until chilled.

7. Beat cream until slightly thickened. Add sugar and continue beating until thickened. Beat in vanilla. Spoon onto pie; spread evenly. Sprinkle with reserved coconut. Refrigerate until served.

9-inch Pie

TIPS • Thawed frozen whipped topping can be substituted for whipped cream topping. Spoon about 4 ozs. (2 cups) topping onto pie and spread evenly.

• Three egg yolks can be substituted for whole eggs.

Yogurt and cream cheese make an easy base for raisin pie. The cool, refreshing flavor will be welcome as a meal finale or a dessert to be served with coffee or iced tea.

RAISIN-YOGURT PIE

- ¼ cup butter or margarine
- 1¼ cups graham cracker crumbs
- 2 tablespoons sugar

Filling:
- 1 package (8 oz.) cream cheese
- ⅓ cup sugar
- ½ teaspoon cinnamon
- ¼ teaspoon nutmeg
- 1 teaspoon vanilla
- 1½ cups plain yogurt
- 1 cup raisins
  Sweetened whipped cream

1. MICROWAVE (high) butter in 9-inch glass pie plate ½ to 1 minute or until melted. Stir in crumbs and 2 tablespoons sugar. Press mixture evenly into bottom and up sides of pie plate.

2. MICROWAVE (high), uncovered, 1½ to 2½ minutes or until heated through, rotating plate once or twice. Set aside.

3. MICROWAVE (high) cream cheese in glass mixing bowl 1 to 1½ minutes or until softened. Blend in ⅓ cup sugar. Mix in cinnamon, nutmeg, vanilla and yogurt until smooth. Stir in raisins. Pour into cooled crust; refrigerate until set, about 3 hours. Serve with whipped cream.

9-inch Pie

TIP • To plump and soften raisins, place them in a glass measuring cup and cover with water. Microwave (high) 1½ to 2 minutes or until steaming hot. Let stand 5 minutes. Drain and cool slightly before adding to yogurt mixture.

Crème De Menthe Cake,
page 126.

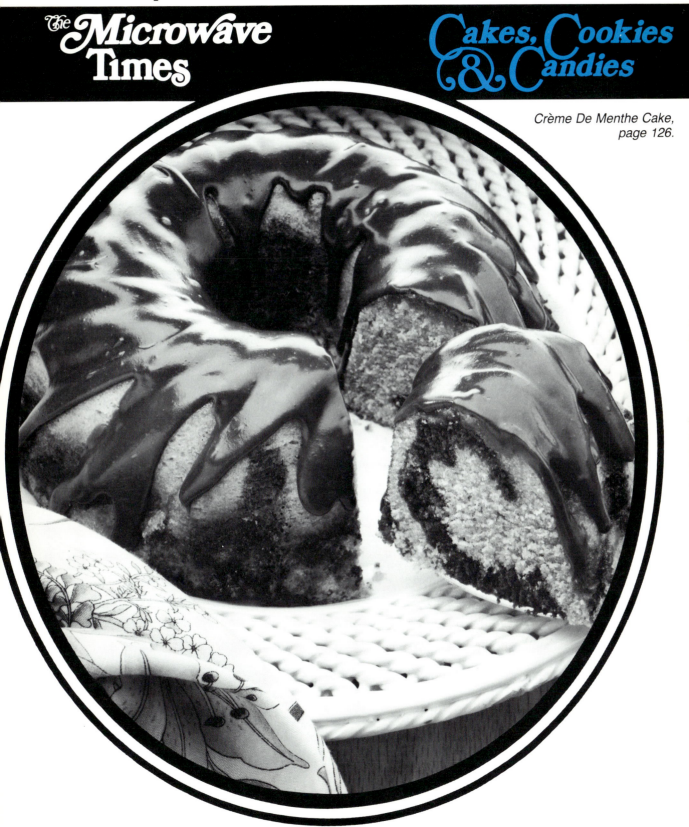

This cake is best when made ahead 12 hours to enhance flavor. It is especially nice for entertaining.

CREME DE MENTHE CAKE

1 package (18.5 oz.) yellow cake mix (without pudding)
1 package (3⅜ oz.) instant pistachio pudding mix
1 cup cooking oil
¾ cup water
¼ cup creme de menthe
4 eggs
 Green food coloring
1 can (5.5 oz.) chocolate ice cream syrup

Frosting:
1 cup sugar
¼ cup butter or margarine
¼ cup milk
⅔ cup (4 ozs.) semi-sweet chocolate pieces

1. Combine cake mix, pudding mix, oil, water, creme de menthe and eggs. Blend at low speed until moistened. Beat at medium speed about 3 minutes. Stir in food coloring until desired color. Reserve one cup of batter for cupcakes.

2. Oil and lightly sugar 10 to 12-cup fluted plastic tube pan. Pour half of batter into pan. Stir chocolate syrup into remaining batter. Pour over green batter and swirl gently with knife for marbling effect.

3. MICROWAVE (medium — 50%), uncovered, 12 minutes, rotating dish once. Rotate dish. Then, MICROWAVE (high) 3 to 4 minutes or until no longer doughy, rotating dish once. Cool 10 minutes. Invert onto serving plate. (See Tips for cooking cupcakes.)

4. Combine sugar, butter and milk in 1-quart glass mix 'n pour bowl.

5. MICROWAVE (high), uncovered, 3½ to 4 minutes or until slightly thickened, stirring twice. Stir in chocolate pieces; cool until thickened, stirring once or twice. Beat well and spoon over cake, reserving some for cupcakes.

About 16 Servings
550 Calories Each

TIPS • Spoon reserved batter into paper-lined microwave muffin pan, filling about half full.

Microwave (high) 6 cupcakes at a time, 1½ to 2 minutes or until no longer doughy.
• With Full Power, microwave 11 to 13 minutes, rotating dish 2 or 3 times in step 3.

Cookie crumbs add flavor and texture to this cake we adapted for a reader.

VANILLA WAFER CAKE

1 cup sugar
½ cup shortening
4 eggs
⅔ cup milk
1 package (10 to 12 oz.) vanilla wafers, crushed (about 3½ cups crumbs)
1 cup flaked coconut
1 cup chopped pecans or other favorite nuts

Frosting:
3 tablespoons butter or margarine
⅓ cup packed brown sugar
2 tablespoons milk
⅔ to ¾ cup powdered sugar

1. Cream together sugar and shortening until combined. Beat in eggs, one at a time. Stir in milk, wafer crumbs, coconut and pecans until well blended.

2. Grease bottom only of 12 x 8-inch glass baking dish. Spoon batter into dish; spread evenly.

3. MICROWAVE (medium — 50%), uncovered, 10 minutes. Rotate dish.

4. MICROWAVE (high), uncovered, 4 to 5 minutes or until cake is no longer doughy, rotating dish once. Cool before frosting.

5. Combine butter, brown sugar and milk for Frosting in 4-cup glass measure.

6. MICROWAVE (high) 2½ to 3 minutes or until mixture boils for about 1 minute, stirring once. Beat in powdered sugar until mixture is of spreading consistency. Spread on cake.

15 to 18 Servings

TIP • With Full Power, microwave (high) 9 to 11 minutes, rotating dish 2 or 3 times.

A delightful flavor combination of pineapple, banana, orange and dates makes this cake extra moist and good. It is just as tasty after storage several days.

FRUITY TUTTY BUNDT CAKE

- 2 cups sugar
- 1 cup cooking oil
- 4 eggs
- 1 can (8 oz.) crushed pineapple, undrained
- 2 cups sliced ripe bananas (2 to 3 med.)
- 1 teaspoon almond extract
- 2 teaspoons grated orange peel
- 2 cups unsifted all-purpose flour
- 1 cup whole wheat flour
- 1 teaspoon salt
- 1 teaspoon baking powder
- ½ teaspoon soda
- 1 cup chopped dates
- 1 to 2 tablespoons graham cracker crumbs

Glaze:
- 1 tablespoon butter or margarine
- 1½ cups unsifted powdered sugar
- 2½ to 3 tablespoons orange juice
- ¼ teaspoon almond extract

1. Blend together sugar and oil in large mixing bowl. Beat in eggs, one at a time. Blend in pineapple, bananas, extract and orange peel.

2. Add flours, salt, baking powder and soda. Blend electric mixer at low speed until well mixed. Stir in half of dates.

3. Grease 12-cup fluted plastic tube pan. Sprinkle with graham cracker crumbs. Shake out excess. Pour batter into pan, spreading evenly. Sprinkle with remaining dates.

4. MICROWAVE (medium — 50%), uncovered, 18 minutes, rotating dish once. Then, MICROWAVE (high) 9 to 10 minutes or until no longer doughy. Let stand 15 minutes. Invert onto serving plate. Cool completely.

5. MICROWAVE (high) butter in small glass bowl 20 to 30 seconds or until softened. Mix in powdered sugar and enough juice until of drizzling consistency. Stir in extract. Spoon onto cooled cake, allowing mixture to drizzle down sides.

About 16 Servings

TIPS • If desired, all-purpose flour can be substituted for whole wheat flour. Add 1 teaspoon cinnamon or nutmeg for additional color if desired.

• With Full Power, microwave in step 4 for 15 to 17 minutes, rotating dish every 3 minutes.

• With Combination Oven, Bake in preheated 350° oven 20 minutes; then, Microwave-Bake 8 to 9 minutes.

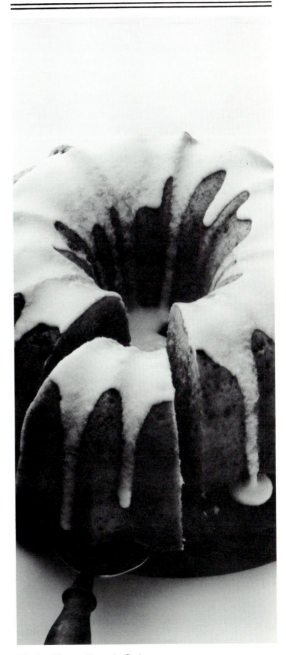

Fruity Tutty Bundt Cake.

Delightful flavors from a favorite coffee are captured in this cake that is just right for special occasions.

CAPPUCCINO CAKE

   1 **package (18½ oz.) pudding-type chocolate cake mix**
   3 **eggs**
   ¾ **cup orange juice**
   ½ **cup cold coffee**
   ⅓ **cup cooking oil**
   1 **tablespoon brandy, if desired**

1. Combine all ingredients in large mixing bowl. Blend on low speed until moistened. Beat at high speed 2 minutes, occasionally scraping sides of bowl.

2. Greases bottom only of 12 x 8-inch glass baking dish. Spoon batter into dish; spread evenly.

3. MICROWAVE (medium — 50%), uncovered, 14 minutes, rotating dish twice. Then, MICROWAVE (high) 4 to 5 minutes or until no longer doughy. Let stand in oven 10 minutes. Cool completely. Frost with Coffee Butter Frosting.

12 x 8-inch Cake

TIPS • Cake can also be microwaved in two layer dishes, lined on bottom with waxed paper. Microwave (medium — 50%), one layer at a time, 5 minutes. Then, microwave (high) 2½ to 3 minutes. Cool 5 minutes before removing from pans.
   • ½ teaspoon instant coffee and ½ cup water can be used for cold coffee.
   • With Full Power, reserve 1½ cups batter and use for cupcakes. Microwave cake in step 3 for 9 to 10 minutes, rotating dish 3 or 4 times. (Cupcakes take about 2 minutes microwave time for 6 cupcakes.)

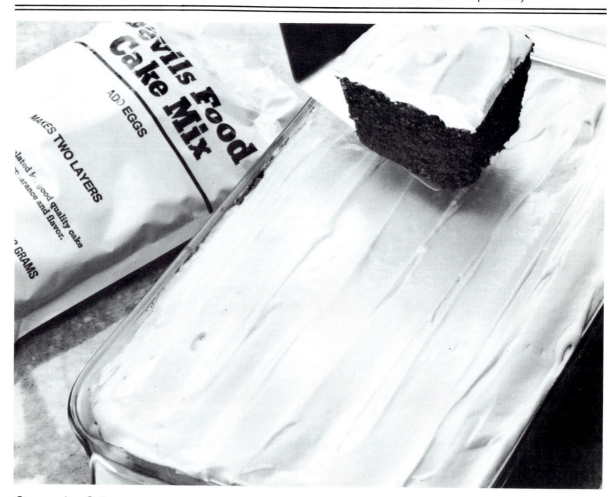

Cappuccino Cake.

This is delicious on Cappuccino Cake or any other favorite chocolate cake.

COFFEE BUTTER FROSTING

- 1 package (3 oz.) cream cheese
- ⅓ cup butter or margarine
- 4 cups (1 lb.) unsifted powdered sugar
- 2 teaspoons instant coffee crystals
- 1 tablespoon hot water
- 3 to 4 tablespoons light cream
- 1 tablespoon brandy, if desired

1. MICROWAVE (high) cream cheese and butter in small glass mixing bowl ¼ to ½ minute or until softened. Mix on medium speed until fluffy. Beat in powdered sugar until light.

2. Dissolve coffee in hot water. Beat into frosting; add enough cream until of spreading consistency. Beat in brandy. Spoon onto cake; spread evenly.

Frosts 12 x 8-inch Cake

The frosting cooks right with the cake for this easy dessert.

SELF-FROSTED GERMAN CHOCOLATE CAKE

- ¼ cup butter or margarine
- ½ cup packed brown sugar
- ⅔ cup chopped pecans or other nuts
- ⅔ cup flaked coconut
- ¼ cup evaporated milk
- 1 bar (4 oz.) German sweet cooking chocolate
- ⅓ cup butter or margarine
- 1⅓ cups unsifted all-purpose flour
- 1 cup sugar
- ½ teaspoon soda
- ½ teaspoon baking powder
- ½ teaspoon salt
- ¾ cup buttermilk or sour milk
- 1 teaspoon vanilla
- 2 eggs

1. Combine ¼ cup butter and the brown sugar in 8-inch square glass baking dish.

2. MICROWAVE (high), uncovered, 1½ to 2 minutes or until bubbly, stirring once. Spread evenly in dish. Sprinkle with pecans and coconut. Pour milk evenly over coconut. Set aside.

3. MICROWAVE (high) chocolate in small glass dish 2 to 2½ minutes or until melted, stirring once.

4. MICROWAVE (high) ⅓ cup butter in glass

mixing bowl ¼ to ½ minute or until softened. Add flour, sugar, soda, baking powder, salt and buttermilk. Beat at medium speed until moistened and combined. Add vanilla, eggs and melted chocolate. Beat at medium speed 2 minutes.

5. MICROWAVE (high) topping mixture in baking dish 2 to 2½ minutes or until bubbly. Stir topping; press evenly into dish. Pour cake batter onto topping.

6. MICROWAVE (medium — 50%), uncovered, 12 minutes. Rotate dish. Then, MICROWAVE (high) 3½ to 4½ minutes or until no longer doughy, rotating dish once. Let stand 5 minutes. Invert onto serving plate. Spread any topping from dish on cake.

8-inch Square Cake

TIPS • This cake freezes well.
• With Full Power, microwave in step 6 for 11 to 12 minutes, rotating dish 3 or 4 times.
• With Combination Oven, microwave in step 2 for 3 to 3½ minutes and in step 3 for 4 to 5 minutes; omit microwaving in step 5. In step 6, bake in preheated 375° oven 15 minutes. Then, microwave-bake for 3 to 5 minutes or until surface springs back when touched lightly.

If you like a fudge-like frosting, we think you will agree this one is perfect for many favorite cakes.

CHOCOLATE FROSTING

- 1 cup sugar
- ½ cup packed brown sugar
- ¾ cup whipping cream
- 2 squares (1 oz. each) unsweetened chocolate
- 1 tablespoon butter or margarine
- 1 teaspoon vanilla, if desired

1. Combine sugars, whipping cream and 1 square of chocolate in 2-quart glass mix 'n pour bowl; mix well. Insert microwave candy thermometer.

2. MICROWAVE (high), uncovered, 7 to 8 minutes or until mixture reaches 235° (soft ball stage), stirring twice. Add remaining chocolate square and butter, but do not stir. Let mixture cool to about 170°, about 30 minutes. Beat until mixture thickens enough to hold shape. Immediately spread on cake. Cut cake with knife dipped in hot water.

Frosts 12 x 8-inch Cake

This super moist and very rich cake is a favorite with our staff.

ZUCCHINI CHOCOLATE CAKE

½ cup butter or margarine
1½ cups sugar
½ cup cooking oil
2 eggs
1 teaspoon vanilla
3 cups shredded, unpeeled zucchini
¼ cup milk
2½ cups unsifted all-purpose flour
¼ cup unsweetened cocoa
1 teaspoon soda
1 teaspoon salt
½ cup semi-sweet chocolate pieces

1. MICROWAVE (high) butter in glass mixing bowl 20 to 30 seconds or until softened. Blend in sugar and oil; beat well. Add eggs, one at a time, beating well after each. Stir in vanilla, zucchini and milk. Add flour, cocoa, soda and salt; mix well. Stir in chocolate pieces.

2. Generously grease a 12-cup fluted plastic tube pan. Sprinkle with sugar; shake out excess sugar. Spoon batter into dish, spreading evenly.

3. MICROWAVE (medium — 50%), uncovered, 12 minutes, rotating dish once. Rotate dish. Then, MICROWAVE (high) 6 to 8 minutes or until no longer doughy, rotating dish once. Cool 10 minutes; invert onto serving plate. If desired, glaze or sprinkle with powdered sugar.

About 16 Servings

TIPS • With Full Power in step 3, microwave 10 to 12 minutes, rotating dish 3 or 4 times.
• Cake can be cooked in 12 x 8-inch glass baking dish using medium and high settings as directed.
• Half a recipe can be cooked in a 10 x 6-inch baking dish microwaving on medium for 9 minutes and then on high for 3 to 4 minutes.

The batter for this cake is very thin, but produces an excellent microwave cake.

CHOCOLATE CAKE

2½ cups unsifted all-purpose flour
2 cups sugar
5 tablespoons unsweetened cocoa
½ teaspoon baking powder
½ teaspoon salt
1 cup buttermilk or sour milk
1 cup cooking oil
2 eggs
1 teaspoon vanilla
¾ cup water
1 teaspoon soda

1. Combine flour, sugar, cocoa, baking powder and salt in large mixing bowl. Add buttermilk, oil, eggs and vanilla; stir until blended.

2. MICROWAVE (high) water in 1-cup glass measure 1½ to 2 minutes or until steaming hot. Stir in soda. Add water and soda to flour mixture. Beat at medium speed about 2 minutes. Batter will be thin. Spoon about 1 cup batter into paper-lined muffin cups to make 6 cupcakes. Set aside. Pour remaining batter into 12 x 8-inch glass baking dish, greased on bottom only.

3. MICROWAVE (medium — 50%), uncovered, 15 minutes, rotating dish once. Rotate dish, then MICROWAVE (high) 5 to 7 minutes or until no longer doughy, rotating dish once. Let stand in oven 10 minutes.

4. MICROWAVE (high), uncovered, cupcakes 2 to 2½ minutes or until no longer doughy, rotating pan once or twice. Cool and frost with favorite frosting.

12 x 8-inch Cake and
6 Cupcakes

TIPS • With Full Power, microwave cake 11 to 13 minutes or until no longer doughy, rotating dish 3 or 4 times.
• With Combination Oven, microwave water in step 2 for 2 to 3 minutes. Preheat oven to 375°. Bake all of batter in 12 x 8-inch dish 20 minutes. Then microwave-bake 4 to 5 minutes or until no longer doughy.

A candy thermometer is very helpful with this recipe, but the same cold water test used for conventional cooking can be used. This frosting is attractive and spreads easily on any cake.

WHITE MOUNTAIN FROSTING

- 1 cup sugar
- ¼ cup water
- ½ cup light corn syrup
- 4 egg whites
- 2 teaspoons vanilla

1. Combine sugar, water and corn syrup in 1-quart glass mix 'n pour bowl. Cover with plastic wrap.

2. MICROWAVE (high) 3 to 4 minutes or until sugar is dissolved. Remove plastic wrap. Stir well and place candy thermometer in bowl. Then MICROWAVE (high), uncovered, 2 to 3 minutes or until 242° is reached or syrup spins a 6 to 8-inch thread.

3. Meanwhile, beat egg whites in large bowl until they form stiff peaks. Pour hot syrup in thin stream over egg whites while beating at high speed. Continue beating until mixture forms soft peaks. Beat in vanilla.

Frosts 12 x 8-inch Cake

A moist apple-spice cake to serve topped with yummy caramel sauce.

APPLE DESSERT WEDGES

- 2 cups chopped apple (about 2 medium)
- 1 egg
- ¾ cup packed brown sugar
- ¼ cup cooking oil
- 1 cup unsifted all-purpose flour
- 1 teaspoon cinnamon
- ½ teaspoon soda
- ¼ teaspoon salt
- ¼ cup chopped nuts
  Caramel Sauce (recipe below)

1. Combine all ingredients except Caramel Sauce; stir until moistened and thoroughly combined.

2. Grease 8 or 9-inch round glass baking dish on bottom only. Spread batter evenly in dish.

3. MICROWAVE (high), uncovered, 7 to 8 minutes or until no longer doughy, rotating pan once. Serve warm with Caramel Sauce.

About 8 Servings

TIP • If cake has cooled, just reheat each serving by microwaving about 10 seconds.

This cake is so good that no one minds its reputation as an ugly duckling.

UGLY DUCKLING CAKE

- ½ package (2-layer size) yellow cake mix (about 2 cups)
- 1 can (8¾ oz.) fruit cocktail, undrained
- ½ cup flaked coconut
- 1 egg
- ¼ cup packed brown sugar
- ¼ cup butter or margarine
- ¼ cup evaporated milk
- ¼ cup sugar
- ¾ cup flaked coconut

1. Combine cake mix, fruit cocktail, ½ cup coconut and egg in mixing bowl. Blend at low speed until moistened. Beat at medium speed 2 minutes, occasionally scraping sides of bowl.

2. Grease bottom only of 8-inch square glass baking dish. Spoon batter into dish. Sprinkle evenly with brown sugar.

3. MICROWAVE (high), uncovered, 6 to 7 minutes or until top is no longer doughy, rotating dish once.

4. Combine butter, milk and sugar in 4-cup glass measure.

5. MICROWAVE (high), uncovered, 1½ to 2 minutes or until mixture boils, stirring once. Stir. Then MICROWAVE (high) 2 minutes. Add coconut and pour over cake. Serve warm or cold.

8-inch Square Cake

TIP • If desired, toast coconut before adding to topping. To toast in microwave, place coconut in 9-inch pie plate. Microwave (high), uncovered, 1½ to 2 minutes, stirring frequently.

A good sauce for cake or ice cream

CARAMEL SAUCE

- ⅓ cup sugar
- ⅓ cup packed brown sugar
- 1 tablespoon cornstarch
- ⅓ cup whipping cream
- 1 tablespoon butter or margarine
- 1 teaspoon vanilla

1. Combine all ingredients except vanilla in 2-cup glass measure.

2. MICROWAVE (high), uncovered, 1½ to 2 minutes or until mixture boils, stirring once.

3. Stir in vanilla. Serve warm over Apple Dessert or other favorite cake or ice cream.

About ¾ Cup

Cake, fresh strawberries and yogurt cream combine for a melt-in-your-mouth dessert. It will be a natural to serve throughout the fresh fruit season as you vary the fruit using what is available.

STRAWBERRIES AND CREAM CAKE

  1 **package (about 9 oz.) one-layer size yellow cake mix**
  ¼ **cup sugar**
  1½ **tablespoons cornstarch**
  1 **cup milk**
  1 **egg, slightly beaten**
  ½ **teaspoon vanilla**
  ¼ **cup strawberry or other favorite jam**
  2 **tablespoons Grand Marnier or other orange-flavored liqueur, if desired**
  1 **cup plain yogurt**
  1 **cup frozen whipped topping, thawed**
  2 **cups sliced fresh strawberries or other favorite fruit**

1. Prepare cake mix as directed on package. Pour into 12 x 8-inch glass baking dish, greased on bottom only. Spread evenly in dish.

2. MICROWAVE (medium — 50%), uncovered, 7 minutes. Rotate dish and MICROWAVE (high) 2 to 3 minutes or until no longer doughy, rotating dish once. Cool.

3. Combine sugar, cornstarch and milk in 4-cup glass measure. Stir until smooth.

4. MICROWAVE (high), uncovered, 3½ to 4 minutes or until mixture boils and thickens, stirring once or twice during last half of cooking time. Blend in egg.

5. MICROWAVE (high) ½ to 1 minute or until mixture just begins to bubble, stirring once or twice. Stir in vanilla. Cool.

6. Combine jam and liqueur; spoon over cake, spreading evenly. Combine cooled pudding mixture and yogurt. Fold in whipped topping until combined. Fold in strawberries. Spoon onto cake, carefully spreading to cover. Refrigerate several hours or overnight. Cut into squares to serve.

12 to 15 Servings

TIPS • With Full Power, microwave in step 2 for 5½ to 6½ minutes or until no longer doughy, rotating 2 or 3 times.

• Unsweetened frozen strawberries can be substituted for fresh.

Strawberries and Cream Cake.

This is an excellent microwave cake with a rich, buttery flavor that was adapted from a reader's favorite.

SHERRY-PECAN BUNDT CAKE

- 1 package (18 oz.) pudding-type yellow cake mix
- 1 package (3 oz.) vanilla instant pudding mix
- ¾ cup dry sherry
- ¾ cup cooking oil
- 1 teaspoon butter flavoring
- 4 eggs
- ¼ cup sugar
- 2 teaspoons cinnamon
- ½ cup chopped pecans

1. Combine cake mix, pudding mix, sherry, oil, flavoring and eggs. Blend at low speed until moistened. Beat at medium speed about 3 minutes.

2. Oil a 12-cup fluted plastic tube pan. Combine sugar, cinnamon and pecans. Sprinkle half of sugar mixture in bottom of cake dish. Pour half of batter over sugar; top with remaining sugar mixture. Pour in remaining batter.

3. MICROWAVE (medium — 50%), uncovered, 12 minutes, rotating dish once. Rotate dish and then MICROWAVE (high) 3 to 4 minutes or until no longer doughy, rotating dish once. Cool 10 minutes; invert onto serving plate.

About 16 Servings

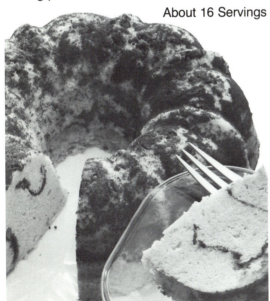

Sherry-Pecan Bundt Cake.

TIPS • Part water can be substituted for sherry.
• With Full Power, microwave in step 3, 11 to 13 minutes, rotating dish often.

To reduce cholesterol, this deliciously moist cake uses Neufchatel cheese in the frosting in place of cream cheese. An egg equivalent is substituted for a whole egg to further lower the cholesterol.

CARROT CAKE

Cake:
- ¾ cup packed brown sugar
- ½ cup cooking oil
- 1 egg equivalent (¼ cup) or 1 egg
- ½ teaspoon vanilla
- 1 cup unsifted all-purpose flour
- ½ teaspoon salt
- ½ teaspoon soda
- ½ teaspoon baking powder
- ½ teaspoon cinnamon
- 1 cup shredded carrot (about 1 medium)
- ½ cup crushed pineapple (with juice)
- ½ cup chopped walnuts

Frosting:
- 1½ ozs. Neufchatel cheese
- 1 tablespoon margarine
- 1 cup unsifted powdered sugar
- ½ teaspoon vanilla
- ¼ cup chopped walnuts, if desired

1. Combine brown sugar and oil in mixing bowl. Beat in egg equivalent and vanilla. Mix in remaining cake ingredients until thoroughly combined.

2. Grease 8-inch square glass baking dish on bottom only. Pour batter into pan; spread evenly.

3. MICROWAVE (medium — 50%), uncovered, 9 minutes, rotating dish once. Then MICROWAVE (high) 3 to 4 minutes or until no longer doughy, rotating dish twice. Cool.

4. MICROWAVE (high) Neufchatel cheese and margarine for Frosting in glass mixing bowl ½ to ¾ minute or until softened. Beat until smooth; blend in powdered sugar. Stir in vanilla. Spread over cake. If desired, sprinkle with chopped nuts. Cut into squares.

About 9 Servings
Calories: 560 Each
Cholesterol: 4 mg. Each

TIPS • With Full Power, microwave 5 to 6 minutes in step 3, rotating dish 3 or 4 times.
• Leftover pineapple can be frozen for use at a later time.

These miniature tarts are always fun to serve or take to a cookie exchange. Egg cartons make sturdy holders for the miniature paper liners.

MINIATURE MACAROON TARTS

2⅔ **cups flaked coconut (about 7 ozs.)**
 ⅔ **cup sweetened condensed milk (half a 14-oz. can)**
 ½ **teaspoon almond extract**
 2 **sticks pie crust mix**
  Favorite jam, jelly or mincemeat

1. Combine coconut, sweetened condensed milk and extract; set aside.

2. Prepare pie crust sticks as directed on package. Divide dough in half. Roll out each portion on floured, cloth-covered surface to 11-inch circle. Cut 2¼-inch rounds using small cutter, drinking glass or metal lid. Repeat with remaining dough to make about 48 rounds.

3. Place a round in each 1-inch paper petits four liner. Place a liner in each cup of cardboard or plastic egg carton. Spoon ¼ teaspoon favorite jam, jelly or mincemeat into each cup.

4. MICROWAVE (high) 1 carton at a time, uncovered, 1 minute, rotating carton once. Place a rounded teaspoonful of coconut mixture in each cup.

5. MICROWAVE (high) ¾ to 1¼ minutes or until coconut mixture is set, rotating once. Remove from egg carton and cool. Repeat with remaining mixtures.

About 48 Miniature Tarts

This recipe uses fructose, a natural sweetener. Since the body handles it differently than table sugar, it does not create a rapid rise in blood sugar. Fructose is about 1½ times sweeter than sugar, so less can be used. These cookies make good snacks or dessert.

OATMEAL-RAISIN COOKIES

 ⅓ **cup margarine**
 ¼ **cup granular fructose or ⅓ cup sugar**
 1 **egg**
 1 **teaspoon vanilla**
1¼ **cups unsifted all-purpose flour**
 1 **cup quick-cooking rolled oats**
 1 **teaspoon baking powder**
 ½ **teaspoon salt**
 1 **teaspoon cinnamon**
 ½ **cup skim milk**
 ¼ **cup water**
 ½ **cup chopped almonds**
 ½ **cup raisins**

1. MICROWAVE (high) margarine in glass mixing bowl 40 to 50 seconds or until melted. Blend in fructose and egg. Stir in vanilla. Add remaining ingredients; mix until combined.

2. Drop dough by teaspoonsful onto waxed paper-lined cardboard, using ⅓ of dough to form 12 cookies.

3. MICROWAVE (high) 12 cookies at a time, uncovered, 1½ to 1¾ minutes or until no longer doughy, rotating cardboard once. Let stand 2 to 3 minutes. Remove to cooling rack. Repeat with remaining batter.

36 Cookies
71 Calories Each

Oatmeal-Raisin Cookies.

A moist texture is characteristic of these bars. They were part of a low sodium feature, but can be enjoyed by all.

APPLESAUCE BARS

- ¼ **cup unsalted butter or margarine**
- ¾ **cup packed brown sugar**
- ¾ **cup sweetened applesauce**
- 1 **cup unsifted all-purpose flour**
- ½ **teaspoon soda**
- ½ **teaspoon cinnamon**
- ⅛ **teaspoon nutmeg**
- ⅛ **teaspoon cloves**
- ¼ **cup chopped nuts**
- ¼ **cup raisins**
- 2 **tablespoons powdered sugar**

1. MICROWAVE (high) butter in glass mixing bowl ¼ to ½ minute or until softened. Blend in brown sugar; beat in applesauce. Stir in flour, soda, cinnamon, nutmeg and cloves. Mix in nuts and raisins.

2. Grease 8-inch square glass baking dish on bottom only. Spread batter in dish.

3. MICROWAVE (high), uncovered, 6 to 7 minutes or until no longer doughy, rotating dish twice. Cool; sprinkle with powdered sugar. Cut into bars.

16 Bars
126 Calories Each
21.5 mg. Sodium or 1 Point

Make a special dessert or snack with a minimum of fuss. Purchased crackers sandwich a delicious date filling and are topped with cream cheese frosting.

DATE NUT COOKIES

- 1 **can (14 oz.) sweetened condensed milk**
- 1 **package (8 oz.) chopped dates**
- ½ **cup chopped nuts**
- 1 **package (12 oz.) butter-flavored crackers (i.e. Ritz)**

Frosting:
- 1 **package (3 oz.) cream cheese**
- 2 **cups unsifted powdered sugar**
- 1 **teaspoon vanilla**
- ½ **to 1 tablespoon milk**

1. Combine sweetened condensed milk and dates in 1-quart glass mix 'n pour bowl.

2. MICROWAVE (high), uncovered, 5½ to 6 minutes or until mixture becomes very thick, stirring twice. Stir in nuts. Arrange half of crackers on tray. Spoon about a teaspoon of filling onto each; top with another cracker pressing gently until filling comes to edge. Repeat with remaining filling and crackers.

3. MICROWAVE (high) cream cheese in 1-quart glass mix 'n pour bowl ½ to 1 minute or until softened. Mix in powdered sugar and vanilla until smooth. Stir in milk until of spreading consistency. Spread frosting atop each cookie. Store in air-tight container or freeze cookies.

About 5 Dozen Cookies

TIP • These cookies are also delicious served frozen.

Date Nut Cookies.

Two favorites — chocolate and mint — combine for colorful bars.

MINT BROWNIES

     2 **squares (1 oz. each) unsweetened chocolate**
    ⅓ **cup butter or margarine**
     1 **cup sugar**
     2 **eggs**
    ½ **teaspoon vanilla**
    ¼ **teaspoon peppermint extract**
    1¼ **cups unsifted all-purpose flour**
    ½ **teaspoon baking powder**
    ¼ **teaspoon salt**
    ½ **cup chopped nuts, if desired**

Frosting:
    ¼ **cup butter or margarine**
     1 **package (3 oz.) cream cheese**
     2 **cups unsifted powdered sugar**
    ½ **teaspoon vanilla**
    ¼ **teaspoon peppermint extract**
      Green food coloring

1. Combine chocolate and butter in large glass mixing bowl.

2. MICROWAVE (high), uncovered, 1½ to 2 minutes or until chocolate and butter are melted. Blend in sugar. Add eggs, one at a time, beating after each. Blend in vanilla and peppermint extract. Add flour, baking powder and salt; mix well. Stir in nuts. Spread in greased 8-inch square glass baking dish.

3. MICROWAVE (high), uncovered, 4½ to 5½ minutes or until no longer doughy, rotating dish once or twice. Cool.

4. Combine butter and cream cheese for Frosting in glass bowl.

5. MICROWAVE (high) ½ to ¾ minute or until softened. Blend until creamy. Beat in powdered sugar. Blend in vanilla and peppermint extract. Stir in food coloring until desired color. Spread on cooled brownies. Refrigerate until set; cut into 1-inch squares.

About 49 Bars

Dried apricots and pecans make a pecan pie-like topping for these bars.

APRICOT-PECAN BARS

    ¾ **cup chopped dried apricots**
    ¾ **cup water**
    ½ **cup quick-cooking rolled oats**
    ¾ **cup unsifted all-purpose flour**
    ½ **cup sugar**
    ½ **cup butter or margarine**
     2 **eggs**
     1 **cup packed brown sugar**
    ½ **teaspoon vanilla**
    ¼ **cup all-purpose flour**
    ¼ **teaspoon salt**
    ½ **cup chopped pecans**
      Powdered sugar

1. Combine apricots and water in 2-cup glass measure.

2. MICROWAVE (high), uncovered, 2 to 2½ minutes or until mixture boils. Let stand 5 minutes to soften. Drain.

3. Combine rolled oats, flour and sugar in mixing bowl. Cut in butter with pastry blender until crumbly. Press into bottom of greased 10 x 6-inch glass baking dish.

4. MICROWAVE (high), uncovered, 3 to 3½ minutes or until mixture is heated and set, rotating dish once or twice.

5. Beat eggs in mixing bowl. Gradually beat in brown sugar and vanilla. Blend in flour and salt. Stir in drained apricots and pecans. Spoon onto baked crust, spreading evenly.

6. MICROWAVE (high), uncovered, 5 to 6 minutes or until set, rotating dish once or twice. Cool and refrigerate. Cut into 1-inch squares, occasionally dipping knife in hot water. Just before serving, sprinkle with powdered sugar.

About 40 Bars

TIP • With Combination Oven, omit cooking in step 4. In step 6, microwave-bake at 350° for 7 or 8 minutes or until toothpick inserted in center comes out clean and crust is set.

Most bars can be prepared easily in the microwave. These blend rich, creamy caramel with chocolate for a treat that is simply delicious.

CHOCO-CARAMEL BARS

- ¾ **cup butter or margarine**
- ¾ **cup packed brown sugar**
- 1¼ **cups unsifted all-purpose flour**
- 1¼ **cups quick-cooking rolled oats**
- ½ **teaspoon soda**
- ¼ **teaspoon salt**
- 24 **caramels (7 ozs.)**
- ¼ **cup milk or light cream**
- 1 **cup (6 ozs.) semi-sweet chocolate pieces**
- ½ **cup chopped nuts**

1. MICROWAVE (high) butter in glass bowl ¼ to ½ minute or until softened. Mix in brown sugar, flour, rolled oats, soda and salt until well mixed. Press ⅔ of mixture into bottom of 8-inch square glass baking dish.

2. MICROWAVE (high), uncovered, 2½ to 3 minutes or until bubbly, rotating dish 2 or 3 times. Set aside.

3. Combine unwrapped caramels and milk in 4-cup glass measure.

4. MICROWAVE (high), uncovered, 2 to 2½ minutes or until melted, stirring once. Mix until smooth.

5. Sprinkle chocolate pieces and nuts onto baked crust. Pour melted caramel mixture evenly over chocolate and nuts. Sprinkle with remaining crumb mixture.

6. MICROWAVE (high), uncovered, 4 to 4½ minutes or until bubbly throughout, rotating dish 2 or 3 times. Cool completely. Cut into 1-inch squares.

About 49 Bars

TIP • When time for cooling is at a minimum, refrigerate bars just long enough to chill and set chocolate.

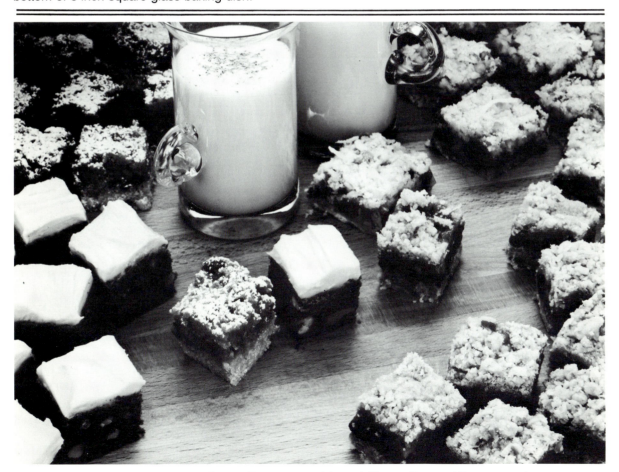

Mint Brownies, page 136, Apricot-Pecan Bars, page 136, and Choco-Caramel Bars.

This simple, yet delicious recipe was sent to us for adaptation by one of our readers. Kids of all ages are sure to enjoy the bars.

NO-BAKE SPECIAL BARS

- 1 **cup sugar**
- 1 **cup light corn syrup**
- ½ **cup peanut butter**
- 5 **cups high protein cereal**
- 1 **cup thin-stick pretzels, broken into pieces**

1. Combine sugar and corn syrup in 2-quart glass mix 'n pour bowl.

2. MICROWAVE (high), uncovered, 4 to 5 minutes or until mixture boils hard and sugar is dissolved, stirring once or twice. Blend in peanut butter until smooth. Stir in cereal and pretzels until evenly coated.

3. Press mixture into greased 12 x 8-inch or 13 or 9-inch baking pan. Cool. Cut into squares.

About 5 Dozen Squares

TIPS • A greased or wet spoon or spatula helps press bars into pan without the mixture sticking to the spoon.

• For special variation, try frosting bars with the following: Combine 1 cup (6 ozs.) semi-sweet chocolate pieces and 1 cup (6 ozs.) butterscotch pieces in 2-cup glass measure. Microwave (high) 2 to 3 minutes or until softened, stirring once. Stir until smooth. Spoon onto bars; spread to cover. Refrigerate to set frosting.

This easy-to-fix snack combines nutritious peanuts and cereal with good to eat chocolate and caramel flavors. If you watch the time carefully and stir halfway through the heating time, the caramels and chocolate melt easily.

YUMMY GRAHAM BARS

- 14 **caramels**
- 3 **tablespoons milk**
- 1 **cup (6 ozs.) butterscotch pieces**
- 4 **cups crisp graham cereal**
- ½ **cup (2½ ozs.) salted blanched peanuts**
- ½ **cup semi-sweet chocolate pieces**

1. Butter an 8-inch square baking dish; set aside.

2. Unwrap caramels and place in 2-quart glass mix 'n pour bowl. Add milk.

3. MICROWAVE (high), uncovered, 2 to 2½ minutes or until melted, stirring once or twice. Add ½ cup of the butterscotch pieces; stir until melted. Add cereal and peanuts; mix until evenly coated. Spoon mixture into buttered dish. Press firmly with buttered fork or fingers to flatten and smooth mixture in pan. Set aside.

4. Combine remaining ½ cup butterscotch pieces and the chocolate pieces in 2-cup glass measure.

5. MICROWAVE (high), uncovered, 1½ to 2 minutes or until softened, stirring twice. Stir until smooth. Pour evenly onto bars; spread with back of spoon to cover bars. Refrigerate 1 to 2 hours to set chocolate. Cut into squares.

About 25 Bars

Use homemade or purchased granola to make these bars that are great for packing in lunches.

GRANOLA BARS

- 2 **cups granola cereal**
- 1 **egg, beaten**
- ½ **cup chopped dates**
- ½ **cup chopped dried apricots**
- ½ **cup dry roasted peanuts**
- ¼ **cup packed brown sugar**
- ½ **teaspoon vanilla**
- ¼ **teaspoon salt**

1. Combine all ingredients in 2-quart glass mix 'n pour bowl. Mix well. Line 8-inch square glass baking dish with waxed paper, allowing paper to extend over edges. Press mixture firmly into waxed paper-lined pan.

2. MICROWAVE (high), uncovered, 3½ to 4 minutes or until set, rotating dish once or twice. Cool 5 minutes; remove from pan. Cool completely; cut into bars.

About 16 Bars
145 Calories Each

TIP • Raisins, coconut, almonds and other dried fruits can be used in place of dates, apricots and peanuts.

The moist cream filling in these bars tastes like raisin pie.

RAISIN CREAM BARS

- 1¼ cups raisins
- ¼ cup water
- ½ cup butter or margarine
- ½ cup sugar
- ¾ cup unsifted all-purpose flour
- ¾ cup rolled oats
- ½ teaspoon soda
- ½ teaspoon vanilla

Filling:
- 1 cup sugar
- 3 tablespoons cornstarch
- ⅛ teaspoon salt
- 1½ cups half & half or evaporated milk
- 2 egg yolks

1. Combine raisins and water in 2-cup glass measure.

2. MICROWAVE (high), uncovered, 1½ to 2 minutes or until heated, stirring once. Set aside.

3. MICROWAVE (high) butter in glass mixing bowl 20 to 30 seconds or until softened. Mix in ½ cup sugar, the flour, oats, soda and vanilla until crumbly. Press half of mixture into bottom of 12 x 8-inch glass baking dish. (Set aside remainder in glass dish.)

4. MICROWAVE (high), uncovered, 3½ to 4 minutes or until crust has a dry appearance, rotating dish once or twice. Set aside.

5. Combine sugar, cornstarch and salt for Filling in 1-quart glass mix 'n pour bowl. Blend in half & half.

6. MICROWAVE (high), uncovered, 4½ to 5 minutes or until mixture boils and thickens, stirring 2 or 3 times. Beat egg yolks with fork; slowly mix in some of hot mixture. Return egg yolk mixture to Filling mixture in bowl. Drain raisins and stir into Filling. Pour over crust in pan. Set aside.

7. MICROWAVE (high) remaining crumb mixture in bowl, uncovered, 2½ to 3 minutes or until lightly toasted, stirring twice. Spoon onto filling.

8. MICROWAVE (high), uncovered, 3 to 3½ minutes or until mixture is bubbly throughout, rotating dish once. Cool and refrigerate until served. Cut into bars.

About 60 Bars

These bars are great to have on hand for friends of all ages.

CRISPY FUDGE LAYER BARS

- ½ cup peanut butter
- ¼ cup butter or margarine
- 4 cups miniature marshmallows
- 5 cups crisp rice cereal
- 1 cup (6 ozs.) semi-sweet chocolate pieces
- ⅔ cup (half a 14-oz. can) sweetened condensed milk
- 2 tablespoons butter or margarine

1. Combine peanut butter, ¼ cup butter and the marshmallows in 2-quart glass mix 'n pour bowl.

2. MICROWAVE (high), uncovered, 1½ to 2 minutes or until melted, stirring once. Stir in cereal until evenly coated. Set aside.

3. MICROWAVE (high) chocolate pieces in 2-cup glass measure 1½ to 2 minutes or until melted, stirring once. Blend in sweetened condensed milk and the butter.

4. Press half of cereal mixture evenly into buttered 12 x 8-inch glass baking dish. Spoon chocolate mixture onto cereal layer; spread evenly. Spoon remaining cereal mixture over chocolate. Carefully press evenly over chocolate. Refrigerate about 1 hour before cutting into squares.

24 to 30 Bars

Crispy Fudge Layer Bars.

Serve these as a dessert to dip at the table. Or, dip them ahead for a candy tray.

MIXED UP BON BONS

1 **square (1 oz.) unsweetened chocolate**
½ **cup sweetened condensed milk**
1 **cup flaked coconut**
¾ **cup chopped pecans or other nuts**
8 **ozs. white almond bark coating**

1. Combine chocolate and sweetened condensed milk in 1-quart glass mix 'n pour bowl.

2. MICROWAVE (high), uncovered, 2½ to 3 minutes or until chocolate is melted, stirring once. Stir in coconut and pecans. Chill several hours.

3. Shape mixture into ¾-inch balls. Arrange on serving plate. Refrigerate until served.

4. MICROWAVE (high) coating in 2-cup glass dish, uncovered, 2½ to 3 minutes or until coating is melted, stirring once. Place coating over warming candle and dip bon bons in warm coating.

About 36 Bon Bons

TIPS • Fruits and nuts are also good dipped in the warm coating. Strawberries, cherries, grapes and apple wedges can be used as well as whole almonds, filberts or walnut halves.

• For candies, dip bon bons in warm coating, covering about ¾ of chocolate. Set on waxed paper, chocolate-part-up. Let stand until coating is set. Store in covered container.

This super-easy candy is sure to be a favorite, and it mails nicely to faraway friends.

SNOWFLAKE-MINT DROPS

1 **lb. (16 ozs.) white almond bark coating**
1½ **cups flaked coconut**
⅓ **cup crushed peppermint candy**

1. Place coating in 1-quart glass mix 'n pour bowl.

2. MICROWAVE (high), uncovered, 2 to 2½ minutes or until candy is softened, stirring once. Stir in coconut and candy. Drop by teaspoonful onto waxed paper. Cool until set. Remove from paper.

About 1 Pound Candy

TIP • Candy can be spread on waxed paper. After it is set, break into pieces.

This fudge is prepared with minimal effort.

QUICK FUDGE

2 **cups sugar**
1 **can (5⅓ oz.) evaporated milk (⅔ cup)**
½ **cup butter or margarine**
10 **large marshmallows**
1 **package (6 oz.) semi-sweet chocolate pieces (1 cup)**
1 **cup chopped nuts, if desired**

1. Combine sugar and milk in 2-quart glass mix 'n pour bowl; stir until blended. Add butter.

2. MICROWAVE (high), uncovered, 3½ to 4½ minutes or until mixture begins to boil, stirring once.

3. MICROWAVE (high) 5 minutes. Stir in marshmallows, chocolate pieces and nuts until blended. Pour into buttered 10 x 6-inch dish. Cool until set; cut into squares.

About 30 Squares

TIP • This type of candy is not recommended for the Combination Oven unless you have the faster 650-watt model.

Sunflower seeds make an interesting and nutritional addition to a candy such as this.

SUNFLOWER BRITTLE

2 **cups sugar**
⅔ **cup light corn syrup**
⅔ **cup water**
¼ **teaspoon salt**
2 **cups raw sunflower seeds**
1 **tablespoon butter or margarine**
1 **teaspoon soda**
1 **teaspoon vanilla**

1. Combine sugar, corn syrup, water, salt and sunflower seeds in 2-quart glass mix 'n pour bowl.

2. MICROWAVE (high), uncovered, 6 minutes. Stir and insert microwave candy thermometer. Then, MICROWAVE (high), uncovered, 16 to 18 minutes or until about 295° (hard crack stage).

3. Stir in butter, soda and vanilla just until light and bubbly. Pour onto large (or 2 small) buttered cookie sheet and spread to desired thickness. Cool. Break into pieces. Store in covered container.

About 1½ Pounds

TIP • If sunflower seeds are toasted, add during last 5 minutes of cooking time. Otherwise, they may toast too much and scorch.

Here the crust is baked in the oven and the microwave is used for the caramel filling and chocolate frosting.

CARAMEL THINS

- ½ **cup butter or margarine**
- ½ **cup powdered sugar, unsifted**
- 1 **cup unsifted all-purpose flour**
- 1 **package (14 oz.) caramels**
- ¼ **cup evaporated milk or light cream**
- ¼ **cup butter or margarine**
- ¾ **cup sifted powdered sugar**
- 1 **cup (6 ozs.) semi-sweet chocolate pieces**
- 3 **tablespoons butter or margarine**

1. MICROWAVE (high) butter in glass mixing bowl ¼ to ½ minute or until softened. Blend in powdered sugar. Mix in flour until crumbly.

2. Butter a 13 x 9-inch baking pan. Press crumb mixture evenly into bottom of pan.

3. BAKE in preheated 350° oven 10 to 12 minutes or until lightly browned.

4. Unwrap caramels and place in 2-quart glass mix 'n pour bowl. Add evaporated milk and ¼ cup butter.

5. MICROWAVE (high), uncovered, 3 to 3½ minutes or until caramels are melted, stirring twice. Stir until smooth. Stir in powdered sugar. Pour over crust; spread evenly. Cool 15 minutes.

6. Combine chocolate pieces and butter in 2-cup glass measure.

7. MICROWAVE (high), uncovered, 1 to 1½ minutes or until chocolate is glossy. Stir until smooth. Spoon onto caramel layer; spread evenly. Refrigerate several hours before cutting into squares.

About 84 Squares

TIP • When preparing in the combination oven, be sure to allow oven to cool between steps 3 and 5.

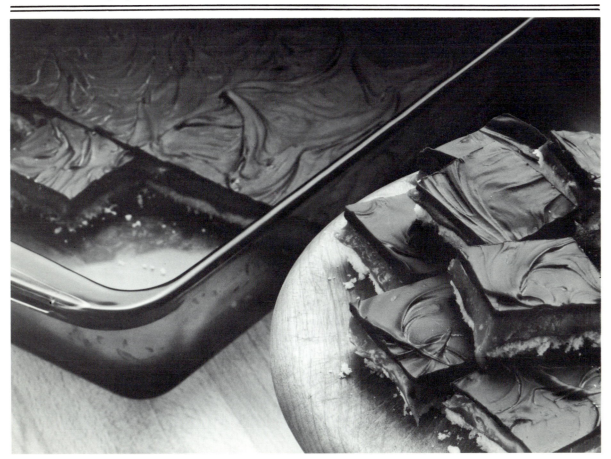

Caramel Thins.

This recipe was adapted from a reader's recipe that came from Mackinac Island. It makes a delicious, creamy, light fudge.

MACKINAC ISLAND VANILLA FUDGE

- ½ **cup milk**
- ½ **cup butter or margarine**
- ½ **cup packed brown sugar**
- ½ **cup sugar**
- ⅛ **teaspoon salt**
- 2½ **cups unsifted powdered sugar**
- 1 **teaspoon vanilla**
- ¼ **cup chopped pecans**

1. Mix together milk, butter, brown sugar, sugar and salt in 2-quart glass mix 'n pour bowl.

2. MICROWAVE (high), uncovered, 3 minutes. Stir, scraping sides of bowl to dissolve sugar. Insert microwave candy thermomometer. Then, MICROWAVE (high), uncovered, 6 to 7 minutes or until mixture reaches 235° (soft ball stage), stirring once or twice.

3. Add powdered sugar and vanilla. Beat on medium speed until thickened, about 8 minutes. Stir in pecans; spread in buttered 9 x 5-inch loaf dish. Let stand until set. Cut into squares.

About 27 One-inch Pieces

TIPS • For Chocolate Fudge, add 1 oz. unsweetened chocolate in step 1.

• For Peanut Butter Fudge, reduce butter to ¼ cup and add ½ cup peanut butter in step 1.

Pecan lovers will enjoy this easy recipe that requires only four ingredients.

PECAN DANDY

- 2½ **cups sugar**
- ⅔ **cup milk**
- ½ **teaspoon soda**
- 2 **cups (8 ozs.) chopped pecans**

1. Mix together sugar, milk and soda in 3-quart glass casserole.

2. MICROWAVE (high), uncovered, 4 minutes. Stir, scraping sides of bowl to dissolve sugar. Then, MICROWAVE (medium — 50%) uncovered, 10 to 12 minutes or until mixture reaches 235° (soft ball stage), stirring when necessary to prevent boilover. Beat mixture slightly; stir in pecans.

3. Drop by teaspoonsful onto waxed paper. When set, remove from paper and store in tightly covered container.

About 50 Pieces

TIPS • For added flavor, toast pecans. Place whole pecans in pie plate. Microwave (high) 2½ to 3 minutes or until toasted, stirring 2 or 3 times.

• Whole pecans can be substituted for chopped.

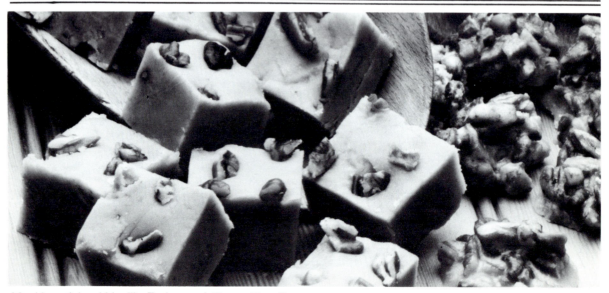

Mackinac Island Vanilla Fudge and Pecan Dandies.

This delightfully soft and chewy candy keeps you going back for more.

CHEWY CHOCOLATE CANDY

   1 **cup dry roasted peanuts, chopped**
   1 **cup sugar**
   1 **cup light corn syrup**
   ½ **cup butter or margarine**
   ¼ **cup light cream**
   3 **squares (3 ozs.) unsweetened chocolate**
   1½ **teaspoons vanilla**

1. Grease a 15 x 10-inch metal jelly roll pan or baking sheet. Sprinkle with peanuts; set aside. Combine sugar, corn syrup, butter, cream and chocolate in 2-quart glass mix 'n pour bowl.

2. MICROWAVE (high), uncovered, 6 to 7 minutes or until boiling, stirring twice. Insert microwave candy thermometer.

3. MICROWAVE (high), uncovered, 6 to 7 minutes or until mixture reaches 260° (hard ball stage). Stir in vanilla. Immediately pour over peanuts in pan. Allow to cool completely — about 2 hours. Cut into squares and wrap in waxed paper.

About 1½ lbs.

These are chewy, crunchy and chocolaty all in the same delectable bite.

TOFFEE BARS

   15 **saltine crackers**
   ½ **cup packed brown sugar**
   ½ **cup butter or margarine**
   ½ **cup semi-sweet chocolate pieces**
   ¼ **cup chopped nuts, if desired**

1. Line 12 x 8-inch glass baking dish with waxed paper. Place crackers, salted side up, in one layer on waxed paper.

2. Combine brown sugar and butter in 1-quart glass mix 'n pour bowl.

3. MICROWAVE (high), uncovered, 1½ to 2 minutes or until slightly thickened, stirring once. Beat with rotary beater until smooth. Pour brown sugar mixture over crackers.

4. MICROWAVE (high), uncovered, 2 to 2½ minutes or until surface is bubbly, rotating dish once. Sprinkle chocolate pieces over hot bars. Let stand 2 to 3 minutes or until melted. Spread chocolate over bars. Sprinkle with nuts, if desired. Score bars by cutting between cracker squares. Cool until chocolate is set. Invert and remove waxed paper. Break into squares.

About 15 Bars
125 Calories Each

TIP • Omit chocolate for plain toffee bars.

This candy is reminiscent of chocolate-covered cherries, but so much simpler.

CHERRY MASH CANDY

   ¼ **cup butter or margarine**
   1 **package (14.3 oz.) cherry frosting mix**
   ½ **cup sweetened condensed milk**
   1 **jar (10 oz.) maraschino cherries, drained and chopped**

Coating:
   ½ **bar (1.6 ozs.) paraffin**
   2 **packages (12 ozs. each) semi-sweet chocolate pieces**
   2 **packages (8 ozs. each) salted peanuts, finely chopped**

1. Place butter in glass mixing bowl.

2. MICROWAVE (high), uncovered, ¼ to ½ minute or until softened. Stir in frosting mix, sweetened condensed milk and cherries.

3. Drop teaspoonsful onto waxed paper. Refrigerate 24 hours or freeze 3 to 4 hours or until set.

4. Break or cut paraffin into small pieces. Place in 1-quart glass mix 'n pour bowl. Add chocolate pieces.

5. MICROWAVE (high), uncovered, 3 to 4 minutes or until paraffin is melted, stirring well 2 or 3 times. Stir in peanuts.

6. Using a dipping or table fork, lower each ball, one at a time, into chocolate; turn to coat evenly. Lift from chocolate with fork and tap gently to remove excess chocolate. Place on waxed paper. When set, remove from paper. (If chocolate becomes too cool, microwave ½ to 1 minute.)

About 5 Dozen Candies

TIPS • Peanuts can be omitted from chocolate coating.

• If cherry frosting is not available, use vanilla and add ½ teaspoon cherry flavoring and a few drops red food coloring.

This candy is chock full of natural ingredients that increase its nutritional value.

APRICOT-DATE BALLS

- 2 eggs
- ⅓ cup honey
- ½ cup chopped dates
- ½ cup chopped dried apricots
- 1 teaspoon vanilla
- 1 cup flaked coconut
- ½ cup chopped almonds
- 1 cup sunflower seeds
  Powdered sugar or coconut

1. Beat eggs until well mixed in 2-quart glass mix 'n pour bowl. Mix in honey, dates and apricots.

2. MICROWAVE (high), uncovered, 3½ to 4 minutes or until mixture is thickened, stirring twice. Stir in vanilla. Cool.

3. Stir in coconut, almonds and sunflower seeds.

4. Form mixture into balls by dropping rounded teaspoonsful of mixture into powdered sugar and coating with sugar while pressing into balls. Let stand several hours uncovered. Store loosely covered in refrigerator.

About 36 Balls

A refreshing sweet that can be used as a garnish or served on a candy tray.

CANDIED FRUIT PEEL

- 2 oranges
- 1 grapefruit
- 1 lemon
- 2 cups water
- 1½ cups sugar
- ¼ cup water
- 1 stick cinnamon
- ⅔ cup sugar

1. Score oranges, grapefruit and lemon into quarters. Remove peel. Remove white membrane from grapefruit and orange peels. Cut peel into ¼-inch strips.

2. Combine strips of fruit and 2 cups water in 1-quart glass mix 'n pour bowl.

3. MICROWAVE (high), uncovered, 20 to 22 minutes or until fruit starts to look transparent, stirring once. Drain. Add 1½ cups sugar, ¼ cup water and cinnamon stick.

4. MICROWAVE (high), uncovered, 9 to 10 minutes or until fruit is tender. Drain and blot dry with paper towel.

5. Toss peels with sugar. Lay fruit strips out flat to dry. Store in loosely covered container.

About 3 Cups

Just as tempting as candy, but with the added nutrition of raisins. Note the "Tip" for preparing with nuts or other dried fruit.

YOGURT-COVERED RAISINS

- 8 ozs. white almond bark coating
- ¼ cup plain yogurt
- 2½ cups raisins

1. Cut white bark coating into 6 to 8 pieces. Place in 4-cup glass measure.

2. MICROWAVE (medium — 50%), uncovered, 3 to 3½ minutes or until melted, stirring twice.

3. Stir until smooth. Stir in yogurt and raisins. Spoon onto waxed paper; spread with 2 forks to make a single layer. Let stand uncovered overnight. Turn mixture over and allow to dry about 1 hour. Break raisins into pieces and store in covered container.

About 3 Cups
205 Calories/¼ Cup

TIPS • Candy can also be dropped by teaspoonsful onto waxed paper to form raisin clusters.

• For variation, substitute dry roasted peanuts or almonds or other dried fruit for raisins. Or, use a combination of fruit and nuts.

• Be sure raisins are at room temperature when adding to coating. Otherwise, the mixture cools and hardens too quickly.

• With Full Power, microwave 2 to 3 minutes, stirring 2 or 3 times.

Goodie Nut Bars.

Our office staff found these to be real favorites and they disappeared quickly. If you have candy lovers at your house, you too will find them well received.

GOODIE NUT BARS

  1 **cup (6 ozs.) semi-sweet chocolate pieces**
  1 **cup (6 ozs.) butterscotch pieces**
  1 **cup peanut butter**
  1 **cup (8 ozs.) dry roasted peanuts**
  ¼ **cup milk**
  2 **tablespoons vanilla pudding mix**
  ½ **cup butter or margarine**
3¼ **cups unsifted powdered sugar**
  ½ **teaspoon maple flavoring**

1. Combine chocolate and butterscotch pieces and peanut butter in 2-quart glass mix 'n pour bowl.

2. MICROWAVE (high), uncovered, 3 to 3½ minutes or until softened, stirring once. Stir until smooth. Line a 13 x 9 or 12 x 8-inch baking pan with waxed paper. Spoon half of chocolate mixture into pan; spread evenly. Refrigerate until set, about 1 hour or freeze about 15 minutes. Stir peanuts into remaining chocolate mixture and allow to stand at room temperature.

3. When chocolate is just about set, combine milk and pudding mix in 1 or 2-quart glass mix 'n pour bowl. Add butter.

4. MICROWAVE (high), uncovered, 1½ to 2 minutes or until mixture boils, stirring once. Stir in powdered sugar and maple flavoring; blend well. Spread over chocolate layer. spoon remaining chocolate with peanuts over top; spread to cover. Refrigerate until set, about 2 hours. Lift out of pan and peel off paper. Cut into squares. Store in refrigerator.

About 5 Dozen Squares

This crunchy caramel corn is sure to be a treat your family will enjoy.

CARAMEL CORN

　8　**cups unsalted popped corn**
½　**cup packed brown sugar**
¼　**cup butter or margarine**
　2　**tablespoons light corn syrup**
¼　**teaspoon salt**
⅛　**teaspoon soda**

1. Place popped corn in 2-quart glass mix 'n pour bowl; set aside.

2. Combine brown sugar, butter, corn syrup and salt in 4-cup glass measure.

3. MICROWAVE (high), uncovered, 1¼ to 1½ minutes or until mixture boils, stirring once. Stir and continue to MICROWAVE (high) 2½ minutes. Stir in soda.

4. Pour syrup evenly over popped corn; stir to lightly coat.

5. MICROWAVE (medium — 50%), uncovered, 6 to 7 minutes or until lightly toasted, stirring twice. Stir a few times while cooling; store in plastic bag.

8 Cups

TIPS • With Full Power in step 5, microwave 1½ to 2 minutes, stirring frequently.

• For a double recipe, increase first time in step 3 to 2½ to 3 minutes. Then boil 2½ minutes. Cook coated corn, half batch at a time, as directed in step 5.

• One-third cup popcorn in a microwave corn popper yields about 8 cups.

A delightful orange flavor is the secret of these toasted almonds.

SPICED NUTS

　1　**egg white**
¼　**teaspoon salt**
　1　**tablespoon orange juice**
⅔　**cup sugar**
　1　**tablespoon grated orange peel**
　1　**teaspoon cinnamon**
½　**teaspoon ginger**
½　**teaspoon allspice**
　3　**cups whole blanched almonds**

1. Beat egg white until foamy; add salt and orange juice. Gradually beat in sugar. Fold in orange peel, cinnamon, ginger, and allspice. Stir in almonds.

2. Pour mixture into 9-inch round baking dish.

3. MICROWAVE (high), uncovered, 9 to 10 minutes or until almonds are toasted, stirring 5 or 6 times. Spread out on waxed paper. When cool, break nuts apart. Store loosely covered.

About 3 Cups Nuts

Children of all ages will enjoy the crunchy popcorn and peanuts.

POPCORN BALLS

½　**cup packed brown sugar**
¼　**cup butter or margarine**
　2　**tablespoons honey**
¼　**teaspoon salt**
¼　**teaspoon soda**
　6　**cups unsalted popped corn**
⅔　**cup Spanish peanuts**

1. Combine brown sugar, butter, honey, and salt in 1-quart glass mix 'n pour bowl.

2. MICROWAVE (high), uncovered, 2 to 3 minutes or until mixture boils, stirring twice. Stir in soda.

3. Place popped corn in 2-quart glass mix 'n pour bowl. Add peanuts. Pour syrup over popped corn and peanuts. Stir to lightly coat.

4. MICROWAVE (medium — 50%), uncovered, 5 to 6 minutes or until lightly toasted, stirring 3 times. Allow to cool slightly. Spoon mounds of about ¾ cup each onto waxed paper. When cool enough to handle, form into balls with buttered hands. Cool. Wrap in plastic wrap and tie with ribbon.

About 10 Popcorn Balls

TIP • With Full Power, microwave in step 4 for 3½ to 4 minutes, stirring every minute.

The Microwave Times

Potpourri

Yogurt Making, page 151.

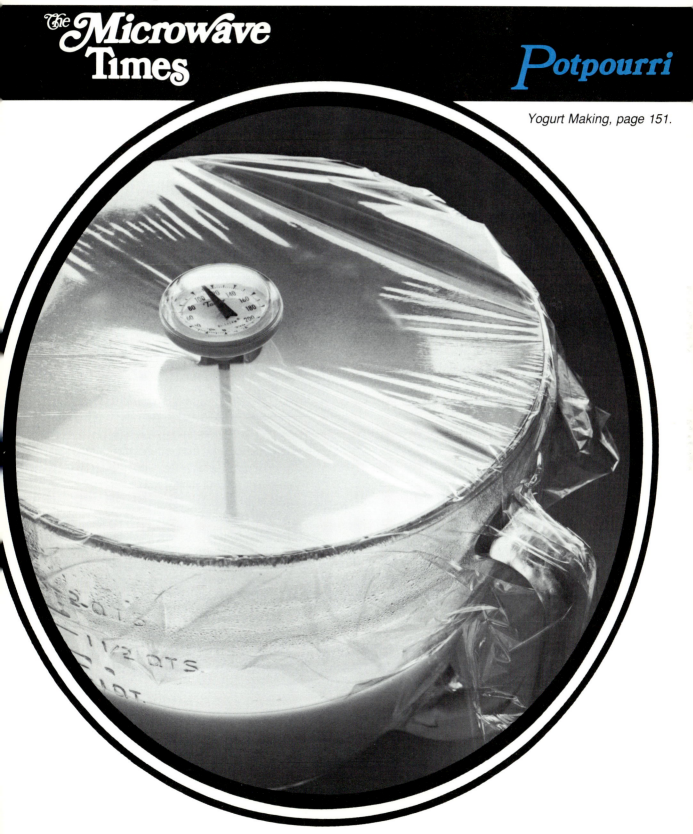

This is a good recipe when you must limit sugar and/or calories.

LOW SUGAR BERRY JAM

  1 **envelope unflavored gelatin**
  ¼ **cup water**
  1 **pint fresh strawberries, raspberries, blueberries or blackberries**
  ½ **cup artificial sweetener**

1. Combine gelatin and water in 1-quart glass mix 'n pour bowl. Let stand a few minutes to soften gelatin.

2. MICROWAVE (high), uncovered, 45 to 60 seconds or until boiling hot. Set aside.

3. Wash and hull berries. Process in blender at medium speed until smooth (should have 1½ cups purée). Stir berries and sweetener into gelatin mixture.

4. MICROWAVE (high), uncovered, 3 to 3½ minutes or until mixture is combined. Pour into containers. Store in freezer.

2 Cups (32 tablespoons)
Calories: 7/tablespoon

TIP • Sugar can be used in place of the artificial sweetener. The calories per tablespoon are still only about 18.

FRESH STRAWBERRY-RHUBARB FREEZER JAM

1½ **pints (3 cups) fresh strawberries**
 2 **cups sliced rhubarb**
 ½ **cup water**
 1 **package (1¾ oz.) powdered fruit pectin**
 5 **cups sugar**

1. Hull and wash strawberries; process in food processor or blender until puréed. Measure out 1½ cups; set aside.

2. Combine rhubarb, water and pectin in 2-quart glass mix 'n pour bowl; mix well.

3. MICROWAVE (high), uncovered, 5 to 6 minutes or until rhubarb is tender and pectin dissolved, stirring twice. Stir in sugar (mixture will become quite thick).

4. MICROWAVE (high,) uncovered, 3 to 4 minutes or until mixture boils, stirring once. Stir in crushed strawberries until well mixed.

Spoon into jars or freezer containers; cover. Let stand at room temperature about 24 hours. Label and store in freezer.

About 6 Cups

TIP • Unsweetened frozen rhubarb and/or strawberries can be substituted for fresh fruits. If rhubarb is frozen, cooking time will be 6 to 7 minutes in step 3. If strawberries are frozen, partially defrost puréed mixture before adding to hot jam.

Combine other fruit flavors with rhubarb for an interesting jam.

FRUIT COMBO JAM

 2 **cups sliced rhubarb**
 2 **cups (16 oz.) frozen unsweetened strawberries**
 1 **can (8¼ oz.) crushed pineapple, undrained**
 1 **package (1¾ oz.) powdered fruit pectin**
 4 **cups sugar**

1. Combine rhubarb, strawberries and pineapple in 2-quart glass mix 'n pour bowl.

2. MICROWAVE (high), uncovered, 9 to 10 minutes or until fruit is tender. Stir in pectin.

3. MICROWAVE (high), uncovered, 3 to 4 minutes or until mixture boils, stirring once. Stir in sugar.

4. MICROWAVE (high), uncovered, 3 to 4 minutes or until mixture boils hard for at least 1 minute, stirring once or twice. Let stand 5 minutes. Ladle into hot sterilized jars; seal.

About 5½ Cups Jam

TIPS • If using already sweetened strawberries, decrease sugar to 3½ cups.
• When fresh strawberries are available, use 2 cups (1 pint). If desired, crush before adding to other fruits.

Here is a colorful relish to serve with poultry.

CRANBERRY-ORANGE RELISH

 4 cups raw cranberries
 1 orange, quartered
1¼ cups sugar
 1 tablespoon lemon juice
 1 cup cold water
 1 package (3 oz.) raspberry-flavored
    gelatin
 ½ cup chopped walnuts, if desired

1. Grind or finely chop half of cranberries and orange in food grinder or processor. Place in food grinder or processor. Place in 2-quart glass mix 'n pour bowl; repeat with remaining fruit. Add sugar, lemon juice and water. Cover with plastic wrap.

2. MICROWAVE (high) 10 to 11 minutes or until mixture boils, stirring once. Stir in gelatin until dissolved. Stir in walnuts. Spoon into covered containers and store in refrigerator up to 2 months.

About 4 Cups

TIPS • For longer storage, place relish in freezer.
 • A blender can also be used to chop the fruits. Add half the water to the blender with each batch of fruit to help it easily pass through the blades.

Here is a special way to season almost any vegetables and other foods without the addition of salt.

NUTTY BUTTER

 ¼ cup unsalted butter or margarine
 ¼ cup coarsely chopped roasted
    unsalted peanuts
 1 teaspoon parsley flakes
 1 teaspoon grated lemon peel
 ⅛ teaspoon sage or ¼ teaspoon thyme
    leaves

1. MICROWAVE (high) butter in small glass dish ¼ to ½ minute or until softened.

2. Blend in peanuts, parsley, lemon peel and sage; beat until fluffy. Serve a rounded tablespoon of butter mixture with favorite frozen or fresh vegetables.

½ Cup
91 Calories/tablespoon
5 mg. Sodium 0 points

These cinnamon apple rings are the perfect garnish for turkey or prime rib. They are so delicious that you will want to pass them as a relish, also.

CANDIED APPLE RINGS

 2 cups water
 ½ cup cinnamon red hot candies
 ¼ cup sugar
 4 medium cooking apples

1. Combine water, candies and sugar in 2-quart glass mix 'n pour bowl.

2. MICROWAVE (high), uncovered, 8 to 9 minutes or until sugar and candies are dissolved, stirring 2 or 3 times.

3. Peel apples and remove core without cutting through apples. Slice apples into ¼-inch rings and add to sugar mixture.

4. MICROWAVE (high), uncovered, 4 to 5 minutes or until apples are almost tender, carefully stirring once. Remove from microwave. Let apples stand in hot syrup until cooled (about 2 to 3 hours); stir once, being careful not to break rings.

About 25 Rings

TIP • Apples such as Jonathan, McIntosh and Rome Beauty are suggested since they retain their shape after cooking.

This sauce has the flavor and consistency of Hollandaise, but is much easier to prepare. Serve over favorite vegetables, fish or poached eggs.

QUICK HOLLANDAISE SAUCE

 ½ cup mayonnaise
 1 egg
 1 tablespoon lemon juice
 ¼ teaspoon tarragon leaves
 ¼ teaspoon prepared mustard

1. Beat together mayonnaise and egg with fork in small glass dish. Mix in lemon juice, tarragon and mustard.

2. MICROWAVE (medium —50%), uncovered, 1¼ to 1¾ minutes or until slightly thickened, stirring twice. Serve warm.

About ¾ Cup Sauce

TIP • With Full Power, microwave 30 to 45 seconds, stirring every 10 seconds.

An overabundance of zucchini can be transformed into pickles that will be enjoyed throughout the year.

ZUCCHINI BREAD AND BUTTER PICKLES

8   cups sliced, unpeeled zuchini (¼-inch thick)
2   cups sliced onion
3   tablespoons salt
6   cups water
1   green pepper, seeded and sliced
1¼ cups sugar
1½ cups cider vinegar
1   teaspoon mustard seed
½   teaspoon celery seed
¼   teaspoon tumeric

1. Combine zucchini, onion, salt and water in large container; mix lightly. Let stand 3 hours. Drain.

2. Transfer zucchini and onion to 2-quart glass mix 'n pour bowl. Add green pepper and remaining ingredients; mix lightly.

3. MICROWAVE (high), uncovered, 25 to 30 minutes or until onions are translucent, stirring every 10 minutes. Spoon zucchini mixture into clean pint jars. Fill with liquid to within ½ inch of top of jar. Top with sealable lids. Process in boiling water 10 minutes. Remove from water; cool. Store in dark place.

About 4 Pints

TIPS • Cucumbers can be substituted for zucchini.
  • If desired, a few drops green food coloring can be added to pickles before filling jars.

This recipe preserves colorful summer vegetables for enjoyment all winter.

ZUCCHINI-CORN RELISH

8   to 10 ears corn
¼   cup water
6   cups chopped, unpeeled zucchini
1   cup chopped onion
1   large green pepper, chopped
1½ cups sugar
1¾ cups white vinegar
1   cup water
1   tablespoon salt
1   tablespoon mustard seed
1   teaspoon celery seed

1. Remove husks and silk from corn. Wash and trim ears. Place in 3-quart glass casserole. Add ¼ cup water. Cover with plastic wrap.

2. MICROWAVE (high) 9 to 10 minutes or until corn is set. Cool in cold water; drain. Cut corn from cob into 3-quart casserole to make 3 cups. Add remaining ingredients; mix well.

3. MICROWAVE (high), uncovered, 25 to 30 minutes or until vegetables are tender-crisp, stirring twice. Spoon corn mixture into clean pint jars. Fill with liquid to within ½ inch of top of jar. Top with sealable lids. Process in boiling water 10 minutes. Remove from water; cool. Store in dark place.

About 6 Pints

A half of pumpkin can be cooked easily in the microwave.

FRESH PUMPKIN

1. Cut a medium-sized pumpkin (about 28 inches around) in half vertically. Scoop out seeds and membranes. Place one half cut-side-down in 12 x 8-inch glass baking dish.

2. MICROWAVE (high), uncovered, 18 to 22 minutes or until tender, rotating dish once or twice. Repeat cooking for other half. Cool until easy to handle. Scoop out pulp and place in blender or food processor container. Process on medium speed until smooth. Spoon into freezer containers and freeze until ready to use.

This yogurt recipe combines dry milk, and fresh milk for a creamy yogurt. Other favorite milk combinations can be used with the same method.

YOGURT

1½ cups non-fat dry milk crystals
    Water
 1 **cup whole or 2% milk**
 1 **can (5.3 fl. oz.) evaporated milk**
    (⅔ cup)
⅓ **cup plain yogurt**

1. Combine dry milk crystals and enough water in 2-quart glass mixing bowl to make 2 cups of milk. Add whole milk.

2. MICROWAVE (high), uncovered 6 to 8 minutes or until steaming hot (190°). Stir in evaporated milk. Cool mixture to 115°.

3. Blend a small amount of cooled mixture into yogurt, mixing until smooth. Return mixture to milk and stir until well blended. Cover with plastic wrap. Insert thermometer or probe through plastic so it rests in center of milk mixture. Place in microwave oven.

4. MICROWAVE (low — 30%) 1½ to 2 minutes or until 115° is reached. Turn off oven and allow mixture to set undisturbed inside microwave oven. Periodically check temperature and when it goes below 110°, again microwave on low power 1½ to 2 minutes or until it reaches 115°. (Usually it will hold temperature for about 1 to 1½ hours.) Allow mixture to stand at this 110° to 115° temperature for about 3 hours or until set. Transfer to refrigerator and chill thoroughly. If desired, stir yogurt and store in smaller containers.

About 4 Cups

TIPS • Medium — 50% power or full power can be used in step 4. With medium power, microwave 1 to 1½ minutes; with full power, microwave ¾ to 1 minute or until temperature is reached.

• When using the probe, check the temperature about every hour and microwave until the 115° temperature is reached. If possible, use the low power setting.

FRESH FRUIT YOGURT

Mix ¼ to ½ cup finely chopped or crushed fruit with each 1 cup yogurt. If desired, sweeten with ½ to 1 tablespoon sugar.

HONEY YOGURT

Mix ½ to 1 tablespoon honey with each 1 cup yogurt. If desired, sprinkle with cinnamon or nutmeg.

FRUIT JAM YOGURT

Mix 1 to 2 tablespoons favorite jam with each 1 cup yogurt.

YOGURT SLICES

Spoon sweetened yogurt (with or without fruit) into small paper drink cups. Insert a wooden stick or plastic spoon into each. Freeze until firm, 2 to 3 hours. Peel off paper when ready to serve.

YOGURT MAKING TIPS:

• A small amount of plain yogurt is required each time as a starter. The first time, purchase a plain yogurt (without additives). For future batches, you can use some from your last homemade batch. After about 5 batches, it is good to again start with commercial yogurt.

• The thickness and tartness depends upon the incubation time. Three hours give a medium-thick, creamy, mild-flavored product. For a thicker product with more tartness increase the incubation time.

• Retain a temperature between 110° and 115°. Lower temperatures mean longer incubation time; higher temperatures cause separating, curdling and can destroy the yogurt bacteria.

• Use of a thermometer or probe is essential to maintain the proper temperature.

• To assure the proper setting and a creamy consistency, do not stir or manipulate the milk mixture during the incubation or chilling period.

• Once the yogurt is the right consistency, refrigerate immediately to quickly chill. After chilling and stirring, the consistency will be slightly softer.

• Yogurt keeps in the refrigerator for 10 days to 2 weeks. The longer the storage the more tart the flavor.

• Yogurt has many uses. Try it in recipes and/or use as a substitute for sour cream; serve with fruit or granola as a snack or dessert; use as a substitute for buttermilk by diluting with equal amounts of water; give to babies as a pudding substitute.

A

A-Lot-Like Lasagna 49

Acorn Squash:
Cheese 'N Apple Acorns 90
Sausage-Stuffed Acorns 90
Almond Float 106

Appetizers:
Chicken Nuggets 7
Fondue Mexicana 8
Liver Paté 6
Oriental Fondue 9
Pizza Fondue 8
Pizza Snacks 10
Potato Nachos 7
Seafood Fondue 9
Spinach Herb Balls 6
Steak Kabobs 6
Stuffed Celery 8
Tortilla Chip Fiesta 7

Apples:
Apple Dessert Wedges 131
Apple Jonathan 106
Apple Kuchen 98
Apple-Nut Torte 108
Candied Apple Rings 149
Cheese 'N Apple Acorns 90
Cinnamon-Apple Bread 97
Cran-Apple Crisp 108
Crumb-Topped Baked
Apples 107
Honey-Glazed Apple
Slices 107
Pork Chops and Apples 32
Simple Apple Dessert 107
Sour Cream-Apple Pie 122
Applesauce Bars 135
Apricot-Date Balls 144
Apricot-Pecan Bars 136

Asparagus:
Asparagus-Topped Pacific
Salmon 15
Sunny Vegetable Combo 80

Avocados:
Chicken-Avocado
Sandwiches 68
Chilled Avocado-Chicken
Soup 74
Shrimp-Avocado
Sandwiches 64

B

Bacon 'N Vegies 82
Baked Apples, Crumb-
Topped 107
Baked Potatoes with Beef
Burgundy Sauce 38

Banana:
Banana-Nut Bread 96
Bananas Foster 111
Choco Banana on a Stick 111
Fruity Tutty Bundt Cake 127

Barbecue:
Barbecued Capon 13
Beef Shish Kabobs 26
Country Barbecued Ribs 35
Marinated Shish Kabobs 36
Micro-Barbecued Turkey 14
Mint-Glazed Leg of Lamb 36
Teriyaki Cornish Hens 14
Zesty Barbecued Chicken 12
Barbecued Beef 30
Barbecued Beef Ribs 29
Barbecued Mini-Loaves 25
Barbecued Wieners 29

Bars:
Applesauce Bars 135
Apricot-Pecan Bars 136
Caramel Thins 141
Choco-Caramel Bars 137
Crispy Fudge Layer Bars 139
Granola Bars 138
Mint Brownies 136
No-Bake Special Bars 138
Raisin Cream Bars 139
Toffee Bars 143
Yummy Graham Bars 138
Bavarian Meatballs and
Noodles 42

Beans:
Bean and Corn Salad 78
Bean and Ham Soup 70
Bean Casserole 52
Corn and Bean Duo 83
Hearty Baked Beans 92
Saucy Triple Bean Bake 52
Spanish Lentils 91

Beef:
A-Lot-Like Lasagna 49
Baked Potatoes with Beef
Burgundy Sauce 38
Barbecued Beef 30
Barbecued Beef Ribs 29

Beef (continued)
Barbecued Mini-Loaves 25
Bavarian Meatballs and
Noodles 42
Beef & Pork Meat Loaf 22
Beef and Potato
Casserole 45
Beef Rolls 22
Beef Rouladen 32
Beef Shish Kabobs 26
Beef Stroganoff 27
Cabbage Casserole 45
Cheese-Filled Meatballs 25
Corned Beef and Cabbage 31
Dried Beef Casserole 61
Easy Beef and Roni
Hot Dish 44
Eggplant Bake 43
Enchilada Casserole 50
Fettuccini Pie 46
Individual Meat and Tator
Casseroles 45
Italian Meat Loaf 22
Lasagna Rolls 48
Lazy Day Lasagna 48
Liver with Stroganoff Sauce 30
Marinated Flank Steak 29
Meat Loaf Dinner 23
Meatball Stew 42
Mexicali Hot Dish 51
Mexican Layer Casserole 50
Mexican Tossed Salad 78
Oven Stroganoff 28
Reuben Pie 24
Saucy Beef Strips 28
Saucy Triple Bean Bake 52
Sauerkraut Balls 24
Spaghetti with Spicy Round
Steak Sauce 38
Steak Kabobs 6
Stuffed Cabbage Rolls 44
Stuffed Flank Steak 28
Taco Bells 26
Tamale Pie 47
Zucchini-Beef Combo 51
Zucchini Meatballs in
Sour Cream Sauce 24
Beer Cheese Soup 75
Beer Muffins 95
Berries: (Also see individual berries)
Berry-Melon Gelatin Salad 75
Fresh Berry Soup 75
Glorified Rice 104
Low-Sugar Berry Jam 148

Beverages:
Fruit Slush ... 10
Old-Fashioned Glogg ... 10
BLT-Cheese Sandwiches ... 64
Blueberry Coffee Cake ... 98
Blueberry Muffins ... 95
Bon Bons, Mixed Up ... 140
Bouillabaisse ... 20
Bread and Butter Pickles,
Zucchini ... 150
Breads:
Apple Kuchen ... 98
Banana-Nut Bread ... 96
Beer Muffins ... 95
Blueberry Coffee Cake ... 98
Blueberry Muffins ... 95
Cheesy French Bread ... 102
Cherry Bread Pudding ... 105
Cinnamon-Apple Bread ... 97
Corn Muffins ... 94
Frozen Bread Dough ... 101
Luncheon Puffs ... 56
Oatmeal Batter Bread or
Rolls ... 100
Quick Caramel Rolls ... 101
Rye Bread ... 102
Versatile Store and Bake
Muffins ... 94
Whole Wheat-Pumpkin
Bread ... 96
Zucchini Spice Muffins ... 95
Brittle, Sunflower ... 140
Broccoli:
Broccoli and Chicken ... 58
Broccoli-Chicken Salad
Puffs ... 56
Broccoli in Sour Cream
Sauce ... 80
Charlie's Super Supper ... 54
Cheesy Broccoli Soup ... 74
Cheesy Vegetable Bake ... 82
Creamy Broccoli Soup ... 73
Ham 'N Turkey Roll-Ups ... 58
Herb-Butter Broccoli ... 80
Mini Vegetable Plate ... 81
Turkey and Broccoli
Casserole ... 59
Brownies, Mint ... 136
Brussels Sprouts with
Seasoned Butter ... 80
Bulgur:
Colorful Cracked Wheat
Salad ... 78
Butter:
Honey-Almond Butter ... 94
Nutty Butter ... 149

C

Cabbage:
Cabbage Casserole ... 45
Corned Beef and
Cabbage ... 31
Pennsylvania Dutch
Cabbage ... 81
Stuffed Cabbage Rolls ... 44

Cakes:
Apple Dessert Wedges ... 131
Capuccino Cake ... 128
Carrot Cake ... 133
Chocolate Cake ... 130
Creme de Menthe Cake ... 126
Delightful Carrot Roll ... 115
Fruity Tutty Bundt Cake ... 127
Self-Frosted German
Chocolate Cake ... 129
Sherry-Pecan Bundt Cake ... 133
Strawberries and Cream
Cake ... 132
Strawberry Ribbon Cake ... 112
Ugly Duckling Cake ... 131
Vanilla Wafer Cake ... 126
Zucchini Chocolate Cake ... 130
Candied Apple Rings ... 149
Candied Fruit Peel ... 144

Candies:
Caramel Corn ... 146
Caramel Thins ... 141
Cherry Mash Candy ... 143
Chewy Chocolate Candy ... 143
Goodie Nut Bars ... 145
Mackinac Island Vanilla
Fudge ... 142
Mixed Up Bon Bons ... 140
Pecan Dandy ... 142
Popcorn Balls ... 146
Quick Fudge ... 140
Snowflake-Mint Drops ... 140
Spiced Nuts ... 146
Sunflower Brittle ... 140
Toffee Bars ... 143
Yogurt-Covered Raisins ... 144
Capon, Barbecued ... 13
Cappuccino Cake ... 128
Caramel Corn ... 146
Caramel-Fudge Sundae
Dessert ... 117
Caramel Rolls, Quick ... 101
Caramel Sauce ... 131
Caramel Thins ... 141
Caramel Upside-Down
Muffins ... 94

Carrots:
Carrot Cake ... 133
Delightful Carrot Roll ... 115
Sherried Carrots ... 81

Casseroles: (See also Main Dishes)
A-Lot-Like Lasagna ... 49
Bean Cassserole ... 52
Beef and Potato
Casserole ... 45
Cabbage Casserole ... 45
Celery Casserole ... 83
Chicken Cantonese
Casserole ... 57
Creamy Tuna and
Noodles ... 54
Dried Beef Casserole ... 61

Casseroles (continued)
Easy Beef and Roni Hot
Dish ... 44
Easy Noodle Bake ... 62
Eggplant Bake ... 43
Enchilada Casserole ... 50
Fettuccini ... 62
Fettuccini Pie ... 46
Frank 'N Bean Biscuit
Bake ... 41
Great Plains Wild Rice ... 62
Ham and Wild Rice ... 40
Hearty Baked Beans ... 92
Individual Meat and Tator
Casserole ... 45
Lasagna Rolls ... 48
Lazy Day Lasagna ... 48
Mexicali Hot Dish ... 51
Mexican Layer Casserole ... 50
Oriental Sprouts 'N Broccoli
Hot Dish ... 39
Pizza-Ghetti Casserole ... 47
Potato Casserole ... 86
Sausage-Rice Oriental ... 39
Seafood Combo ... 53
Seafood Stuffing
Casserole ... 53
Sweet Potato Bake ... 88
Tamale Pie ... 47
Wild Rice Pilaf ... 61
Zucchini-Beef Combo ... 51

Cauliflower:
Cauliflower in Cheese
Sauce ... 82
Cheesy Vegetable Bake ... 82
Italian-Style Cauliflower ... 83
Mini Vegetable Plate ... 81
Velvety Cauliflower-Cheese
Soup ... 73
Celery Casserole ... 83
Celery, Stuffed ... 8
Charlie's Super Supper ... 54
Cheddar Chili Hot Dogs ... 66

Cheese:
Beer Cheese Soup ... 75
BLT-Cheese Sandwiches ... 64
Cauliflower in Cheese
Sauce ... 82
Cheese-Filled Meatballs ... 25
Cheese 'N Apple Acorns ... 90
Cheese Soup ... 74
Mostaccioli and Cheese
Supreme ... 60
Velvety Cauliflower-Cheese
Soup ... 73
Cheesecake Fondue ... 120
Cheesecake, Cherry
Chocolate ... 112
Cheesy Broccoli Soup ... 74
Cheesy French Bread ... 102
Cheesy Micro-Fries ... 87
Cheesy Pears ... 110
Cheesy Vegetable Bake ... 82

Cherry:
Cherry Bread Pudding 105
Cherry Chocolate
  Cheesecake 112
Cherry Mash Candy 143
Chocolate Cherry Tarts 116
Quick Cherry Dessert 105
Chewy Chocolate Candy 143
Chicken:
Broccoli and Chicken 58
Broccoli-Chicken Salad
  Puffs 56
Chicken Almond Ding 57
Chicken and Cantonese
  Vegetables 12
Chicken and Pasta 55
Chicken-Avocado
  Sandwiches 68
Chicken Cantonese
  Casserole 57
Chicken in Creamy Wine
  Sauce 12
Chicken Nuggets 7
Chicken Tacos for Two 65
Chicken with Dumplings 13
Chilled Avocado-Chicken
  Soup 74
Crispy Seasoned Chicken 13
Fruited Chicken Salad 76
Guacomole-Chicken over
  Noodles 55
Liver Paté 6
Zesty Barbecued Chicken 12
Choco Banana on a Stick 111
Choco-Caramel Bars 137
Chocolate:
Capuccino Cake 128
Cherry Chocolate
  Cheesecake 112
Cherry Mash Candy 143
Chewy Chocolate Candy 143
Chocolate Brickle Fondue 119
Chocolate Cake 130
Chocolate Cherry Tarts 116
Chocolate Frosting 129
Goodie Nut Bars 145
Self-Frosted German Chocolate
  Cake 129
Strawberry-Chocolate Pie 121
Zucchini Chocolate Cake 130
Chowders:
New England Clam
  Chowder 71
Tuna-Vegetable Chowder 71
Cinnamon-Apple Bread 97
Cinnamon-Coated Muffins 94
Citrus Pie, Refreshing 123
Clam Chowder, New
  England 71
Coconut Cream Pie 124
Coconut Crunch Pears 109
Coffee Butter Frosting 129

Coffee Cakes:
Apple Kuchen 98
Blueberry Coffee Cake 98
Colorful Cracked Wheat
  Salad 78
Colorful Stuffed Baked
  Potatoes 88
Compote, Hot Fruit 105

Cookies:
Applesauce Bars 135
Apricot-Date Balls 144
Apricot-Pecan Bars 136
Choco-Caramel Bars 137
Crispy Fudge Layer Bars 139
Date Nut Cookies 135
Granola Bars 138
Ice Cream Sandwiches 118
Miniature Macaroon Tarts 134
Mint Brownies 136
No-Bake Special Bars 138
Oatmeal-Raisin Cookies 134
Raisin Cream Bars 139
Yummy Graham Bars 138

Corn:
Bean and Corn Salad 78
Corn and Bean Duo 83
Scalloped Corn and
  Oysters 54
Zucchini-Corn Relish 150
Corn Muffins 94

Corned Beef:
Corned Beef and Cabbage 31
Corned Beef Hash 'N Eggs 66
Tortilla Roll-Ups 65
Cornish Hens, Teriyaki 14
Country Barbecued Ribs 35

Crabmeat:
Crab Quiche 63
Seafood Combo 53
Seafood Stuffing
  Casserole 53
Cran-Apple Crisp 108
Cranberry-Orange Relish 149

Cream Puffs:
Luncheon Puffs 56
Cream Sauce, Fresh
  Peas in 84
Creamy Broccoli Soup 73
Creamy Tuna and Noodles 54
Creamy Yogurt Potatoes 85
Creme de Menthe Cake 126
Crispy Fudge Layer Bars 139
Crispy Seasoned Chicken 13
Crumb-Topped Baked
  Apples 107
Crumb-Topped Onion Slices 84
Custard Pudding 104

D

Date Balls, Apricot 144
Date Nut Cookies 135
Delightful Carrot Roll 115
Desserts:
Almond Float 106
Apple Dessert Wedges 131
Apple Jonathan 106
Apple Kuchen 98
Apple-Nut Torte 108
Bananas Foster 111
Caramel-Fudge Sundae
  Dessert 117
Cheesecake Fondue 120
Cheesy Pears 110
Cherry Bread Pudding 105
Cherry Chocolate
  Cheesecake 112
Choco Banana on a Stick 111
Chocolate-Brickle Fondue 119
Chocolate Cherry Tarts 116
Coconut Crunch Pears 109
Cran-Apple Crisp 108
Crumb-Topped Baked
  Apples 107
Custard Pudding 104
Delightful Carrot Roll 115
Fresh Berry Soup 75
Fresh Pineapple Topping 109
Frozen Yogurt 119
Glorified Rice 104
Granola Ice Cream Pie 119
Honey-Glazed Apple
  Slices 107
Hot Fruit Compote 105
Ice Cream Sandwiches 118
Instant Rice Pudding 104
Pineapple Cream Pudding 104
Pink Squirrel Soufflé 114
Quick Cherry Dessert 105
Raspberry Delight 114
Rhubarb Creme 117
Simple Apple Dessert 107
Strawberries and Cream
  Cake 132
Strawberry Cream
  Dessert 113
Strawberry Creme Melon 110
Strawberry Crunch 113
Strawberry Ribbon Cake 112
Sunshine Sorbet 118
Tangy Rhubarb Sauce 111
Ugly Duckling Cake 131
Dried Beef Casserole 61
Dumplings, Chicken with 13

E

Easy Beef and Roni
  Hot Dish 44
Easy Noodle Bake 62

Eggplant Bake 43
Eggs:
Corned Beef Hash
'N Eggs 66
Crab Quiche 63
Fix-Ahead Scrambled
Eggs 63
Enchilada Casserole 50

F

Far East Vegetable Combo 84
Fast 'N Easy Salad 77
Fettuccini 62
Fettuccini Pie 46
Fish:
Asparagus-Topped Pacific
Salmon 15
Bouillabaisse 20
Fish Divine 19
Individual Salmon Loaves 16
No-Hassle Baked Fish 18
Oriental Scampi 18
Salmon Loaf Florentine 17
Sole Florentine 18
Stuffed Mountain Trout 16
Fix-Ahead Scrambled Eggs 63
Flank Steak:
Marinated Flank Steak 29
Stuffed Flank Steak 28
Florentine:
Salmon Loaf Florentine 17
Sole Florentine 18
Spaghetti Florentine 60
Fondues:
Cheesecake Fondue 120
Chocolate-Brickle Fondue 119
Fondue Mexicana 8
Oriental Fondue 9
Pizza Fondue 8
Seafood Fondue 9
Frank 'N Bean Biscuit Bake 41
French Bread, Cheesy 102
Fresh Berry Soup 75
Fresh Mushroom Soup 73
Fresh Peas in Cream Sauce 84
Fresh Pineapple Topping 109
Fresh Pumpkin 150
Fresh Strawberry-Rhubarb Freezer
Jam 148
Fries, Cheesy Micro 87
Frosted Fruit Salad 75
Frostings:
Chocolate Frosting 129
Coffee Butter Frosting 129
White Mountain Frosting 131
Frozen Bread Dough 101
Frozen Yogurt 119
Fruits: (Also see individual fruits)
Almond Float 106
Candied Fruit Peel 144

Fruits (continued)
Frosted Fruit Salad 75
Fruit Combo Jam 148
Fruit Slush 10
Hot Fruit Compote 105
Sunshine Sorbet 118
Fruited Chicken Salad 76
Fruity Tutty Bundt Cake 127
Fudge:
Caramel-Fudge Sundae
Dessert 117
Crispy Fudge Layer Bars 139
Fudge Sauce 120
Mackinac Island Vanilla
Fudge 142
Quick Fudge 140

G

Gazpacho 70
Gelatin:
Almond Float 106
Berry-Melon Gelatin Salad 75
Glorified Rice 104
Key Lime Chiffon Pie 122
Pink Squirrel Soufflé 114
Raspberry Delight 114
Rhubarb Creme 117
Strawberry Cream
Dessert 113
Strawberry Crunch 113
Glogg, Old-Fashioned 10
Glorified Rice 104
Goodie Nut Bars 145
Graham Bars, Yummy 138
Granola Bars 138
Granola Ice Cream Pie 119
Great Plains Wild Rice 62
Ground Beef:
A-Lot-Like Lasagna 49
Barbecued Mini-Loaves 25
Bavarian Meatballs and
Noodles 42
Beef & Pork Meat Loaf 22
Beef and Potato
Casserole 45
Beef Rolls 22
Cabbage Casserole 45
Cheese-Filled Meatballs 25
Easy Beef and Roni Hot
Dish 44
Eggplant Bake 43
Enchilada Casserole 50
Fettuccini Pie 46
Individual Meat and Tator
Casseroles 45
Italian Meat Loaf 22
Lasagna Rolls 48
Lazy Day Lasagna 48
Meat Loaf Dinner 23
Meatball Stew 42

Ground Beef (continued)
Mexicali Hot Dish 51
Mexican Layer Casserole 50
Mexican Tossed Salad 78
Saucy Triple Bean Bake 52
Sauerkraut Balls 24
Sausage-Stuffed Green
Peppers 27
Stuffed Cabbage Rolls 44
Taco Bells 26
Tamale Pie 47
Zucchini-Beef Combo 51
Zucchini Meatballs in
Sour Cream Sauce 24
Guacamole-Chicken over
Noodles 55
Gumbo, Louisiana 20

H

Ham:
Bean and Ham Soup 70
Ham and Wild Rice 40
Ham 'N Turkey Roll-Ups 58
Hearty Baked Beans 92
Hamburger (see Ground Beef)
Hash 'N Eggs, Corned Beef 66
Hearty Baked Beans 92
Herb-Butter Broccoli 80
Hollandaise Sauce, Quick 149
Honey-Almond Butter 94
Honey-Glazed Apple Slices 107
Hong Kong Chops 34
Hors d'Oeuvres (see Appetizers)
Hot Fruit Compote 105
Hot Tuna Sandwiches 65

I

Ice Cream:
Caramel-Fudge Sundae
Dessert 117
Frozen Yogurt 119
Granola Ice Cream Pie 119
Ice Cream Sandwiches 118
Individual Meat and Tator
Casseroles 45
Individual Salmon Loaves 16
Instant Rice Pudding 104
Italian Hot Dogs 41
Italian Meat Loaf 22
Italian-Style Cauliflower 83

J

Jam-Topped Muffins 94
Jams:
Fresh Strawberry-Rhubarb
Freezer Jam 148
Fruit Combo Jam 148
Low-Sugar Berry Jam 148
Jonathan, Apple 106

K

Kabobs:
Beef Shish Kabobs 26
Marinated Shish Kabobs 36
Steak Kabobs 6
Key Lime Chiffon Pie 122

L

Lamb:
Marinated Shish Kabobs 36
Mint-Glazed Leg of Lamb 36
Lasagna:
A-Lot-Like Lasagna 49
Lasagna Rolls 48
Lazy Day Lasagna 48
Lemon-Butter Potatoes 87
Lentils, Spanish 91
Lime Chiffon Pie, Key 122
Liver Paté 6
Liver with Stroganoff Sauce 30
Louisiana Gumbo 20
Low Calorie:
Cabbage Casserole 45
Low-Sugar Berry Jam 148
Marinated Flank Steak 29
Reuben Pie 24
Sauerkraut Balls 24
Low Cholesterol:
Carrot Cake 133
Chicken Almond Ding 57
Low Sodium:
Beer Cheese Soup 75
Gazpacho 70
Spaghetti Squash Pasta 89
Low-Sugar Berry Jam 148
Luncheon Puffs 56

M

Macaroni:
Dried Beef Casserole 61
Easy Beef and Roni Hot
Dish 44
Mostaccioli and Cheese
Supreme 60
Macaroon Tarts, Miniature 134
Mackinac Island Vanilla
Fudge 142
Main Dishes: (Also see Casseroles)
Baked Potatoes with Beef
Burgundy Sauce 38
Bavarian Meatballs and
Noodles 42
Bouillabaisse 20
Broccoli and Chicken 58
Broccoli-Chicken Salad
Puffs 56
Charlie's Super Supper 54
Chicken Almond Ding 57

Main Dishes (continued)
Chicken and Cantonese
Vegetables 12
Chicken and Pasta 55
Chicken with Dumplings 13
Crab Quiche 63
Fix-Ahead Scrambled
Eggs 63
Guacamole-Chicken over
Noodles 55
Ham 'N Turkey Roll-Ups 58
Italian Hot Dogs 41
Louisiana Gumbo 20
Meat Loaf Dinner 23
Meatball Stew 42
Mostaccioli and Cheese
Supreme 60
Oriental Scampi 18
Pork Chops and Dressing 34
Pork Chops and Rice 33
Pork Stroganoff with
Stuffing Balls 35
Pork Tenderloin Platter 33
Scalloped Corn and
Oysters 54
Sherried Turkey
Casserole 59
Spaghetti Florentine 60
Spaghetti with Spicy Round
Steak Sauce 38
Stuffed Cabbage Rolls 44
Sweet-Sour Links
over Rice 40
Turkey and Broccoli
Casserole 59
Manicotti:
Italian Hot Dogs 41
Marinated Flank Steak 29
Marinated Garden Salad 77
Marinated Shish Kabobs 36
Meat Loaf:
Barbecued Mini Loaves 25
Beef & Pork Meat Loaf 22
Beef and Potato
Casserole 45
Individual Meat and Tator
Casseroles 45
Italian Meat Loaf 22
Meat Loaf Dinner 23
Reuben Pie 24
Meatballs:
Bavarian Meatballs and
Noodles 42
Cheese-Filled Meatballs 25
Meatball Stew 42
Sauerkraut Balls 24
Zucchini Meatballs in
Sour Cream Sauce 24
Meatless Pocket
Sandwiches 68
Melon:
Berry-Melon Gelatin Salad 75
Strawberry Creme Melon 110

Mexican:
Enchilada Casserole 50
Fondue Mexicana 8
Mexicali Hot Dish 51
Mexican Layer Casserole 50
Mexican Tossed Salad 78
Tortilla Chip Fiesta 7
Micro-Barbecued Turkey 14
Mini Vegetable Plate 81
Miniature Macaroon Tarts 134
Mint Brownies 136
Mint Drops, Snowflake 140
Mint-Glazed Leg of Lamb 36
Mixed Up Bon Bons 140
Mostaccioli and Cheese
Supreme 60

Muffins:
Beer Muffins 95
Blueberry Muffins 95
Caramel Upside-Down
Muffins 94
Cinnamon-Coated Muffins 94
Corn Muffins 94
Jam-Topped Muffins 94
Streusel Muffins 94
Versatile Store and
Bake Muffins 94
Zucchini Spice Muffins 95
Mushroom Soup, Fresh 73

N

New England Clam
Chowder 71
No-Bake Special Bars 138
No-Hassle Baked Fish 18
Noodles:
Bavarian Meatballs and
Noodles 42
Chicken and Pasta 55
Creamy Tuna and
Noodles 54
Easy Noodle Bake 62
Fettuccini 62
Fettuccini Pie 46
Guacamole-Chicken over
Noodles 55
Nuts, Spiced 146
Nutty Butter 149

O

Oatmeal Batter Bread or
Rolls 100
Oatmeal-Raisin Cookies 134
Old-Fashioned Glogg 10
Onion Slices, Crumb-
Topped 84
Onion Soup Potatoes 85
Orange Relish, Cranberry 149

Oriental:
Almond Float 106
Chicken Almond Ding 57
Chicken and Cantonese
  Vegetables 12
Chicken Cantonese
  Casserole 57
Far East Vegetable
  Combo 84
Hong Kong Chops 34
Oriental Fondue 9
Oriental Scampi 18
Oriental Sprouts 'N Broccoli
  Hot Dish 39
Sausage-Rice Oriental 39
Other Potatoes 87
Oven Stroganoff 28
Oysters:
Louisiana Gumbo 20
Oyster Stew 71
Scalloped Corn and
  Oysters 54

P

Paris Potatoes 87
Paté, Liver 6
Pea Pods:
Far East Vegetable
  Combo 84
Sunny Vegetable Combo 80
Pears:
Cheesy Pears 110
Coconut Crunch Pears 109
Peas in Cream Sauce,
  Fresh 84
Pecan Dandy 142
Peel, Candied Fruit 144
Pennsylvania Dutch
  Cabbage 81
Peppers:
Sausage-Stuffed Green
  Peppers 27
Taco Bells 26
Pickles:
Zucchini Bread and
  Butter Pickles 150
Pies:
Coconut Cream Pie 124
Granola Ice Cream Pie 119
Key Lime Chiffon Pie 122
Raisin-Yogurt Pie 124
Refreshing Citrus Pie 123
Rhubarb Cream Pie 121
Sour Cream-Apple Pie 122
Strawberry-Chocolate Pie 121
Pilaf, Wild Rice 61
Pineapple:
Fresh Pineapple Topping 109
Pineapple Cream Pudding 104
Pink Squirrel Soufflé 114
Pizza Fondue 8

Pizza-Ghetti Casserole 47
Pizza Snacks 10
Pizza, Zucchini 67
Popcorn:
Caramel Corn 146
Popcorn Balls 146
Pork: (Also see Ham and Sausage)
Beef & Pork Meat Loaf 22
Country Barbecued Ribs 35
Hong Kong Chops 34
Oriental Sprouts 'N Broccoli
  Hot Dish 39
Pork Chops and Apples 32
Pork Chops and Dressing 34
Pork Chops and Rice 33
Pork Stroganoff with
  Stuffing Balls 35
Pork Tenderloin Platter 33
Potatoes:
Baked Potatoes with Beef
  Burgundy Sauce 38
Cheesy Micro-Fries 87
Colorful Stuffed Baked
  Potatoes 88
Creamy Yogurt Potatoes 85
Lemon-Butter Potatoes 87
Onion Soup Potatoes 85
Other Potatoes 87
Paris Potatoes 87
Potato Casserole 86
Potato Nachos 7
Potatoes Romanoff 88
Twice Baked Potatoes 85
Zippy Buttered Potatoes 88
Poultry:
Barbecued Capon 13
Broccoli and Chicken 58
Broccoli-Chicken Salad
  Puffs 56
Chicken Almond Ding 57
Chicken and Cantonese
  Vegetables 12
Chicken and Pasta 55
Chicken-Avocado
  Sandwiches 68
Chicken Cantonese
  Casserole 57
Chicken in Creamy Wine
  Sauce 12
Chicken Nuggets 7
Chicken with Dumplings 13
Crispy Seasoned Chicken 13
Fruited Chicken Salad 76
Guacamole-Chicken over
  Noodles 55
Ham 'N Turkey Roll-Ups 58
Micro-Barbecued Turkey 14
Sherried Turkey
  Casserole 59
Teriyaki Cornish Hens 14
Turkey and Broccoli
  Casserole 59
Zesty Barbecued Chicken 12

Puddings:
Cherry Bread Pudding 105
Custard Pudding 104
Instant Rice Pudding 104
Pineapple Cream Pudding 104
Pumpkin:
Fresh Pumpkin 150
Whole Wheat-Pumpkin
  Bread 96

Q

Quiche, Crab 63
Quick Caramel Rolls 101
Quick Cherry Dessert 105
Quick Fudge 140
Quick Hollandaise Sauce 149
Quick Orange Sweet
  Potatoes 89

R

Raisin Cream Bars 139
Raisin-Yogurt Pie 124
Raisins, Yogurt-Covered 144
Raspberry Delight 114
Refreshing Citrus Pie 123
Relishes:
Cranberry-Orange Relish 149
Zucchini-Corn Relish 150
Reuben Pie 24
Rhubarb:
Fresh Strawberry-Rhubarb
  Jam 148
Fruit Combo Jam 148
Tangy Rhubarb Sauce 111
Rhubarb Cream Pie 121
Rhubarb Creme 117
Ribs:
Barbecued Beef Ribs 29
Country Barbecued Ribs 35
Rice:
Glorified Rice 104
Great Plains Wild Rice 62
Ham and Wild Rice 40
Instant Rice Pudding 104
Pork Chops and Rice 33
Sausage-Rice Oriental 39
Sweet-Sour Links over
  Rice 40
Wild and White Rice
  Stuffing 14
Wild Rice Pilaf 61
Rolls:
Oatmeal Batter Bread
  or Rolls 100
Quick Caramel Rolls 101
Rouladen, Beef 32
Rye Bread 102

S

Salads:
Bean and Corn Salad 78
Berry-Melon Gelatin Salad 75
Broccoli-Chicken Salad
Puffs 56
Colorful Cracked Wheat
Salad 78
Fast 'N Easy Salad 77
Frosted Fruit Salad 75
Fruited Chicken Salad 76
Marinated Garden Salad 77
Mexican Tossed Salad 78

Salmon:
Asparagus-Topped Pacific
Salmon 15
Individual Salmon Loaves 16
Salmon Loaf Florentine 17

Sandwiches:
Barbecued Beef 30
BLT-Cheese Sandwiches 64
Cheddar Chili Hot Dogs 66
Chicken-Avocado
Sandwiches 68
Chicken Tacos for Two 65
Hot Tuna Sandwiches 65
Meatless Pocket
Sandwiches 68
Shrimp-Avocado
Sandwiches 64
Tortilla Roll-Ups 65
Zucchini Pizza 67
Zucchini Pockets 66

Sauces:
Bananas Foster 111
Caramel Sauce 131
Fudge Sauce 120
Nutty Butter 149
Quick Hollandaise Sauce 149
Tangy Rhubarb Sauce 111
Saucy Beef Strips 28
Saucy Triple Bean Bake 52

Sauerkraut:
Reuben Pie 24
Sauerkraut Balls 24

Sausage:
Bean Casserole 52
Sausage-Rice Oriental 39
Sausage-Stuffed Acorns 90
Sausage-Stuffed Green
Peppers 27
Sweet-Sour Links over
Rice 40
Zucchini Pizza 67
Scalloped Corn and Oysters 54
Scampi, Oriental 18

Seafood:
Bouillabaise 20
Louisiana Gumbo 20
Seafood Combo 53
Seafood Fondue 9
Seafood Stuffing
Casserole 53
Seafood Supreme 19
Seasoned Butter, Brussels
Sprouts with, ... 80
Self-Frosted German Chocolate
Cake 129
Sherried Carrots 81
Sherried Turkey Casserole 59
Sherry-Pecan Bundt Cake 133

Shrimp:
Bouillabaise 20
Louisiana Gumbo 20
Oriental Scampi 18
Seafood Combo 53
Seafood Stuffing
Casserole 53
Seafood Supreme 19
Shrimp-Avocado
Sandwiches 64
Simple Apple Dessert 107
Snowflake-Mint Drops 140
Sole Florentine 18
Sorbet, Sunshine 118
Soufflé-Topped Tomatoes 92

Soups:
Bean and Ham Soup 70
Beer Cheese Soup 75
Cheese Soup 74
Cheesy Broccoli Soup 74
Chilled Avocado-Chicken
Soup 74
Creamy Broccoli Soup 73
Fresh Berry Soup 75
Fresh Mushroom Soup 73
Gazpacho 70
New England Clam
Chowder 71
Oyster Stew 71
Tuna-Vegetable Chowder 71
Velvety Cauliflower-Cheese
Soup 73
Sour Cream-Apple Pie 122
Sour Cream Sauce,
Broccoli in 80

Spaghetti:
A-Lot-Like Lasagna 49
Pizza-Ghetti Casserole 47
Spaghetti Florentine 60
Spaghetti Squash Pasta 89
Spaghetti with Spicy Round
Steak Sauce 38
Spanish Lentils 91
Spiced Nuts 146

Spinach:
Fast 'N Easy Salad 77
Soufle-Topped Tomatoes 92
Spinach Herb Balls 6
Squash Pasta, Spaghetti 89

Steak:
Baked Potatoes with Beef
Burgundy Sauce 38
Beef Rouladen 32
Beef Shish Kabobs 26
Beef Stroganoff 27
Marinated Flank Steak 29
Oven Stroganoff 28
Saucy Beef Strips 28
Spaghetti with Spicy Round
Steak Sauce 38
Steak Kabobs 6
Stuffed Flank Steak 28
Stew, Oyster 71

Strawberries:
Fresh Strawberry-Rhubarb
Jam 148
Fruit Combo Jam 148
Strawberries and Cream
Cake 132
Strawberry-Chocolate Pie 121
Strawberry Cream Dessert 113
Strawberry Creme Melon 110
Strawberry Crunch 113
Strawberry Ribbon Cake 112
Streusel Muffins 94

Stroganoff:
Beef Stroganoff 27
Liver with Stroganoff
Sauce 30
Oven Stroganoff 28
Pork Stroganoff with Stuffing
Balls 35
Stuffed Cabbage Rolls 44
Stuffed Celery 8
Stuffed Flank Steak 28
Stuffed Mountain Trout 16

Stuffings:
Pork Chops and Dressing 34
Pork Stroganoff with Stuffing
Balls 35
Seafood Stuffing Casserole 53
Sherried Turkey Casserole 59
Wild and White Rice
Stuffing 14
Sunflower Brittle 140
Sunny Vegetable Combo 80
Sunshine Sorbet 118

Sweet Potatoes:
Quick Orange Sweet
Potatoes 89
Sweet Potato Bake 88
Yam Boats 89
Sweet-Sour Links over Rice 40

T

Taco Bells 26
Tacos for Two, Chicken 65
Tamale Pie 47
Tangy Rhubarb Sauce 111
Tarts:
  Chocolate Cherry Tarts 116
  Miniature Macaroon Tarts 134
Tenderloin Platter, Pork 33
Teriyaki Cornish Hens 14
Toffee Bars 143
Tomatoes:
  BLT-Cheese Sandwiches 64
  Soufflé-Topped Tomatoes 92
Torte, Apple-Nut 108
Tortilla Chip Fiesta 7
Tortilla Roll-Ups 65
Trout, Stuffed Mountain 16
Tuna:
  Charlie's Super Supper 54
  Creamy Tuna and Noodles 54
  Hot Tuna Sandwiches 65
  Tuna-Vegetable Chowder 71
Turkey:
  Ham 'N Turkey Roll-Ups 58
  Micro-Barbecued Turkey 14
  Sherried Turkey Casserole 59
  Turkey and Broccoli
    Casserole 59
Twice Baked Potatoes 85
Two Servings:
  Bacon 'N Vegies 82
  Bananas Foster 111
  BLT-Cheese Sandwiches 64
  Cheese 'N Apple Acorns 90
  Chicken Tacos for Two 65
  Fruited Chicken Salad 76

Two Servings (continued)
  Lasagna Rolls 48
  Mini Vegetable Plate 81
  Shrimp-Avocado
    Sandwiches 64
  Spaghetti Squash Pasta 89
  Twice Baked Potatoes 85

V

Vanilla Wafer Cake 126
Vegetables:
  Bacon 'N Vegies 82
  Cheesy Vegetable Bake 82
  Colorful Cracked Wheat
    Salad 78
  Corn and Bean Duo 83
  Marinated Garden Salad 77
  Mini Vegetable Plate 81
  Sunny Vegetable Combo 80
  Vegetable Saute 90
Velvety Cauliflower-Cheese
  Soup 73
Versatile Store and Bake
  Muffins 94

W

White Mountain Frosting 131
Whole-Wheat Pumpkin
  Bread 96
Wieners:
  Barbeoued Wieners 29
  Cheddar Chili Hot Dogs 66
  Frank 'N Bean Biscuit
    Bake 41
  Italian Hot Dogs 41

Wild and White Rice
  Stuffing 14
Wild Rice Pilaf 61

Y

Yams:
  Quick Orange Sweet
    Potatoes 89
  Sweet Potato Bake 88
  Yam Boats 89
Yogurt:
  Frozen Yogurt 119
  Raisin-Yogurt Pie 124
  Yogurt 151
  Yogurt-Covered Raisins 144
Yummy Graham Bars 138

Z

Zesty Barbecued Chicken 12
Zippy Buttered Potatoes 88
Zucchini:
  Vegetable Saute 90
  Zucchini-Beef Combo 51
  Zucchini Bread and Butter
    Pickles 150
  Zucchini Chocolate Cake 130
  Zucchini-Corn Relish 150
  Zucchini Meatballs in Sour
    Cream Sauce 24
  Zucchini Pizza 67
  Zucchini Pockets 66
  Zucchini Special 91
  Zucchini Spice Muffins 95

Handy Order Form

Use the form below for ordering additional copies of this book or other offerings published by Recipes Unlimited. The books are printed on excellent quality stock and contain exciting photography and recipes created and tested for perfection in our kitchens.

Favorite Recipes from The Microwave Times, Volume I.

Our popular cookbook, filled with favorite recipes from the first 5 years of "The Microwave Times." Organized in easy-to-use chapters. 160 pages, large 8x10-inch format, spiral bound so the book always lies flat. Black and white photography throughout. Handy to use, filled with delicious, interesting recipes.

Volume II.

The sequel to our popular Volume I. Same easy-to-use format but with all new recipes from volumes 6, 7, 8 and 9 of "The Times." 160 pages. Attractive spiral binding. Black and white photography throughout.

Enjoying Microwave Cooking.

This all-time best seller includes easy to understand basics on microwave cooking and special "Tips" throughout the book. Full color photography. Over 200 recipes. 96 pages. Great reference for the beginner and experienced microwave cook, alike.

Microwave Meals Made Easy.

37 complete meal plans arranged for top efficiency. All recipes for each menu are printed on the same pages. A step-by-step Time Guide is given for each menu so you'll know at a glance how much time is needed and the sequence for preparing each recipe resulting in perfectly coordinated meals.

The Microwave Times.

Six valuable issues of this informative publication will keep you up-to-date over the coming year with new recipes, time and moneysaving tips, new developments in the use and manufacture of microwave ovens, creative ideas and projects, plus questions and answers from fellow readers.
